Mr J. Eden
9 Greenway
Middleton
Manchester
M24 1WR
Tel. 061-643-5967

GW01372441

ELITE ATTACK FORCES

DESERT ADVERSARIES

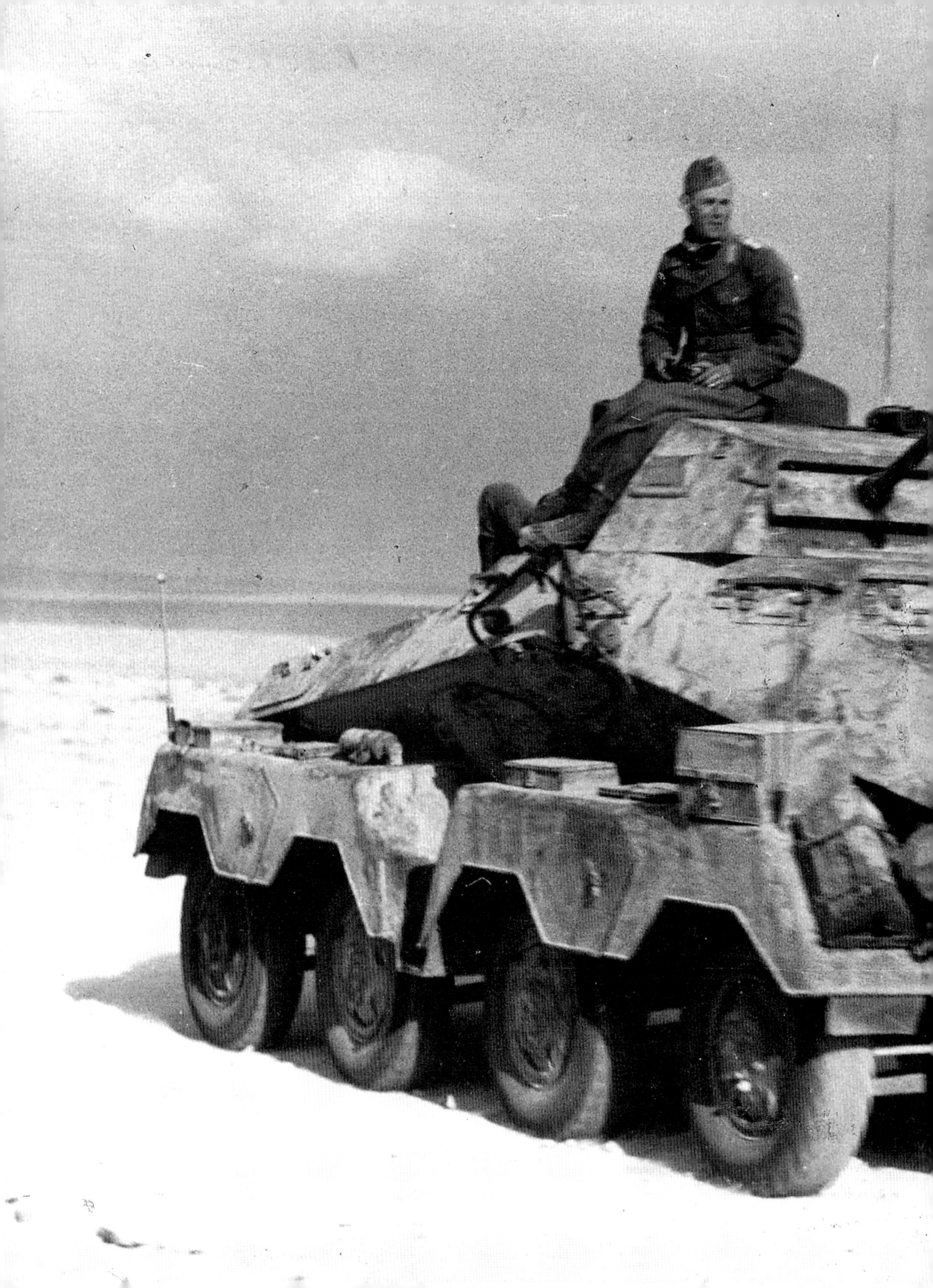

ELITE ATTACK FORCES

DESERT ADVERSARIES

Chris Ellis and George Forty

CHARTWELL
BOOKS, INC.

This edition published by 2007 by

CHARTWELL BOOKS, INC.
A Division of
BOOK SALES, INC.
114 Northfield Avenue
Edison, New Jersey 08837

ISBN: 978-1-84013-829-0

© 2007 Compendium Publishing Ltd, 43 Frith Street, London, W1D 4SA
Previously published in the Spearhead series

Cataloging-in-Publication data is available from the Library of Congress

All rights reserved. No part of this publication may be reproduced, stored in a retrieval system or transmitted in any form or by any means, electronic, mechanical, photocopying, recording or otherwise without the prior permission of Compendium Publishing Ltd. All correspondence concerning the content of this volume should be addressed to Compendium Publishing Ltd

Printed in China through Printworks Int. Ltd

Acknowledgements
Maps on page 64 are taken from *D-Day* by Robert Kershaw (Ian Allan Publishing). Photos on pages 97 to 192 are from the collection of George Forty, except for those on pages 158, 162-163, 166-167 and 170-171, which were supplied by Martin Brayley. The publishers thank Peter Chamberlain, Brian L. Davis, Jonathan Forty, and Simon Forty for information and many of the illustrations used in this book

Previous page: Sd Kfz 231 armoured car of 3rd Reconnaissance Battalion on patrol in the 1941 advance into Cyrenaica.

Right: An Sd Kfz 251/6 halftrack command vehicle of the 21st Panzer Division.

CONTENTS

21st PANZER DIVISION	5
Origins & History	6
Ready for War	10
In Action	16
Insignia & Markings	70
People	82
Assessment	89
Reference	92
7th ARMOURED DIVISION	97
Origins & History	98
Ready for War	102
In Action	107
Insignia, Clothing & Equipment	158
People	172
Postwar	178
Assessment	181
Reference	184
Glossary & Abbreviations	188
Index	189

21st PANZER DIVISION
Rommel's Afrika Korps Spearhead
Chris Ellis

ORIGINS & HISTORY

Not all famous fighting formations have a long tradition of battles and campaigns stretching over many years and more than one war. Some become famous for their exploits in only one hard-fought campaign—of these, 21st Panzer Division is an excellent example. Before the year 1941 it did not exist; yet two years later it had become one of the best-known fighting divisions of the war. The spearhead of Rommel's Deutsches Afrika Korps (DAK), there was no part of the war in the Western Desert in which it did not have some involvement. In most of the notable events of the North African campaign, 21st Panzer Division was in the thick of the fighting, the key to success—or failure—in the fortunes of the DAK.

None of the activities or actions in which 21st Panzer Division became involved had been anticipated even a year before it came into existence. Prior to the outbreak of World War 2, the German High Command (differentiated in this book as OKW=command of all German forces; OKH=command of the German Army) had made no provision for operations outside Europe or Russia—in spite of the highly developed and disciplined staff tradition of the German Army which might have been expected to plan for all contingencies. There appeared to be no official appreciation by either the OKH or staff that the British and their Commonwealth forces had vast experience of colonial operations in hot and arid climates, not least in World War 1, when the British had been so active in Egypt from which they launched the campaigns in Palestine, Syria and Mesopotamia. Between the wars, too, British mandates in Palestine and Egypt, and peacekeeping in the Gulf states gave valuable expertise in Middle East operations. During the Abyssinian campaign by Italy in 1936, the British had even established a modest but balanced Mobile Force (based at Mersa Matruh) which provided early experience of desert operations with modern vehicles and weapons. Hence, when war was declared against Germany in September 1939, the British not only had a useful tradition of desert fighting knowledge, but there was a British military force already in place in Egypt.

During the momentous year of 1940, German military ambitions were fully occupied in Hitler's bold European campaigns. The invasion of Denmark and Norway in April 1940, the latter involving weak and fragmented opposition by a Franco-British expeditionary force, was quickly followed by the swift and well-planned invasion of France and Flanders, starting on 10 May, which conquered Luxembourg, Holland and Belgium in short order and swept the British Expeditionary Force out of Northern France via Dunkirk all within three weeks. The French, demoralised and outfought, sued for peace on 17 June, and on 21 June were forced into a humiliating armistice. This did, however, leave more than a third of the southern part of the country unoccupied, run by a puppet government based at Vichy under the veteran World War 1 hero Marshal Pétain.

Above: PzKpfw 38(t) tanks of 7th Panzer Division waiting to move forward during the advance in France, May 1940. Rommel, later the Afrika Korps commander, obtained his first major experience of handling tank forces at this time as commander of 7th Panzer Division.

During the German campaign in France and Flanders, one of the German divisional commanders, whose fast-moving 7th Panzer Division gave distinguished and effective service, was Generalmajor Erwin Rommel, and his skill as an armoured force commander impressed Hitler. By now Hitler was master of most of Europe with only Great Britain standing in his way. So the summer and early autumn of 1940 was taken up largely with the attempt of the Luftwaffe to gain air superiority over British skies—in what became known as the Battle of Britain—while the German army and navy made preparations for a projected, but much delayed seaborne assault on southeast England, Operation 'Sealion' (*Seelöwe*).

Against all this activity in Europe, the Mediterranean and Middle East were of much less significance to the German High Command in the spring and early summer of 1940. Hitler's Italian ally, Benito Mussolini, already had colonial interests in Africa including the major colony of Cyrenaica (Libya) to the west of Egypt. At the time of his conquest of Abyssinia (Ethiopia) in 1936, Mussolini had actually been a more feared dictator than Adolf Hitler. However, for most of the time after that Mussolini postured and boasted but did little that was effective. In April 1939 he annexed neighbouring Albania in a 24-hour campaign, soon after Hitler had taken over the whole of Czechoslovakia and annexed Memel from Lithuania.

Even after Britain and France declared war on Germany in September 1939, Mussolini held back until he saw the way fortunes were going. On 10 June 1940, however, with France about to fall, he declared war on Britain and France, and just before the French armistice he sent a military invasion force into Southern France, via the Alpine front and centring on Mentone as an objective.

North Africa first entered German High Command thoughts on 24 July 1940, a few days after the decision to invade Great Britain was taken. The staff considered possible options in case Operation 'Sealion' was postponed or abandoned, and one idea was to back up the Italian Army in Libya with German armoured forces in case it undertook operations against the British in Egypt. The German Army C-in-C, Generalfeldmarschall Walter von Brauchitsch, put this up to Hitler who liked the idea. 3rd Panzer Division, therefore, fresh from its triumphs in the French campaign, was told to prepare for service in North Africa. Meanwhile the Chief of Mobile Forces, General Wilhelm Ritter von Thoma, was sent to Libya to sound out the Italian C-in-C, Marshal Graziani, on this prospect of German assistance. He got a lukewarm reception, however, and Graziani showed no enthusiasm at all, confident of the strength of his own forces.

This was emphasised further when Hitler and Mussolini had their famous 'summit' meeting at the Brenner Pass on 4 October. Hitler brought up again the prospect of German assistance in North Africa, and Mussolini flippantly replied that he would need no assistance until his North African army had pushed the British back to Mersa Matruh, at which time some German tanks and Stuka dive-bombers might come in useful.

Von Thoma's own assessment of the situation was produced about that time. He concluded that any operations in North Africa would best be carried out by German troops alone and thought four panzer divisions would be necessary, not withstanding the difficulty of transporting them and supplying them across the Mediterranean and having to run the gauntlet of the British Royal Navy to do so. This proposal was politically and logistically impossible at the time (not least because four panzer divisions could not be spared). When Mussolini carried out his sudden invasion of Greece on 28 October 1940 without consulting or forewarning Germany, Hitler was sufficiently disillusioned to order the postponement of any German plans for involvement in North Africa. As a result 3rd Panzer Division was diverted to another project, Operation 'Felix', the plan—never realised, of course— to attack Gibraltar.

Less than two months later, however, all this had changed. The war in the Western Desert had actually started in a modest way in June 1940, soon after Italy had declared war on Great Britain. At that time Egypt was being guarded by quite

Below: The success of Rommel and his fellow armoured division generals in sweeping away the British and French forces in his path led to the debacle of Dunkirk and a severe weakening of British fighting strength and equipment in 1940. Here British troops come back from France in May 1940.

a small British force, but British troops took part in active reconnaissance patrols along the Libya-Egypt border. In mid-September 1940 the Tenth Italian Army moved ponderously 60 miles into Egypt under the command of Marshal Graziani. British strength in Egypt had expanded meanwhile from the original 7th Armoured Division by the addition of three Commonwealth divisions, forming what was called the Western Desert Force under command of Lt-Gen R. N. O'Connor. On 9 December 1940, O'Connor started a well-planned and brilliantly conducted offensive against the numerically superior Italian Army and this resulted in a sweeping conquest of Cyrenaica, including the taking of of the important towns of Bardia, Tobruk and Benghazi. The Italian Army was virtually eliminated by the first week in February with the capture of 130,000 men and a big haul of equipment.

While this campaign was at its height, Hitler became alarmed at the political consequences of this defeat and realised that German reinforcements would be needed. Not least of his worries was that the British conquest of the whole of North Africa, plus command of the seas in the Mediterranean, would be a strategic disaster for Germany. Therefore, on 11 January 1941 Hitler signed his Military Directive No 22 ordering the Army Command to raise a 'special blocking force' (*Sperrverband*) for dispatch to Tripoli, while the Luftwaffe Command was ordered to transfer Fliegerkorps X to Sicily for operations against British shipping and bases in the Mediterranean. Hitler met Mussolini on 19 January to discuss this. Mussolini accepted the idea of the blocking force, but on 22 January the important base of Tobruk fell to the British who now looked set fair to take the whole of Cyrenaica. It now seemed likely that a modest blocking force would be insufficient on its own and a force with offensive capability would be needed instead. Hitler may have been influenced in this by a comment made by the Army Chief of General Staff, General Franz Halder, in October 1940 that a single German division could probably push the British back to the Nile if Germany did have to get involved in North Africa. (As it happened this prediction had a bigger element of truth in it than anyone thought at the time.)

The Army General Staff acted quickly. The move to Tripoli was designated Operation 'Sunflower' (*Sonnenblume*) in orders issued on 10 February 1941, and the commander of German military forces in North Africa was to be Generalleutnant Erwin Rommel who had been picked and appointed personally by Hitler on 6 February. From his exploits as a panzer division commander in both the Polish and French campaigns, Hitler considered Rommel to be the best man for a post which would demand considerable on the spot decision-making a long way from home.

Despite the powerful size and strength of the German Army early in 1941, the forces allocated the Rommel's command were relatively scanty and weak. The main reason for this was that North Africa was still considered something of a sideshow despite the massive defeat of the Italian forces and, more importantly, the invasion of Russia scheduled for early summer 1941 was already in its advanced planning stages and took priority of allocation over all other considerations.

Nonetheless, advance members of staff for the special blocking force were appointed by 31 January and sent to Naples to await early passage to Tripoli. On 12 February, Rommel and his chief adjutant Rudolf Schmundt, plus other key staff members, reached Tripoli to set up their HQ. On 19 February the German expeditionary force to North Africa was given the name that was to become famous, Deutsches Afrika Korps, and the order stipulated that all German forces were to remain at all times under control of their commander and not to be put under Italian command except for periods of tactical co-operation when necessary.

Above: Rommel, in characteristic pose, directs troop movements from his staff car early in the Cyrenaica campaign. A staff officer with map case stands alongside. This photo dates from soon after the capture of Mechili.

READY FOR WAR

Right: PzKpfw III tanks of 5th Panzer Regiment move along the coast road towards the Cyrenaica frontier in March 1941.

Below right: 5th Panzer Regiment's PzKpfw IIIs parade in front of an admiring crowd on arrival in Africa.

*German staff officer numbers—similar to our GSO (General Staff Officer) 1 etc—

5th LIGHT DIVISION

The division that was later to become 21st Panzer Division had a very modest birth indeed. As originally conceived the special blocking force was seen as having an anti-tank and defence function. It was to be made up mainly from elements drawn from 3rd Panzer Division, which had been the formation originally earmarked for North Africa back in the summer of 1940. There was no intention at this stage of sending a full-strength panzer division.

The first unit designated to to move was 39th Panzerjäger (anti-tank) Battalion from 3rd Panzer Division. This was a motorised unit with halftracks and trucks towing anti-tank guns, three companies each with nine Pak 36 37mm guns and two Pak 50mm guns. However, events already dictated that an armour, reconnaissance and infantry presence would be needed. 5th Panzer Regiment of 3rd Panzer Division was chosen as the armour element, having at the time an under-strength establishment of 20 PzKpfw IVs, 75 PzKpfw IIIs, 45 PzKpfw IIs and 25 Pzkpfw I Ausf B tanks (including command and observation vehicles).

Also from 3rd Panzer Division came 3rd Reconnaissance (*Aufklärung*) Battalion with a light and heavy armoured car company, a motorcycle company and heavy weapons support platoons. Even this was under strength, for one of the light armoured car platoons had VW Kübelwagens substituted. The infantry element was 200th Rifle (Schützen) Regiment from 3rd Panzer Division, and artillery support came from one battalion only of 75th Artillery Regiment, also from 3rd Panzer. Divisional staff was drawn from the staff of 3rd Panzer Brigade within 3rd Panzer Division, the chief staff officer (1a)* being Major Hauser and the intelligence officer (1c) being Hauptmann von Kluge.

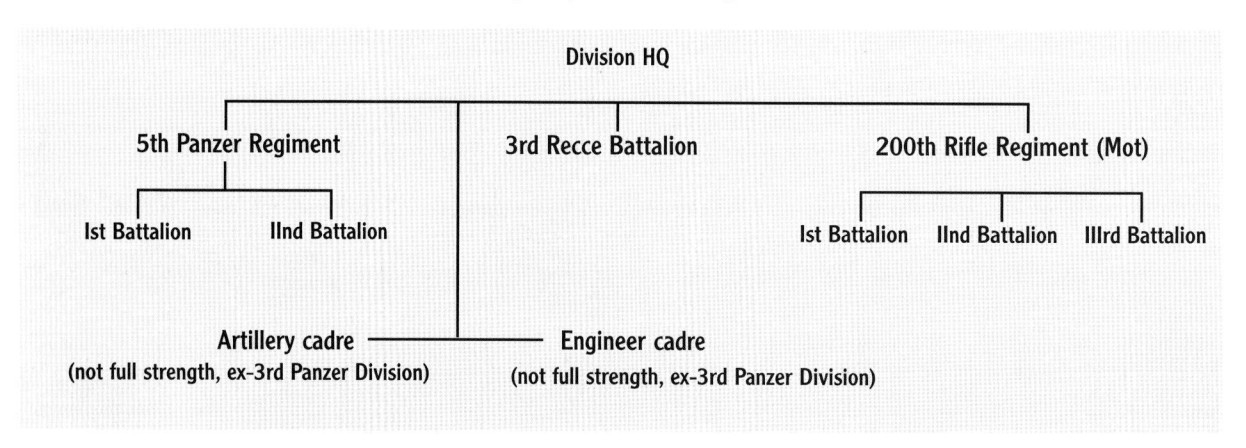

```
                            Division HQ
         ┌──────────────────────┼──────────────────────┐
  5th Panzer Regiment    3rd Recce Battalion    200th Rifle Regiment (Mot)
    ┌────┴────┐                                  ┌──────┼──────┐
Ist Battalion IInd Battalion                 Ist Battalion IInd Battalion IIIrd Battalion

          Artillery cadre ─────────── Engineer cadre
  (not full strength, ex-3rd Panzer Division)  (not full strength, ex-3rd Panzer Division)
```

READY FOR WAR

To these ex-3rd Panzer Division units were added army troops from various depots and formations comprising 606th Flak Battalion (with 20mm guns), 605th Panzerjäger Battalion with three companies each of nine 4.7cm *Pak(t)(Sf) auf PzKpfw I Ausf B*—an ex-Czech 47mm anti-tank gun on a PzKpfw I Ausf B chassis (see photo page 16)—plus the 2nd and 8th Machine Gun Battalions.

This scratch formation was officially named 5th Light Division (Motorised) on 18 February 1941 and its divisional commander, effective from that date, was Generalmajor Johannes Streich, who had been awarded the Knight's Cross for distinguished service while commanding 15th Panzer Regiment within 5th Panzer Division (as an *Oberst*—colonel) during the 1940 French campaign. By this date the first elements of the division were already in Tripoli, arriving in the February period, though the last of the tanks did not finally arrive until 11 March, by which time the division had already seen action.

UNIT STRENGTHS

Light divisions were established by the Wehrmacht in 1938 and were essentially reduced-scale tank divisions. The full establishment was one tank (Panzer) battalion, with four motor rifle battalions (originally called *Kavallerie Schützen* to reflect the 'light' nature of the division) and recce, engineer and artillery battalions. However, 5th Light Division when formed departed from this establishment by having a tank regiment of two battalions, only three motor rifle battalions, and other units initially in only cadre strength. The bulk of the units allocated to 5th Light Division were taken from 3rd Panzer Division which had taken part in the campaign in France and Flanders in 1940. The tank regiment was 5th Panzer Regiment and the reconnaissance battalion that played an important part in early operations was 3rd Recce Battalion.

The ad hoc nature of 5th Light Division was such that it never had a full establishment of tanks as laid down on paper. The two panzer battalions in theory would have had between them 105 PzKpfw III and IV medium tanks and 51 PzKpfw I and II light tanks. In the 5th Panzer Regiment there were only 130 tanks of all types of which two-thirds were gun tanks, the rest being unarmed observation or command tanks.

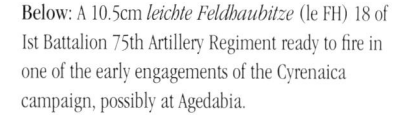

Below: A 10.5cm *leichte Feldhaubitze* (le FH) 18 of Ist Battalion 75th Artillery Regiment ready to fire in one of the early engagements of the Cyrenaica campaign, possibly at Agedabia.

By September 1941 the 5th Light Division had been brought up to Panzer division strength insofar as supplies would allow and was then redesignated 21st Panzer Division. While there were theoretical establishments laid down for the size, equipment and manning of all German units, including armoured divisions, the exigencies of war meant that there were many understrength units or ad hoc units made up from whatever equipment and men were available. This was true of the war in the Western Desert as it was later in Northwest Europe. The following tables, however, taken from US Intelligence Reports give the theoretical full strength allocations, though they were rarely achieved.

1. Composition, armament and manpower of a tank regiment in the early part of World War II.

Units	Men	MCs	Other Vehs	PzII	PzIII	PzIV	MG	20mm	50mm	75mm
Two Bns of three Coys	1,700	120	255	21	77	28	263	21	71	28
Two Bns of four Coys	2,011	134	284	21	111	28	331	21	105	28
Three Bns of three Coys	2,416	170	353	28	114	30	400	28	106	30

2. Composition, armament and manpower of a tank regiment in the later part of the war (1943-44)

Units	Men	MCs	Other Vehs	PzII	PzIII	PzIV	MG	20mm	50mm	75mm
RHQ (inc Sig Pl, Lt Tk Pl and repair platoon)	128	10	15	7	3	0	13	7	1	0
Three Bn HQs	63	9	15	0	0	0	0	0	0	0
Three Bn HQ Coys	666	78	135	21	9	0	87	21	3	0
Three Battalions	1,251	63	108	0	102	30	288	0	102	30
Supply column	56	4	18	0	0	0	0	0	0	0
Workshop Coy	252	6	62	0	0	0	0	0	0	0
Total	2,416	170	353	28	114	30	388	28	106	30

3. Composition of a tank battalion in a Panzer Division

Units	Men	MCs	Other Vehs	PzII	PzIII	PzIV	MG	20mm	50mm	75mm
Bn HQs	21	3	5	0	0	0	0	0	0	0
Bn HQ Coy (inc Sig Pl, Lt Tk Pl, MC Pl, AA Pl and repair platoon)	222	26	45	7	3	0	40	7	1	0
Two light Coys	288	14	24	0	34	0	68	0	34	0
One medium Coy	129	7	12	0	0	14	28	0	0	14
Total	660	50	86	7	37	14	136	7	35	14

4. Composition of a tank battalion in a light division (theoretical)

Units	Men	MCs	Other Vehs	PzII	PzIII	PzIV	MG	20mm	50mm	75mm
Battalion HQ	232	29	50	7	3	0	99	7	3	0
Two light Coys	288	14	24	0	34	0	0	0	34	0
One medium Coy	129	7	12	0	0	10	0	0	0	10
Total	649	50	86	7	37	10	99	7	37	10

5. Composition, armament, and manpower of an anti-tank battalion in a Panzer division.

Units	Men	MCs	Other	MG	20mm ATk	50mm ATk
Battalion HQ	76	5	23	0	0	0
Two Coys (each 9 x 50mm ATk guns)	276	22	52	6	0	18
One Coy (20mm AA/ATk guns on SP mounts)	200	17	18	4	12	0
Total	552	44	93	10	12	18

Left: In their brand-new tropical uniforms, men of 5th Light Division line up on parade in Tripoli on the day they arrived in North Africa, ready for inspection by Rommel.

Opposite page: Equipment for 5th Light Division is put ashore from transports in Tripoli. This is an 88mm Flak 18 of Ist Battalion 33rd Flak Regiment.

6. Organisation, equipment, and manpower of a full-strength Panzer Division, 1943.

Units	Men	Mtrcl	Other	Lt AC	Hy AC	PzII	PzIII	PzIV
Division HQ	185	39	31	0	0	0	0	0
Panzer Regiment	2,416	170	353	0	0	28	114	30
Motorcycle Battalion	1,153	236	150	18	6	0	0	0
Motorised Infantry Brigade	4,409	314	713	0	0	0	0	0
Panzer Artillery Regiment	2,102	132	455	0	0	0	0	0
Panzer Engineer Battalion	979	101	220	0	0	2	0	0
Panzerjäger Battalion	552	44	93	0	0	0	0	0
Panzer Signal Battalion	420	27	85	0	0	0	0	0
Services	2,157	120	446	0	0	0	0	0
TOTAL	14,373	1,183	2,546	18	6	30	114	30

Weapons	Panzer Regt	MC Bn	Mot Inf Brig	Panzer Arty Regt	Panzer Engr Bn	ATk Bn	Panzer Sig Bn	TOTAL
Machine pistols	0	0	156	0	0	0	0	156
Machine guns, light	376	87	358	24	48	16	22	931
Machine guns, heavy	24	12	48	0	0	0	0	84
ATk rifles	0	9	36	0	0	0	0	45
20mm AA/ATk guns	28	18	0	0	2	12	0	60
37mm ATk guns	0	0	18	0	0	0	0	18
50mm tank guns	106	0	0	0	0	0	0	106
50mm ATk guns	0	3	18	0	0	18	0	39
81mm mortars	0	6	24	0	0	0	0	30
75mm inf howitzers	30	2	16	0	0	0	0	48
150mm inf howitzers	0	0	8	0	0	0	0	8
105mm gun-howitzers	0	0	0	24	0	0	0	24
105mm guns	0	0	0	4	0	0	0	4
150mm gun-howitzers	0	0	0	8	0	0	0	8

IN ACTION

Right: The complete order of battle for 5th Light Division when all elements had arrived in North Africa.

The 'light division' as a concept came about in the newly expanded army of Nazi Germany in an attempt to accommodate the old cavalry tradition in the age of tanks and mechanisation. Many senior officers at staff or command level had been cavalry officers in World War 1, and the German order of battle in World War 2 still included some cavalry regiments and even cavalry divisions with horses. Four light divisions were formed in 1938–39 and the basis for each consisted of one or two mechanised cavalry regiments (known as *Kavallerie Schützen*) which were fully motorised with rifle and heavy support companies, and included motorcycle platoons. There was also a motorcycle battalion or a motorcycle recce regiment, plus a motorised artillery regiment. The armoured element comprised a panzer battalion, though for the invasion of Poland in September 1939 a complete panzer regiment was added to 1st Light Division.

Experience in the Polish campaign suggested that panzer divisions were far more effective, so in October 1939 the 1st, 2nd and 3rd Light Divisions were expanded and reorganised to become the 6th, 7th and 8th Panzer Divisions respectively. In January 1940, 4th Light was similarly converted to become 9th Panzer Division. When the 'blocking force' for North Africa was being swiftly organised in January/February 1941, it was certainly not at panzer division strength, so the methodical bureaucracy at OKH (Army High Command) gave it the next available light division number—making it the 5th Light, even though its establishment did not match that of the original light divisions.

In several ways the fortunes of war were kind to Rommel's newly formed Deutsches Afrika Korps (DAK). It could have been wiped out straight away but it wasn't. For the first two months in North Africa 5th Light Division was, effectively, the entire Afrika Korps, because the next division allocated to the force—15th Panzer—was still being organised. It had not long before converted from an infantry division and was not up to strength until late March 1941, being scheduled to move to Tripoli in April. The third formation that eventually made up the predominantly German component of the Afrika Korps was another 'scratch' assembly of available artillery and infantry units formed by Rommel in August 1941 as Afrika Division zbV (zbV=*zur besonderen Verwendung*=for special purposes), renamed 90th Light Division on 27 November. It had no armoured element at all.

When 5th Light Division troops and equipment started to arrive in only small numbers in the 14–20 February period, they were, on paper and in practice, extremely vulnerable. After the British Western Desert Force had captured Tobruk on 21 January, General O'Connor was poised to sweep the Italians out of the rest of Cyrenaica and move on into Tripolitania (the northwestern province of Libya), taking

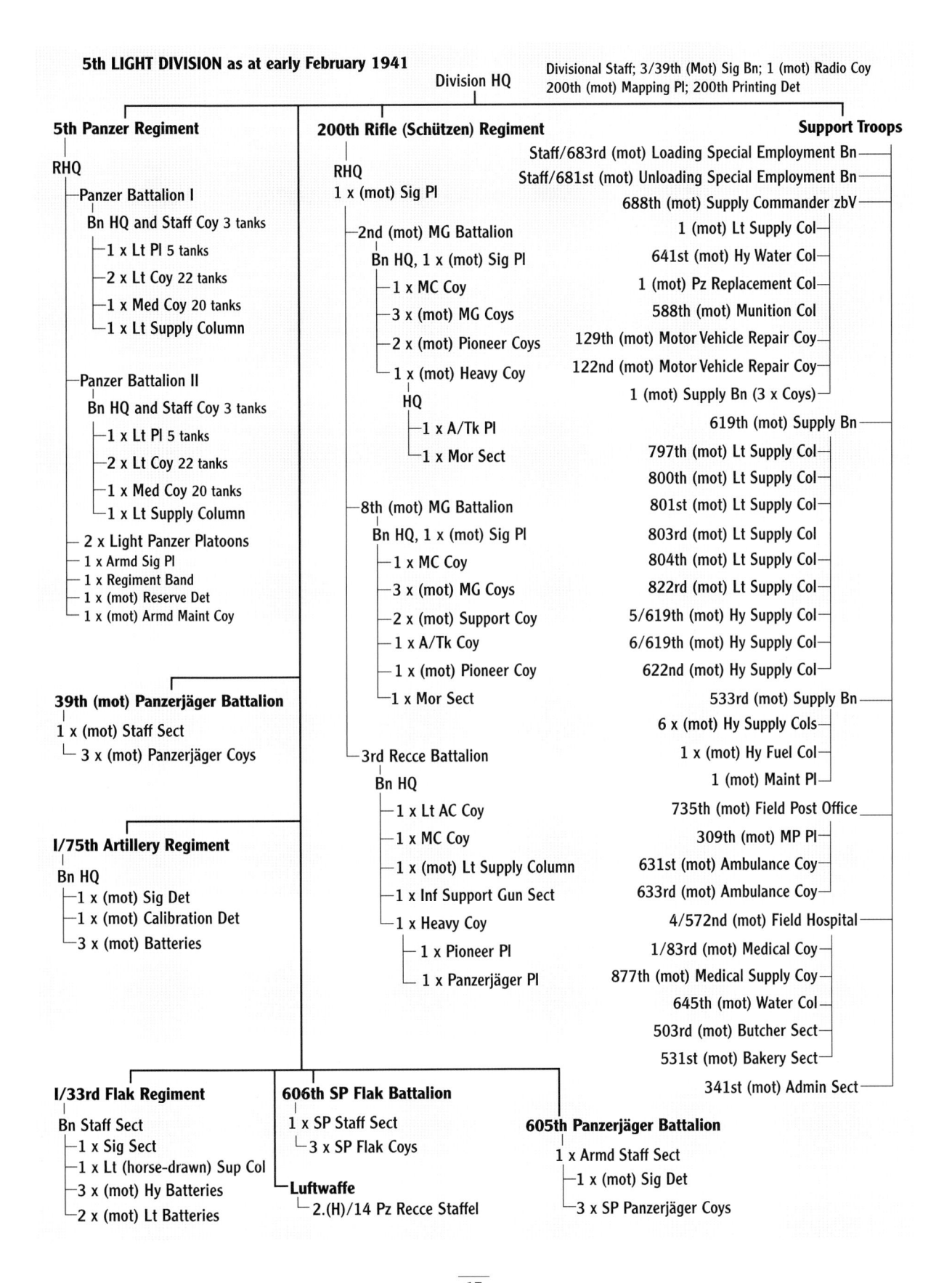

5th LIGHT DIVISION as at early February 1941

Division HQ — Divisional Staff; 3/39th (Mot) Sig Bn; 1 (mot) Radio Coy; 200th (mot) Mapping Pl; 200th Printing Det

5th Panzer Regiment
- RHQ
  - Panzer Battalion I
    - Bn HQ and Staff Coy 3 tanks
      - 1 x Lt Pl 5 tanks
      - 2 x Lt Coy 22 tanks
      - 1 x Med Coy 20 tanks
      - 1 x Lt Supply Column
  - Panzer Battalion II
    - Bn HQ and Staff Coy 3 tanks
      - 1 x Lt Pl 5 tanks
      - 2 x Lt Coy 22 tanks
      - 1 x Med Coy 20 tanks
      - 1 x Lt Supply Column
  - 2 x Light Panzer Platoons
  - 1 x Armd Sig Pl
  - 1 x Regiment Band
  - 1 x (mot) Reserve Det
  - 1 x (mot) Armd Maint Coy

39th (mot) Panzerjäger Battalion
- 1 x (mot) Staff Sect
  - 3 x (mot) Panzerjäger Coys

I/75th Artillery Regiment
- Bn HQ
  - 1 x (mot) Sig Det
  - 1 x (mot) Calibration Det
  - 3 x (mot) Batteries

I/33rd Flak Regiment
- Bn Staff Sect
  - 1 x Sig Sect
  - 1 x Lt (horse-drawn) Sup Col
  - 3 x (mot) Hy Batteries
  - 2 x (mot) Lt Batteries

200th Rifle (Schützen) Regiment
- RHQ
  - 1 x (mot) Sig Pl
  - 2nd (mot) MG Battalion
    - Bn HQ, 1 x (mot) Sig Pl
      - 1 x MC Coy
      - 3 x (mot) MG Coys
      - 2 x (mot) Pioneer Coys
      - 1 x (mot) Heavy Coy
        - HQ
          - 1 x A/Tk Pl
          - 1 x Mor Sect
  - 8th (mot) MG Battalion
    - Bn HQ, 1 x (mot) Sig Pl
      - 1 x MC Coy
      - 3 x (mot) MG Coys
      - 2 x (mot) Support Coy
      - 1 x A/Tk Coy
      - 1 x (mot) Pioneer Coy
      - 1 x Mor Sect
  - 3rd Recce Battalion
    - Bn HQ
      - 1 x Lt AC Coy
      - 1 x MC Coy
      - 1 x (mot) Lt Supply Column
      - 1 x Inf Support Gun Sect
      - 1 x Heavy Coy
        - 1 x Pioneer Pl
        - 1 x Panzerjäger Pl

606th SP Flak Battalion
- 1 x SP Staff Sect
  - 3 x SP Flak Coys

Luftwaffe
- 2.(H)/14 Pz Recce Staffel

605th Panzerjäger Battalion
- 1 x Armd Staff Sect
  - 1 x (mot) Sig Det
  - 3 x SP Panzerjäger Coys

Support Troops
- Staff/683rd (mot) Loading Special Employment Bn
- Staff/681st (mot) Unloading Special Employment Bn
- 688th (mot) Supply Commander zbV
- 1 (mot) Lt Supply Col
- 641st (mot) Hy Water Col
- 1 (mot) Pz Replacement Col
- 588th (mot) Munition Col
- 129th (mot) Motor Vehicle Repair Coy
- 122nd (mot) Motor Vehicle Repair Coy
- 1 (mot) Supply Bn (3 x Coys)
- 619th (mot) Supply Bn
- 797th (mot) Lt Supply Col
- 800th (mot) Lt Supply Col
- 801st (mot) Lt Supply Col
- 803rd (mot) Lt Supply Col
- 804th (mot) Lt Supply Col
- 822rd (mot) Lt Supply Col
- 5/619th (mot) Hy Supply Col
- 6/619th (mot) Hy Supply Col
- 622nd (mot) Hy Supply Col
- 533rd (mot) Supply Bn
- 6 x (mot) Hy Supply Cols
- 1 x (mot) Hy Fuel Col
- 1 (mot) Maint Pl
- 735th (mot) Field Post Office
- 309th (mot) MP Pl
- 631st (mot) Ambulance Coy
- 633rd (mot) Ambulance Coy
- 4/572nd (mot) Field Hospital
- 1/83rd (mot) Medical Coy
- 877th (mot) Medical Supply Coy
- 645th (mot) Water Col
- 503rd (mot) Butcher Sect
- 531st (mot) Bakery Sect
- 341st (mot) Admin Sect

Official tank strength at February 1941

PzKpfw I	25
PzKpfw II	45
PzKpfw III	75
PzKpfw IV	20
Total	165

the Gulf of Sirte and Tripoli and eliminating all Italian forces from North Africa. But fortune changed all this. With stretched lines of communication and the need to resupply and repair damaged equipment, O'Connor was ordered by General Sir Archibald Wavell, the British C-in-C, to rest and replenish for two weeks. Thus it was not until 4 February that the advance was resumed, with Benghazi and Beda Fomm taken after spirited fighting on 7 February, and El Agheila secured on 8 February. General O'Connor now planned his final push, scheduled to start on 12 February. His 7th Armoured Division would move along the coast road to take Sirte and then head towards Tripoli, co-ordinating with the possible landing of a British infantry brigade from the sea at Tripoli itself on 20 February, so clearing Tripolitania of the enemy. It would not have been too formidable a task—save for the lengthened supply lines — for the remaining Italian forces were demoralised, disorganised and poorly equipped.

However, at the end of January 1941 the British government was asked by the Greek government for urgent assistance against the threat of a German invasion. As a result, Prime Minister Churchill asked the Middle East C-in-C to transfer the bulk of the Western Desert Force (by now renamed XIII Corps) to Greece while further operations in Libya were suspended. Despite pleas to be allowed to take Tripoli, Churchill was insistent and on 13 February, the day after Rommel arrived at Tripoli, the Libyan campaign was officially halted, XIII Corps was withdrawn and dispersed. A week later, Cyrenaica Command was set up at little more than brigade strength as an army of occupation.

This mistake was further compounded by complacency. The British Ultra decrypting organisation was reading German signal traffic from the moment Rommel arrived in Tripoli. A key order came from General Halder at OKH telling him not to contemplate any offensive action until May after 15th Panzer Division had arrived in Tripolitania. The British, like OKH, believed this would be the case (so giving the light British forces in Cyrenaica time to train and organise defences), but nobody reckoned with Rommel's own military instincts.

Rommel was surprised by the turn of events by the time he arrived in Tripoli. In his diary he wrote: 'On 8 February leading troops of the British Army occupied El Agheila. Graziani's army had virtually ceased to exist. All that remained of it were a few lorry columns and hordes of unarmed soldiers in full flight to the west. If Wavell had now continued his advance into Tripolitania no resistance worthy of the name could be mounted against him.'

There was no time for 5th Light to relax and all arrangements, including provision of tropical clothing and briefing the troops about conditions in North Africa, were done literally at the last minute—on the ships crossing to Tripoli. The hastily produced supply of reed-green cotton uniforms—breeches, shirt and tunic —and cork sun helmets were worn for the first time after the men landed. For publicity purposes, Rommel had the first arrivals (3rd Reconnaissance Battalion) parade in front of the Governor's Palace in Tripoli as soon as they were landed. Because there were so few of them, Rommel had each platoon go around the corner and tag on again at the back, four times, so that for newsreel cameras and photographers the force appeared much bigger than it actually was. As the tanks were not due to arrived for some time, he engaged all the local carpenters to make 200 dummy wooden tanks and placed them on commandeered car chassis so that any photo-recce operations by the British would assume that a massive armoured force was already present. In fact, it would be another month before 5th Light's tank component (5th Panzer Regiment) would be in place, and logically Rommel would conserve his forces until then. However, the expected British advance into Tripolitania did not happen, so Rommel decided to test out the opposition without

Right: PzKpfw I Ausf A of 5th Panzer Regiment is hoisted ashore from a transport on arrival at Tripoli, still in grey European camouflage finish.

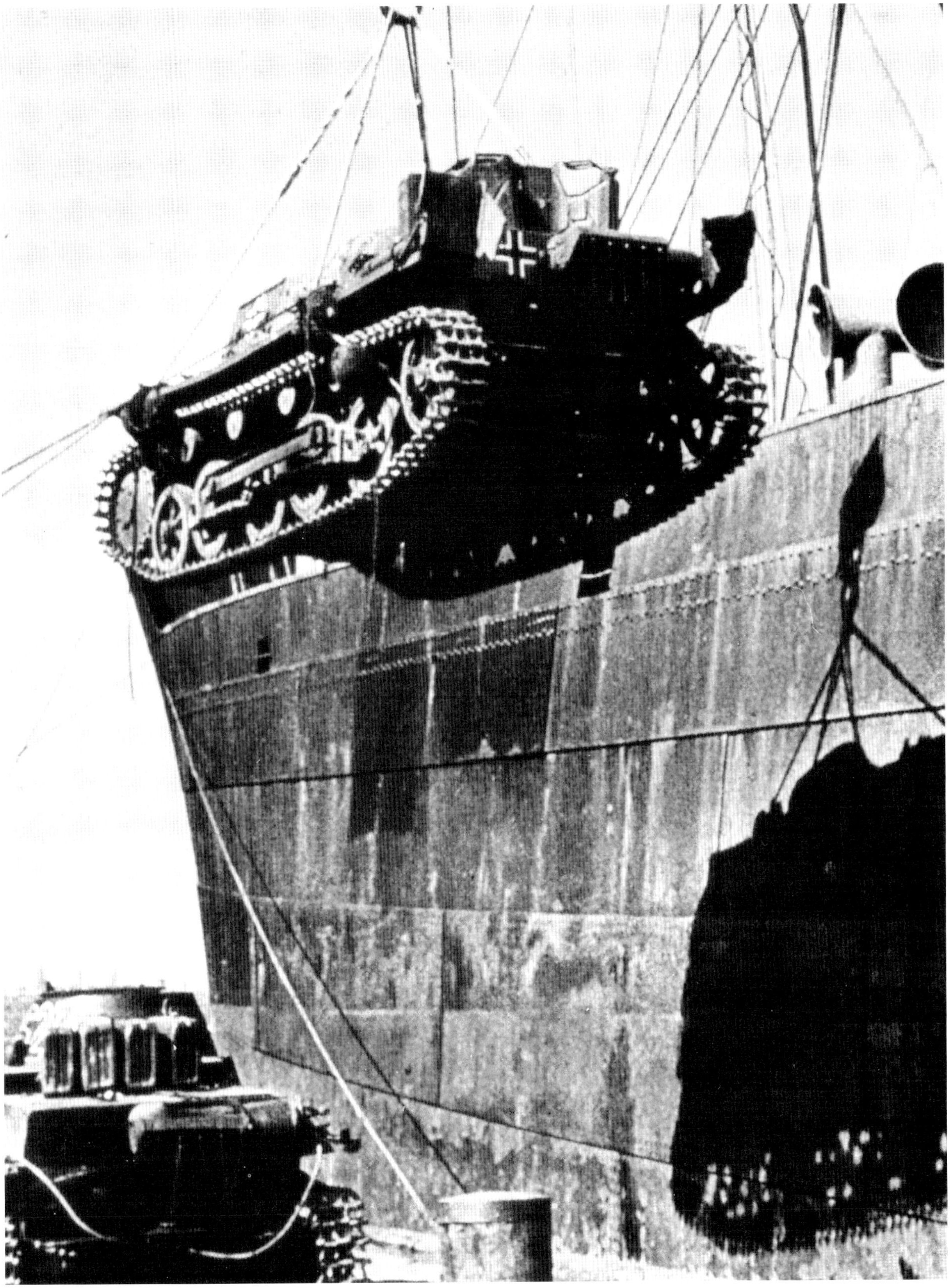

waiting. Together with his chief adjutant, Rudolf Schmundt, he made several flights along the coast towards Sirte and saw disorganised retreating Italian units but no sign of the British. He sent Schmundt straight back to Germany to report personally to Hitler on 19 February, asking for more anti-tank guns, mines and air support. The latter request was met personally by Goering, who arranged for a composite squadron of Heinkel He111 bombers, Junkers Ju52 transports and six Fieseler Fi156 Storch spotter planes to be sent at once.

Meanwhile, Rommel sent the armoured cars of 3rd Reconnaissance Battalion along the coast road to Sirte and beyond to probe the enemy—if the enemy was there. It was on 20 February, within a week of landing in Tripoli, that first contact was made, on the Tripolitania-Cyrenaica border. A troop of three Marmon-Harrington armoured cars of the King's Dragoon Guards, patrolling the border near El Agheila, spotted on an opposite hilltop a big eight-wheeled armoured car of a type they'd never seen before. Reaching the coast road at 15.00hrs they encountered near the border fort a platoon of three of the eight-wheeled armoured cars—Sd Kfz 232s—together with an armed truck and a motorcycle combination. Fire was exchanged and the British cars tried to outflank the German vehicles but got stuck in the sand. By the time they got out the Germans had gone. As dusk fell they moved back along the coast road and saw another armoured car near the border fort blocking the road. They presumed this to be British, but as they drew close they saw it was another Sd Kfz 232. There was an exchange of fire as the cars raced away. On 24 February there was another clash when the same British armoured car troop again approached the border fort and was ambushed by another platoon of 3rd Recce Battalion who were hidden in wait. In the close range exchange of fire one of the Marmon-Harrington cars was knocked out and its crew taken prisoner, while the driver of another car was killed—first blood to 5th Light. The British troop commander in both these engagements was Lt E. T. Williams who later (as a Brigadier) was famous as General Montgomery's chief intelligence officer. German propaganda made great play of what they called the Battle of Fort El Agheila, but this also prompted the British to take offensive action. They started to set up an ambush alongside the fort with 25pdr and 2pdr anti-tank guns, heavy infantry weapons and a minefield in the road, but they were spotted by the Germans, They called in an air strike that knocked several British vehicles and caused major casualties before the mission was aborted. No German ground forces were seen.

At dawn on 2 March, 5th Light struck back with an ambush on the coast road. They now had the first '88' to arrive in North Africa, and this was well sited to pick off approaching British vehicles. The leading Marmon-Harrington armoured car was attacked, cut off and blocked by two 3rd Recce eight-wheel armoured cars, and its crew captured. They were surprised to find themselves being interviewed shortly afterwards by Generalmajor Streich, the divisional commander, who was personally directing this operation and had occupied the border fort.

Meanwhile Rommel had ordered the rest of 5th Light to move up the coast road of the Gulf of Sirte towards the Cyrenaica border. By mid-March 8,000 men of the division had landed as had all the tanks of 5th Panzer Regiment. British patrols on 28 March saw the

Below: Some of the follow-up shipments of tanks later in 1941 arrived already painted in desert camouflage, as shown on these newly landed PzKpfw IIIs. The wheeled transport, however, is still in field grey finish.

first German tanks approaching the border and one of them ran over one of the British mines, killing two crewmen—the first casualties in 5th Light. By now the Italian Ariete Division, a fresh armoured formation, had been put under Rommel's command and events were about to speed up.

There was still wariness on both sides in early March 1941. British intelligence now thought a limited German advance was likely in early April, information gleaned by Ultra from German signal traffic. The King's Dragoon Guards, who held the Cyrenaica frontier area, were told to make a fighting withdrawal if that happened. At the same time, Rommel was still worried that the British would resume their offensive and push into Tripolitania. He sent a report to OKH on 9 March stating that he preferred to attack the British sooner rather than later to avoid the really hot weather of June, though he was still prepared to await the arrival of 15th Panzer Division before he made a move. At this stage he only contemplated attempting to take Cyrenaica, not least because of problems of supply and lines of communications. OKH thinking at that time was that moving beyond Cyrenaica into Egypt would best be put off until autumn 1941 when the hoped-for conquest of Russia should be completed, thus freeing many more troops and tanks for North Africa. On 20 March Rommel flew back to Berlin to report on progress. The Army C-in-C, von Brauchitsch, took a typically cautious view, suggesting that with 15th Panzer in place, DAK could strike out for Agedabia using that as a base for any further advances. At that stage OKH was sure that there must still be powerful British armoured divisions in place in Cyrenaica.

The fighting patrols of late February and March, which had led to only a limited British response, convinced Rommel that a modest offensive advance was possible, certainly now that 5th Light Division had the tanks of 5th Panzer Regiment. He ordered Generalmajor Streich to mount a set-piece attack by 5th Light on 31 March to take the Mersa Brega gap, which was the key to the coastal route into Cyrenaica.

The British forces available to guard Mersa Brega amounted to little more than the newly arrived 2nd Armoured Division, which had just replaced the experienced 7th Armoured Division. 2nd Armoured was under strength, not fully trained or acclimatised, short of transport and armed with a motley mix of older cruiser tanks, light tanks and captured M13 Italian tanks, not all of them radio-equipped. Nonetheless, when 5th Light launched its attack, the attackers had a hard time of it. A regiment of 25pdrs held off two attacks by 5th Panzer Regiment tanks, damaging several, and forcing others off the road into the sand where they got stuck. Even Streich's command post was almost made untenable by accurate 25pdr fire. Streich called in Stukas to try to dislodge the effective British batteries but the British gunners held fast. Streich realised that if the British put in a counter-attack with tanks at that moment, 5th Light would have to withdraw.

Fortunately, nothing like that happened, and at dusk Streich had the idea of sending 8th Machine Gun Battalion up the coast, through the sand dunes beyond the coast road, to get behind and attack the British right flank. This unexpected surprise assault at night caused mayhem in the British rear and the British commander quickly pulled out. Streich was surprised and delighted at this successful outcome, and without reference to his corps commander he send his tanks, 3rd Recce Battalion, the two machine gun battalions and his only artillery—12 guns—in close pursuit. He gleefully told Major Hauser, his 1a (see page 10), that they were going to Agedabia, and they moved so fast the next day that some of the German tanks caught up, cut off and ran amok among the British rear units who were still withdrawing to Agedabia. Three German tanks were lost in this

Above: The crew of one of 5th Panzer Regiment's PzKpfw IIIs takes a meal break parked at the roadside. Note the jerricans of fuel or water and the spare wheels carried on the track covers.

Official tank strength at end March 1941	
PzKpfw I	25
PzKpfw II	45
PzKpfw III	71
PzKpfw IV	20
Total	161

Below: Rommel's map caravan, still in the markings for the Polish campaign of 1939, and his Sd Kfz 251/6 command vehicle, still in French campaign markings, parked on the beach at El Agheila during the opening stages of the advance into Cyrenaica. Note the camouflage from local beach plants added on top of each vehicle.

action and two broke down, but a numerically small number of German tanks, only 12 at the finish, caused much damage and chaos. An immediate lesson learned was that the 2pdr guns on the British cruiser tanks could not penetrate a German PzKpfw III at 1,000m (c3,000ft), but at the same range the 50mm gun of the German tank could penetrate the thickest front armour of a British cruiser tank. This valuable lesson was put to good use in the weeks and months ahead.

The British now abandoned Agedabia, leaving it in Streich's hands, and withdrew fast in the direction of Antelat (inland) and Beda Fomm along the coast. Though Rommel is generally credited with this swift advance that set the German offensive moving, he only found out about it after it happened. It was Streich's initiative as a divisional commander (and drawing on his experience as a tank regiment commander in France in 1940) that got the advance started, though it was approved by Rommel in retrospect when he saw the opportunity that the move provided. Air reconnaissance now showed British units moving east generally. So on 3 April, the day after the capture of Agedabia, Rommel decided that the British had no determination to stand and fight. He realised now that he had the chance to keep the momentum going and take the whole of Cyrenaica in one bold operation.

British misfortunes were compounded by several further command decisions. General O'Connor had been succeeded by Lt-Gen Phillip Neame VC, an officer of great reputation but with no previous experience of the desert. The battle-hardened 7th Armoured Division had been withdrawn to Egypt and replaced by the newly formed 2nd Armoured Division, which together with its commander, Maj-Gen M. D. Gambier-Parry, was fresh from England. Because of the complacent assumption that no big German offensive would begin before May, the British C-in-C, Wavell, had given written orders to Neame that in the event of any German light probing, his forces were to withdraw and yield the ground. Neame obeyed this order quite literally and ordered his forces to pull back when the first German forces appeared on 31 March—but the speed and zeal of Rommel's advance meant that what in normal circumstances might have been an orderly withdrawal, soon became a chaotic rout.

Rommel had organised his relatively meagre forces to cover every possible route into Cyrenaica. The armoured cars of 5th Light's hard-worked 3rd Recce Battalion were sent racing up the coast road towards Benghazi, which they reached that same evening of 3 April. To their surprise they found it abandoned with the military stores burning and the two brigades of Australian infantry who were based there already departed, following orders, and joining the general retreat eastwards.

In a typically unorthodox move, Rommel contacted Generalmajor Heinrich Kirchheim, a staff officer from OKH on a fact-finding tour of Libya, and put him in charge of some assorted units of the Italian Brescia Division to follow up the 3rd Recce Battalion and carry on round the coast road to Derna. Meanwhile, Generalmajor Streich took

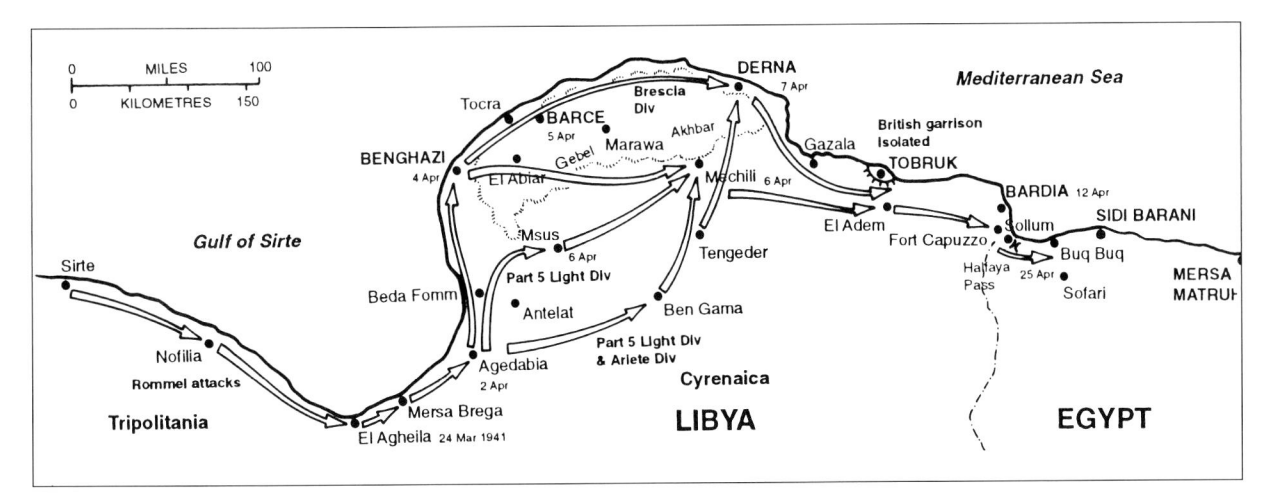

Above: The advance into Egypt: operations in March/April 1941.

the remaining units of the division across a southerly route towards Tobruk, though on 5 April they were ordered to divert to Mechili instead. Some units of the Italian Ariete Division were also under command.

From the main body, 8th Machine Gun Battalion, commanded by Oberstleutnant Gustav Ponath, was sent northwards towards Mechili and Derna in a 450km (280-mile) dash to cut the coast road west of Tobruk, and a detachment of 5th Panzer Regiment, under its commander Oberst Olrich, plus the 2nd Machine Gun Battalion, the artillery and some Italian Ariete Division tanks, went north to head for Mechili via Msus where there was known to be a British supply dump. From Benghazi a 5th Light force, commanded by Oberst Gerhard Graf von Schwerin, comprising the 3rd Recce Battalion, the Panzerjäger battalions and some Italian Ariete Division tanks, headed due east towards Mechili skirting the southern edge of the Gebel Akhbar. Thus every possible route across Cyrenaica was being taken by 5th Light Division and Italian troops and all were converging on Mechili and Derna with Tobruk as an objective beyond.

The region called the Gebel Akhbar was a key feature of Cyrenaica, a hilly region with some fertile areas which restricted possible transport routes to the coastal area to the north or the desert hinterland to the south. Rommel speedily set up a Tactical HQ (*Führungsstaffel*) in the sand dunes at Agedabia where his map caravan, command half-tracks and support vehicles were based. From here, too, he could operate his newly arrived Storch liaison aircraft. Supplies were always going to be a problem in desert operations, and Rommel ordered the setting up of a major forward supply dump on the Via Balbia coast road near 'Marble Arch' (actually the Arco Philaenorum), the grand archway which Mussolini had built at El Agheila on the Tripolitania-Cyrenaica border.

Streich's column was heading for Ben Gania on the following day, 4 April, and already beginning to run out of fuel and water. He had his first clash with Rommel over this, for Streich wanted to wait for a supply column, which might well have taken three or four days. Rommel was enraged at this lack of urgency and ordered Streich to unload all his own trucks and send them back to Marble Arch overnight and there 'to collect sufficient fuel, rations, and ammunition for the advance through Cyrenaica within 24 hours'.

Rommel's fast offensive was surprising his own side as well as the British. His divisional commander, Streich, and the individual regimental and unit commanders were urged on, often against their better judgement and usually by Rommel dropping literally from the sky to tell them, for he was using his Storch aircraft incessantly over the battlefield. If he didn't actually land alongside a unit he flew low over it and dropped a hand-written message. Even Hitler was upstaged. On 3 April he sent a telegram to Rommel reminding him not to launch any large scale offensive until the 15th Panzer Division was in place, and not to expose his flank by advancing to Benghazi. But by the time this telegram was was received Benghazi had already been occupied by 3rd Recce Battalion and the three-pronged offensive was already under way across the Cyrenaica 'Bulge'. When the Italian General Gariboldi, nominally the area commander and senior to Rommel, questioned the wisdom of what he was doing, Rommel simply told him the opportunity was too good to miss!

British fortunes were aggravated by poor and confused communications (or sometimes none at all), the ever-troubling shortage of fuel which caused some tanks to be abandoned, and faulty intelligence or misinterpretation of events. A major mistake occurred on 3 April when a large enemy column was reported to be heading for Msus, a major fuel dump. The fuel was destroyed and the post abandoned, but the 'enemy force' was then discovered to be a returning patrol of the Long Range Desert Group. On the same day, 5th Royal Tank Regiment (RTR) were ordered to engage approaching 'enemy tanks' near Antelat but these turned out to be 6RTR withdrawing to the same position.

On 6 April 5th Panzer Regiment and units under command took Msus, with its romantic 'Beau Geste' fort already abandoned by the British and headed on for Mechili. Between Msus and Mechili, however, the going got rough. Fuel was running out and the stony ground to the south of the Gebel Akhbar played havoc with the tank tracks, so only a few tanks, trucks and halftracks made it unscathed to Mechili. Streich's main party suffered similarly, largely due to shortage of fuel for the tanks. By the time it reached Mechili, Streich had left his tank detachment behind because of breakdowns or lack of fuel, and the heaviest equipment he had with him were a few of the trucks armed with 20mm flak guns. Von Schwerin's 3rd Recce and units under command, coming across from Benghazi, were similarly afflicted. One good reason for all this, of course, is that all the vehicles, from trucks to tanks, had been designed for European conditions and not for the extremes of

Below: The British strongholds of Msus and Mechili, both 'Beau Geste' style forts, were swiftly captured by the DAK's desert columns. Here an Sd Kfz 251 halftrack is seen at Msus with a battalion commander and his staff, while the German flag is hoisted on the fort in the background.

Left: Hard going over the Gebel Akhbar's rocky slopes for one of the small Sd Kfz 222 armoured cars during the advance on Mechili in April 1941.

heat, sand and rock they were now traversing, nor for the very long distances being travelled.

Rommel, buzzing over the area in his Storch, was frustrated by the delays. He had noted British forces gathering around Mechili and was keen to get among them. He landed alongside Streich on the late afternoon of April 6 to urge the division on, and was very displeased at the excuses for the delays. He flew off to find the stragglers and the next day the surviving runners of Streich's tank detachment, a PzKpfw IV and seven PzKpfw IIs, caught up, as did an artillery battery of the Italian Ariete Division which Rommel had rounded up. Von Schwerin's 3rd Recce Battalion finally caught up, too, on 7 April and by that evening a somewhat reduced 5th Light Division had finally drawn up on the low hills looking down on the fort at Mechili. Rommel was in better mood. In the gathering dusk he landed his Storch alongside Streich's command car and shouted, 'Tomorrow we attack.'

What had undoubtedly lifted Rommel's spirits was an unexpected coup on the night of 6/7 April. Because of the disarray among the British forces, Wavell had sent General O'Connor up from Egypt, where he had been on leave, to advise General Neame. They met at Marua, a British base in the Gebel Akhbar, to confer with Maj-Gen Leslie Morshead, commander of 9th Australian Infantry Division, whose brigades had been stretched between Benghazi and Tobruk. Spirited resistance by an Australian infantry battalion had held up the 3rd Recce Battalion for a day east of Benghazi. O'Connor suggested a defence line be set up between Mechili and Gazala, and Morshead set off east in his staff car past Derna and on to Gazala. Neame and O'Connor followed a short time later in another staff car, but in the dark the driver took a wrong turning and ran into the leading troops of Ponath's 8th Machine Gun Battalion who had just arrived on the outskirts of Derna. The Germans were surprised to find they had captured the two senior British generals in Cyrenaica, and they went on to capture quite a few more British troops that night including a complete mobile field hospital and the commander and some staff officers of 3rd Armoured Brigade.

Seeking to take Derna airfield, 8th Machine Gun Battalion were counter-attacked, first by the armoured cars of the King's Dragoon Guards who were withdrawing east, then on the afternoon of 7 April by the remnants of 5RTR whose few remaining A13 cruiser tanks were lost in the engagement, though not before knocking out several 8th Battalion vehicles.

By rights 8th Machine Gun Battalion was too weak and tired to achieve success at Derna, but they were undoubtedly helped by the demoralisation and confusion of the British. This certainly helped the next day when Streich's much depleted main force put in its attack on Mechili. The base was actually held by 3rd Indian Motor Brigade, but Maj-Gen Gambier-Parry had also moved in his 2nd Armoured Division HQ and support units, and ordered the remnants of 3rd Armoured Brigade to join them. On the evening of 7 April, however, Gambier-Parry received orders to pull out of Mechili at dawn the next day and withdraw eastwards on Tobruk. At that time 2nd Armoured Division was down to its last tank, an A13 cruiser of divisional HQ.

As soon as the British started to move out things went wrong for them, for 5th Light was waiting to attack. A company of 3rd Indian Motor Brigade was first out, but it ran into an artillery column of the Italian Ariete Division emplaced to the east. The Indians dispersed the Italians with a bayonet charge, but they soon regrouped and destroyed the sole A13 tank as soon as it appeared, leading a British motorised column. The column moved on but right into the path of Streich's divisional HQ, whose personnel, including Streich, engaged it with small-arms fire and the truck-mounted 20mm cannon. While this was happening, Streich's small tank force attacked from the side. A lucky shot by a courageous 2pdr anti-tank gun crew knocked out the sole PzKpfw IV, hitting the tank's undersides as it climbed the anti-tank mound around the fort. The attacking force now comprised only the seven PzKpfw IIs and a few trucks carrying infantry, but some of the trucks were fitted with rakes to raise extra dust and sand—not only to to conceal them from enemy gunners but to make the force look much bigger than it actually was. Over all this dust and gunfire flew Rommel in his Storch. Gambier-Parry, viewing the apparent size of the attacking force and the confusion all around him, decided to surrender, though several groups—including one column of 60 vehicles—managed to break out and make a run for it to Tobruk or Sollum. Over 2,000 British and Indian troops were captured at Mechili, though not before the British had set fire to the fuel dump. The smoke from this, however, acted as a beacon for the many small elements of 5th Light who were struggling to catch up, broken down vehicles, tanks awaiting fuel, and the like.

Rommel's own mobility in his Storch caused problems for his staff. On 7 April it became clear from intelligence reports to Rommel's chief of staff and operations officer at the Tactical HQ in Agedabia that the ad hoc and disorganised assembly of British forces at Mechili offered no threat to the advance and could be bypassed for the more important objective of Tobruk. But they could not pass this appreciation on

Below: Rommel swooped over the battlefield in his Storch liaison aircraft, landing to direct operations when he needed to. Here he talks with his personal Luftwaffe pilot, soon after the capture of Mechili.

to their chief who was flying here, there and everywhere in his Storch, completely out of touch with Tactical HQ. So they sent Rommel's ADC, Lt H. W. Schmidt, in another Storch either to track down Rommel or, failing that, to reach Generalmajor Streich and pass the order straight to him. However, Schmidt himself got lost (there were sandstorms about) and did not arrive at Streich's divisional HQ until the early morning of 8 April, by which time the attack on Mechili was already under way. Commentators on the desert war have speculated that, had Rommel not lost touch with his Tactical HQ and received the staff's advice, the outcome of the Cyrenaica campaign might have been even more successful, culminating in the speedy capture of Tobruk, which in the event did not happen.

On the positive side, in spite of the burning of the fuel, the taking of Mechili did yield a good supply of stores and rations and vehicles to boost Afrika Korps stocks. Included in the haul were two AEC armoured command trucks, one of which was appropriated by Rommel for his personal use and named *Mammut* (mammoth).

Prudently, Johannes Streich requested two days for rest and maintenance before proceeding, but Rommel ordered him to press straight on to Tobruk no matter what the state of the men or equipment, 'Every man and vehicle that can move, must move.' However, a fierce sandstorm raged on 9 and 10 April and severely restricted movement and reconnaissance. This did not stop the Australian and British troops who were in Tobruk, with General Morshead as garrison commander, working non-stop to make good the defences on the perimeter. Morshead took a typically tough line, promising a policy of 'no surrender, no retreat' to his unit commanders.

Above: Evenings and nights could be cold in the desert and the army overcoat was welcome wear, as shown by the crew of this self-propelled 4.7cm *Pak(t) (Sf) auf PzKpfw I Ausf B* of 605th Panzerjäger Battalion in April 1941.

AN OBJECTIVE TOO FAR

For Rommel, Tobruk proved an objective too far. Morshead had around 25,000 troops under command, half of them Australian. 1RTR, with 27 assorted cruiser and light tanks, had arrived from Egypt just before Tobruk was besieged, and various other tanks were found and repaired to make up another squadron. After a week, a squadron of 7RTR arrived by sea making up a unit of 14 Matilda tanks when those already at Tobruk were included. There were also the surviving KDG armoured cars. Artillery was better provided for with four field regiments with 72 25pdrs in all, and further batteries had 18pdr and 60pdr guns.

The town and seaport of Tobruk lay at the foot of a low natural escarpment emanating from the eastern foothills of the Gebel Akhbar. The Italians had built an anti-tank ditch all round the landward perimeter up on the escarpment, reinforced with barbed wire and minefields. Concrete emplacements had been built in a double row inside the perimeter with others sited at the heads of the many wadis worn into the escarpment. Priority had been given to repairing the perimeter defences so that by April 11 the perimeter was reasonably complete and fully covered by infantry. The perimeter was a considerable 45km (30 miles) in length, and the garrison troops were fully stretched guarding it. As there was only a limited number of anti-tank guns available—all 2pdrs of limited value—there was great dependency on the 25pdrs to hold off enemy tanks. The plan was to hold them well back, so that if any German armour broke through it could be engaged over open sights.

Rommel sent Ponath's 8th Machine Gun Battalion on along the coast road from Derna towards Tobruk, but for two days (9 and 10 April) they were forced to fight for every inch of the way against a determined Australian rearguard backed up by KDG's armoured cars. Rommel had the idea of shelling the Tobruk port area from the west if he could find a high enough gun position. He asked Generalmajor Kirchheim, who had been shepherding along the the units from the Italian Brescia Division, to go forward to find a suitable position. While doing so, his car was strafed by an RAF fighter coming in over the coast and Kirchheim was wounded. As it happened the newly arrived commander of 15th Panzer Division, Generalmajor Heinrich von Prittwitz und Gaffron, had arrived on the scene to see the battlefront while he awaited the arrival of his division. Rommel asked him to take Kirchheim's place. Von Prittwitz did so, but his car was completely destroyed when he was ambushed, just 6km (less than four miles) from Tobruk by the

Right: The coast road between Bardia and Sollum at the time of the German advance in April 1941, as photographed from a German aircraft.

Australian rearguard who were using a captured Italian 47mm anti-tank gun. Von Prittwitz died in this attack and 15th Panzer Division had lost its commander even before the main units had arrived in North Africa.

The next day, 11 April, the German attack began. The 3rd Recce Battalion was detached and sent down the coast road east to the border to seize the remainder of Cyrenaica. With them went reinforcements in the shape of three motorcycle companies from 15th Panzer Division's recce battalion. This had been the first 15th Panzer unit to arrive and had been sent immediately on the long haul from Tripoli up to the front. The motorcycle companies took Bardia on 12 April and Sollum, Capuzzo and Halfaya Pass on the 13th to secure the Cyrenaica-Egypt border. Meanwhile, 2nd Machine Gun Battalion, with attached flak and artillery companies, was sent to block the road and hinterland east of Tobruk to prevent any breakout in that direction.

The balance of 5th Light, under Streich's command, comprised the few remaining tanks of 5th Panzer Regiment, a few Italian M13 tanks, the remaining field guns (eight in all and low on ammunition), the rest of the flak units, and 8th Machine Gun Battalion, which had been moved round from the Derna area. This force approached the perimeter from the south, trying the same trick of a heavy dust cloud as had been used at Mechili. But the attack was a failure. It came under heavy artillery fire and the infantrymen of 8th Machine Gun Battalion found it difficult to dig-in on the rocky ground. Cover was poor and casualties were high under the merciless artillery fire. Only the coming of darkness gave some relief. The tanks could do no better than run along the perimeter wire, taking pot shots at the defences, and at one point they were engaged across the wire by cruiser tanks of 1RTR. The major drawback to 5th Light's offensive capability at that moment was lack of artillery, virtually none of which was effective.

Above: The PzKpfw III was numerically the most important tank used by DAK. Here a PzKpfw III Ausf H with retrospectively fitted extra frontal armour is seen during Rommel's big offensive of January 1942, which resulted in the retaking of most of Cyrenaica. The white colour of the Afrika Korps symbol—just visible on the front of the vehicle—indicates this is a tank of 5th Panzer Regiment.

Right: This anti-tank ditch formed part of the perimeter defences of Tobruk, as did the extensive barbed wire entanglements seen in the background.

On the following day, 12 April, 5th Light's tanks tried again. Passing through the positions of 8th Machine Gun Battalion at 11.00hrs they reached the wire, again without artillery support, but could not cross the anti-tank ditch, and therefore withdrew. On the following day, Easter Sunday, 13 April, Rommel carried out a leaflet raid over Tobruk, telling the 'British' forces to surrender: '. . . soldiers signalling with a white handkerchief will not be fired on. Strong German forces have surrounded Tobruk. There is no point in trying to escape. Remember Mechili. Our bombers and Stukas lie in wait for your ships in the harbour.'

This bluff got nowhere, for by now it must have been obvious to Tobruk's defenders that the Germans were thinly spread with hardly enough forces to patrol the 45km (30-mile) perimeter, let alone attack it effectively. Also Rommel did not know that there had been a change of policy, and far from trying to escape, the defenders were there to stay.

Rommel now had an argument with Streich over the interpretation of air recce photos and intelligence reports. Rommel thought the forces in Tobruk were being evacuated by sea; Streich and his 1a, Major Hauser, took the opposite view, thinking that the forces were being reinforced. As it happened they were correct: the small convoy of lighters and ships seen arriving were bringing Matilda tanks, 25pdrs, more stores and ammunition, and more troops; they were not an evacuation fleet. In view of this, Streich thought that yet another attack on the perimeter at present strength would be ineffective and wasteful. Ponath, commanding 8th Machine Gun Battalion, was of the same opinion. His men had already suffered many casualties, and in their present position in front of the wire were still exposed to heavy artillery and small-arms fire from the Australians.

Rommel was enraged at what he called the 'pessimism' of his senior commanders, and decided to take personal charge of the attack planned for next day, 14 April. He promised a 'concentrated artillery' strike to back this attack, which was to start at 18.00hrs in the dusk. However, the artillery support turned out to be just a few 88mm flak guns, certainly powerful and useful, but being emplaced on the flat rocky ground behind 8th Machine Gun Battalion they were fully exposed, with no cover for the crews; consequently, casualties from enemy fire were so heavy that the guns were largely ineffective.

As darkness fell, 8th Machine Gun Battalion under Ponath advanced cautiously and found a gap in the wire which they cleared of mines. Advancing further, they saw nobody, but the bridgehead was tenuous and there were a number of counter-attacks in the dark by small Australian raiding parties which caused 40 casualties. Nonetheless, Rommel thought the penetration of of the perimeter now made a tank attack viable, so he handed operational control back to Streich but detailed his ADC, Lt Schmidt, to stay as a liaison officer with Streich and keep a 'watching brief' on operations.

The tank attack went gravely wrong, however. Streich decided to lead the assault from the top of a PzKpfw II, but as he approached the start line in the dark, the tank and Streich's accompanying Kübelwagen came under artillery and small-arms fire from a British patrol. The Kübelwagen and its driver escaped, but the tank was disabled and Streich and Lt Schmidt had to escape on foot and rejoin the action late. The tank attack itself was a rout in a trap cleverly set up by General Morshead. The bridgehead corridor was under half a mile wide, and the 25pdrs were placed well back at the end of the corridor, with Portee anti-tank guns (guns on the back of lorries to provide mobility) on each flank, and 1RTR on the eastern flank as well. As the German tanks advanced the defenders held fire. Once the Germans were well into the corridor, the British opened up with a withering barrage of 25pdr fire, followed by fire from the flanks. Under this battering the German 5th Panzer Regiment commander, Oberst Olrich, had no real option but to turn and withdraw, leaving behind 17 of the 36 tanks that had started. This withdrawal in turn left 8th Machine Gun Battalion exposed. Ponath—his men running out of ammunition—ordered a fighting withdrawal through the gap. As he led his men back he was killed; later he was awarded a posthumous Knight's Cross for his brave leadership. The battalion by now had only five officers and 92 men left, having lost over 700 in the previous two weeks of action. With Ponath dead, the survivors surrendered to the Australians and the unit was no more.

Rommel blamed both Streich and Olrich for this debacle, and criticised them for not securing the flanks, but in truth they had insufficient infantry to have done this—only the much depleted 8th Machine Gun Battalion—and there was virtually no supporting artillery and too few tanks to sustain the assault. Rommel himself certainly lost some credibility over this unsuccessful attack (though seemingly not with Hitler), for the wounded Generalmajor Kirchheim and other senior officers privately communicated to OKH that continued attacks with DAK at its present low strength would merely deplete and demoralise it further.

Left: Several abortive attempts were made to take Tobruk in April/May 1941. Here a 10.5cm le FH 18/40 L/28 is seen firing against the beleagured garrision during this period.

Above: Infantrymen of 15th Panzer Division leaving a Junkers Ju52 transport that had flown them up to Derna airfield to bolster up the infantry strength of 5th Light Division in April 1941.

Nevertheless, Rommel personally directed another attack on the Tobruk perimeter on 16 April. This time he used Italian forces, tanks of Ariete Division and an infantry regiment of Trente Division. Some officers of 5th Light were attached as advisers, but essentially it was an all-Italian affair. The chosen point was Ras al Madawar, a raised fortified strongpoint on the southwest corner of the perimeter. The attack was a complete fiasco. Many of the M13 tanks broke down on the way from the start line and most others were knocked out. When the Australian defenders counter-attacked, many of the Italian infantry surrendered, and Rommel's HQ troops knocked out two of the retreating Italian tanks thinking them to be captured vehicles used in a counter-attack.

Meanwhile, 5th Light Division was nursing its wounds, trying to repair and overhaul its equipment, and taking some respite for the previous hectic fortnight of combat and movement. With hard work, 5th Panzer Regiment managed to get 74 tanks repaired and running, half of them PzKpfw IIs, the rest PzKpfw IIIs and IVs. Rommel was now trying to beef up the DAK for another attack on Tobruk in force. Further units of 15th Panzer Division arrived in Tripoli, and the infantry regiments of 15th Panzer were flown by Ju52 transport to Derna airfield, then put under command of 5th Light to give much needed infantry support. Artillery had been another priority, and by careful repairs and drawing on Italian equipment, some 35 batteries were scraped together. At that time, also, more Luftwaffe aircraft of all kinds were beginning to arrive to give a boost to air support, though throughout the desert campaign Luftwaffe strength was always vastly outnumbered by the RAF.

The unsuccessful attacks on Tobruk, and the buccaneering taking of Cyrenaica against OKW and OKH advice in the first part of April, were causing alarm amongst the High Command. Army C-in-C von Brauchitsch, and his chief of staff, Halder, were particularly disapproving and regarded Rommel with some disdain, a jumped-up provincial (he was from Schwabia) rather than a 'traditional' Prussian-style officer like themselves. When the complaints from Kirchheim and others reached them, they sent General Friedrich von Paulus, a deputy chief of staff and quartermaster general (later famous as the Sixth Army commander at Stalingrad), out to North Africa to give them a first-hand report on the situation. He arrived on

27 April for a two-week stay, and made a rather conventional report that was more negative than positive. He noted the severe logistics problem. At that time DAK needed 30,000 tons of stores a month just to get going and up to 20,000 tons more if a big strategic reserve was to be built up. Most of the replenishment stores at the time had to be trucked—or occasionally flown—over 1,000 miles from Tripoli, though there were tiny harbours for small cargo boats at Derna and Gazala. Paulus suggested a new defence line at Gazala to reduce the supply distance, and the abandonment of any plans to take Tobruk or advance on to Egypt. He did commend sending out more supplies, more vehicles, more troops and more guns when they could be spared. This report by von Paulus was obviously influenced by his High Command staff thinking and it was what his bosses wanted to hear.

Rommel ignored the commendations. He knew that reinforcing supplies and men would never come in sufficient numbers, and there would be many losses on the way from Sicily to Tripoli because the British dominated the Mediterranean Sea and the skies over it. He was enjoying fame around the world because of his spectacularly fast campaign in Cyrenaica, which was much admired. While von Paulus was in Cyrenaica, he saw first-hand Rommel's next attempt to take Tobruk in a five-day operation from 30 April to 4 May 1941. It proved to be a failure, but was much better controlled and handled than the previous attempts. Once again Rommel had chosen as the point of the attack Ras el Madawar on the southwest corner of the perimeter. Through the night of 30 April/1 May there was an artillery bombardment, and infantry raids with flamethrowers on the forward Australian defensive positions. There was also a fierce bombing raid by Stukas at sunset. By the time dawn broke, the infantry, mainly from 15th Panzer Division, were through the wire and opened up a 2.5km (1.5-mile) breach, backed up by fire from mortars and infantry guns. At first light the first wave of 5th Panzer Regiment tanks went through the gap. About 2.5km (1.5 miles) back from the perimeter gap they noticed a second defence line behind dry stone walls. It concealed the inevitable 25pdr battery. As they approached this, they ran into a minefield which, even worse, was laid in an echelon pattern so that following tanks that veered either right or left also ran into mines. In only minutes all but two of the 22 tanks had lost their tracks and were stuck only about 500 yards in front of the enemy defence line, from where Australian infantry fired on them with small arms. Fortunately, they didn't use the 25pdrs, partly because these tanks were already immobilised and partly because the gunfire set off more mines. The tank company commander ordered some of the immobilised tanks to fire back at the Australians, and he called in other covering fire from the following infantry and assault engineers. Under fire, the tank tracks were repaired and all except five were able to withdraw, though it took until nearly nightfall before the last tank was recovered.

Below: A British Matilda tank captured by 5th Light Division is added to the strength of 5th Panzer Regiment in the early part of the Cyrenaica campaign. Here the Matilda meets a PzKpfw I, probably one of the regimental command tanks. Also present is a motorcycle despatch rider.

Meanwhile, one platoon of tanks had turned left and run westwards inside the perimeter, but these turned back when they were engaged by fire from the 25pdrs behind the dry stone wall. One tank took a direct hit on its engine compartment, and the crew was captured by the Australians from an adjacent defence point. They, in turn, were captured minutes later by the German assault engineers who had seen what had happened and came to the rescue.

Another more significant wave of 34 tanks (mainly PzKpfw IIs but with a few IIIs and IVs) from 5th Panzer Regiment moved forward into the perimeter breach and turned right, putting up a smokescreen as they ran eastwards inside the perimeter, followed by infantry. They engaged and cleared each Australian defence post in turn with heavy fire, under cover of which the infantry attacked. Two squadrons of A13s of 1RTR were brought up from the east to counter-attack, which they did with some success since they were able to fire from hull-down positions. The 5th Panzer Regiment tanks pulled back about midday to refuel and rearm, then returned to the attack. But they were now hammered by the 25pdrs behind the stone defence line, then counter-attacked again by the A13s, plus some Matildas from 7RTR. In a considerable melee, four British tanks were lost and others severely damaged, but the German tank company also suffered losses and damage, and at nightfall they withdrew back to the Ras al Madawar position. By this time only half of the 5th Panzer Regiment's 70 tanks that went into action that day were still battleworthy, and 5th Light had lost 1,200 dead and wounded, many of these

Below: Desert living conditions could be harsh. Here is a tented camp, better placed than some for it is in the sand dunes near the sea somewhere near the coast road in Cyrenaica.

from the newly arrived 15th Panzer Division infantry unit that had been under command. This was such a costly battle that Rommel could not sustain his attack. He realised that Tobruk was too tough a nut to crack without more forces. Though he held on to the Ras al Madawar position for some months to remind the Tobruk garrison of the DAK's presence, the key units of 5th Light withdrew to lick their wounds, and for the next ten days there was a lull in the action.

Above: Once Benghazi was captured, it became an important German command and supply centre since it had some port facilities. For German troops off duty there was a cinema that was a popular attraction.

OPERATION 'BREVITY'

Ultra intercepts gave the British C-in-C, General Wavell, the contents of the von Paulus report which had been transmitted to OKW in Germany on 12 May. In addition reports from Tobruk indicated how weak the DAK appeared to be. The apparent prospects looked good for the British. If the von Paulus recommendations were acted upon, the DAK would pull back to Gazala and it still did not have all of 15th Panzer Division in place to strengthen it. On 13 May, therefore, Wavell ordered an offensive—Operation 'Brevity'—to start on 15 May. This was to be commanded by Brigadier W. H. E. ('Strafer') Gott. He had already had a clash with Combat Group Knabe—the small force named after its commander, comprising 3rd Reconnaissance Battalion and 15th Motorcycle Battalion, sent in early April to secure the Cyrenaica-Egypt frontier. On 25 April this small group had launched a bold attack against Gott's small frontier guard force, which drew back to Buq Buq leaving the Halfaya Pass in German hands.

For Operation 'Brevity' Gott had under command 22nd Guards (Motorised) Brigade, artillery, 11th Hussars, 7th Armoured Division Support Group, 2RTR and 4RTR which together made up 7th Armoured Brigade. The main units involved had to make a 100-mile move up from Mersa Matruh. The ambitious objective was to sweep the German forces from the border, join up with the Tobruk garrison, and use that as a springboard to push the DAK further west. But it was an embarrassing failure for Rommel had under his command a very effective Wireless Intercept Section (*Fernmeldeaufklärung*) commanded by an astute expert in his field, Lt Seebohm, who time and again was was able to interpret British intentions by good monitoring of the radio traffic. By this means Rommel got wind of the British moves and ordered 5th Light's tanks to the frontier area.

The British attack secured Halfaya Pass easily, for it was held by Italian troops, 500 of whom were captured, though not before their guns had knocked out seven Matilda tanks of 7RTR. Sollum, lightly held, was also taken by a tank attack but as the rest of 4RTR, with infantry support, approached Capuzzo, they were attacked on the flanks by Combat Group Knabe, who disabled seven Matildas by aiming at their tracks. 2RTR formed the left wing of the attack and intended to swing round behind Capuzzo and secure Sidi Azei to cut off the expected German retreat from the border. However, they encountered first a 5th Light motorised infantry column heading for Capuzzo, then 5th Panzer Regiment's tanks following up. With this force now outnumbering the British, whose tank losses had been large, Gott called off the offensive and withdrew through Halfaya Pass, which was left guarded by 3rd Battalion Coldstream Guards and the nine remaining 4RTR Matildas.

Halfaya Pass was strategically valuable, however, and as soon as the newly arrived tanks of 15th Panzer Division could be brought up to Cyrenaica, Rommel used them to increase his available tanks to produce his largest tank force yet. On 26 May he put in an assault that involved a 15th Panzer infantry battalion, with artillery support, attacking from the west; a battalion of 8th Panzer Regiment tanks moving south round the Halfaya Pass escarpment and attacking from the east (ie the British rear); and a 5th Panzer Regiment battalion attacking from the southeast. A company of the latter succeeded in overrunning and capturing a British 25pdr battery, by the not infrequently used ploy of ignoring orders. The company commander requested permission from the battalion commander to eliminate the 25pdrs, which were causing trouble. The battalion commander told him to hold back, but the company commander decided to attack anyway because the guns were such a threat to his tanks. Feldwebel Wilhelm Wendt, who led a charge into the 25pdrs with his PzKpfw IV, was awarded the Iron Cross, First Class, in this action.

With Halfaya Pass under threat from all sides, the Coldstream Guards and 4RTR's Matildas had no option but to make a fighting withdrawal, which they did with some losses, including six of the tanks. Halfaya Pass was once again in German hands.

Despite what amounted to valiant and considerate leadership during the hard fighting of April and May 1941, Rommel decided that Generalmajor Streich, the divisional commander, and Oberst Olrich, 5th Panzer Regiment commander, should be dismissed after the Halfaya Pass action. He also ordered the court martial of one of the panzer battalion commanders who had declined to attack Matilda tanks head on. Rommel undoubtedly wanted some 'new brooms' and he had clashed with both Streich and Olrich several times in

Below: German troops in the background approach a British Matilda tank knocked out by one of the 88s in the Halfaya Pass.

Above: German radio intelligence gathering was good. Here is an early observation post of 3rd Reconnaissance Battalion up by the Cyrenaica border on 21 March 1941 waiting for the main elements of 5th Light Division to catch up. Note the radio mast erected from the eight-wheel *Funkwagen* (radio vehicle) Sd Kfz 232.

the past as previously noted. Streich's fellow officers considered he had been unfairly and meanly treated for he had a good reputation for leadership, bravery, tank handling, politeness and humanity, and Olrich was highly regarded, too. Both had demonstrated their qualities well during the Cyrenaica campaign despite the differences with Rommel along the way.

As Streich's replacement Rommel brought in Generalmajor Johann von Ravenstein (confirmed 23 July 1941), promoted from the command of one of the 5th Panzer Regiment battalions. Von Brauchitsch, the Army C-in-C, was disturbed by such high profile dismissals and suggested command problems be handled more coolly and discreetly. Rommel justified his decisions by saying that both Streich and Olrich had 'failed completely' several times and often criticised his orders.

OPERATION 'BATTLEAXE'

Wavell's early May assessment of German strength and intentions in Cyrenaica encouraged Prime Minister Churchill to send much-needed tank reinforcements for the British Western Desert Force by means of a five-ship fast convoy through the Mediterranean to Alexandria. One ship was sunk en route, but the rest delivered 82 of the new Crusader cruiser tanks, 135 Matildas and—of more limited value—21 Vickers light tanks.

Lt-Gen Noel Beresford-Pierce took over command of Western Desert Force and was directed by Wavell to mount a new major offensive, Operation 'Battleaxe', on 15 June, with the objective of relieving Tobruk and pushing the Germans back to the west of it. The British assessed the DAK to have about 300 tanks available at that time, compared with 200 British tanks. Actually DAK had only about 200, not all fit for service, and only about half these were PzKpfw IIIs and IVs, the rest being light IIs and Is.

By this time DAK had been fully joined by 15th Panzer Division (commanded by Generalmajor Walter Neumann-Silkow) so that the 'Brevity' action had been the last where 5th Light had to bear the full brunt of action alone. From now on it would be truly operating as part of a corps command.

After the recapture of Halfaya Pass on 27 May, Rommel left 15th Panzer Division defending the Cyrenaica-Egypt border area, and pulled 5th Light back to join the siege of Tobruk, with some elements at Gambut further east. 15th Panzer had also arrived with the Pak 38 50mm anti-tank gun, which was a useful addition, and these were mostly deployed in positions between Hafid Ridge (south of Capuzzo) round to Halfaya. A key decision, however, was to deploy the Flak 18 88mm guns of 1st Battalion 33rd (Luftwaffe) Flak Regiment dug into well-protected sangars to guard Halfaya Pass. This was the first deliberate deployment by Rommel of the guns in the anti-tank role, though he had used them briefly in emergency in the 1940 Battle of Arras, and at least once in the Cyrenaica campaign a Flak 88 had been aimed at a tank. The Luftwaffe flak unit was attached to 5th Light. It was the 88s that struck the first decisive blow that wrecked the British hopes for 'Battleaxe'.

The British master plan was for the 4th Indian Division on the right flank (with 4th Armoured Brigade giving tank support) to take Halfaya Pass, while 7th Armoured Division (less 4th Armoured Brigade) approached inland above the coastal escarpment towards an area called Hafid Ridge, where 15th Panzer Division was expected to be. Meanwhile, in the centre, 22nd Guards Brigade was to advance and seize Capuzzo and Sollum, backed by 4th Armoured Brigade who would move on to them after the Halfaya Pass action. With all these objectives secured, 7th Armoured Division was to drive on the 80 miles to Tobruk, and they and Tobruk garrison forces would then force the DAK back on the Derna-Mechili line.

On paper this looked good, but British staff work often made wrong assumptions. In this case, understandably perhaps, the deployment and power of the 88mm guns was overlooked. The approach to the Halfaya Pass at dawn on 15 June was met by silence as though the defenders were unaware of the attack. But at 09.00hrs, when the British Matildas advanced, they were decimated by fire from the 88s sunk deep in their sangars. 'They are tearing my tanks to bits,' were the last words heard over the radio from the commander of C Squadron, 4RTR, which had put in the main attack All the Matildas were destroyed except one, and the follow-up infantry never went in. The towed 25pdr battery intended to have given fire support did not arrive as its vehicles got stuck in sand on the approach.

In the centre, 7RTR of 4th Armoured Brigade enjoyed more success. They did successfully take Capuzzo after some close-quarter fighting. It was quite lightly held and some of Rommel's decoy tanks were encountered.

On the left flank 7th Armoured Division, with some of the new Crusaders as well as the old A13s, made a slow late start, ran into well-concealed 50mm anti-tank guns at Hafid Ridge and suffered losses, but counter-attacked. Attacking a

Right: The British made good use of Portees—trucks carrying 2pdr anti-tank guns. The vehicles shown, however, are improvised Portees, being trucks carrying captured Italian 4.7cm anti-tank guns, here well emplaced in one of the defensive boxes much favoured by the British.

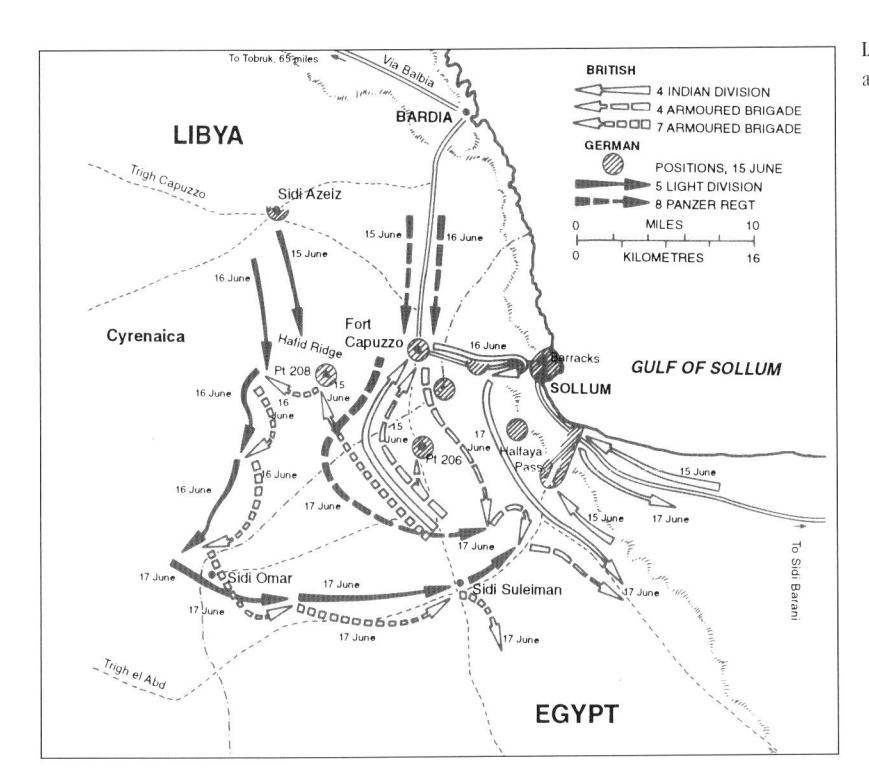

Left: Operation 'Battleaxe'—showing the British attack and the German response.

dummy German leaguer, they were ambushed by some 5th Light tanks and were then counter-attacked again in the evening by a larger 5th Light force before withdrawing back to the border wire to replenish and recover overnight. By now hardly any of the British objectives had been achieved, save for the taking of Capuzzo, and half the British tanks had already been destroyed—some by mines but most by 50mm Pak 38s or the formidable 88s at Halfaya, which could outrange and penetrate any British tank. Rommel had seen British intentions and gained time during the day to rush 5th Light down from Tobruk and Gambut.

Next day, 16 June, Rommel ordered Generalmajor Neumann-Silkow to counter-attack and retake Capuzzo, while von Ravenstein, in his first action as 5th Light commander, was to take his division in a bold swing south of Hafid Ridge to outflank the intended British armoured thrust westward, then circle behind it at Sidi Omar and head for Halfaya Pass to cut off its retreat. This resulted in running battles all day, as the armour of both sides clashed and swerved apart after hard fighting. The British tanks did mighty damage to an unprotected 5th Light supply column, which was virtually destroyed. The hardy Feldwebel Wendt added a Knight's Cross to his Iron Cross that day for spotting and directing fire on a moving British Portee anti-tank battery to prevent it coming into action. A lucky 2pdr shot penetrated his PzKpfw IV and badly wounded his driver and gunner, but did not destroy the tank. Meanwhile, 15th Panzer Division had a tougher time. They found that the British Matilda tanks defending Capuzzo had dug themselves in hull-down during the night and so were well protected. Thirty (out of 80) attacking German tanks were lost.

In view of this, on 17 June Rommel ordered just a token force of 8th Panzer Regiment to stay north of Capuzzo to prevent a breakout, while the balance of the regiment's tanks and other 15th Panzer Division units swept south to join 5th Light in outflanking 7th Armoured Division. The British, fearing a new attack on Capuzzo and being cut off as a result, withdrew from Capuzzo.

All the British units were in confusion and had lost more than half their tanks. DAK's astute radio monitors heard radio traffic calling the Western Desert Force commander, Beresford-Pierce, up to the front for consultation. Rommel interpreted this as meaning that British plans were in disarray, so called on 5th Light to run straight for Halfaya via Sidi Suleman to cut off the withdrawing British, while 15th Panzer Division swung parallel to them south of Hafid Ridge. A determined and stubborn fighting withdrawal and rearguard action by the surviving 15 Matilda tanks of 7RTR, plus bombing attacks by the RAF, slowed up the German advance and gave time for British forces to withdraw along the escarpment—virtually back to where they started. The British lost 80 percent of their tanks to all causes. The German losses were 62 tanks, but 50 of these were recovered and repaired from the battlefield.

This three-day battle was a triumph for Rommel and the DAK and a disaster for the British. Prime Minister Churchill decided a change of command was necessary to bring in new thinking. He appointed General Sir Claude Auchinleck as the new C-in-C Middle East, and sent Sir Archibald Wavell to take Auchinleck's place as C-in-C India.

Both sides made significant changes after 'Battleaxe'. The new British C-in-C took charge on 2 July and staved off Churchill's urgings for a new offensive that summer, calling instead for considerable reinforcements and time to prepare a very large winter offensive. He suggested his expanded forces should include two or three more armoured divisions. This resulted in the setting up of a new command, Eighth Army (effective September 26, but staffed well before that) commanded by General Sir Alan Cunningham. At the time he was a highly regarded national hero, having liberated Italian-occupied Somaliland and Abyssinia (Ethiopia) in spectacular style earlier in 1941. He was also a brother of Admiral Sir Andrew Cunningham, then the successful commander of the British Mediterranean Fleet, whose submarines were making life hard for the DAK by sinking so many of its supply ships. About 270,000 tons of supplies of all kinds were lost in submarine or air attacks through 1941, equivalent to about eight months of basic needs.

Right: A 10.5cm le FH 18 L/28 in action with 75th Artillery Regiment, probably at Mechili in April 1941.

Above: 75th Artillery Regiment Sd Kfz 11 showing sand camouflage roughly applied over the original field grey finish. Note DAK symbol on door.

Cunningham had under command XIII Corps (once Western Desert Force but now reorganised as an infantry corps) and the new XXX Corps, which comprised three armoured divisions or brigades. This segregation into specialised roles at corps level proved to be a basic flaw as tactical flexibility (which was the basis of German success) was severely restricted. In XIII Corps were 1st New Zealand Division, 4th Indian Division, 1st Guards Brigade and 1st Army Tank Brigade, newly arrived from England with one regiment of Valentines and two of Matildas. In XXX Corps were 7th Armoured Division, 4th Armoured Brigade Group, 22nd Guards (Motor) Brigade and 1st South African Division. In reserve was 2nd South African Division.

This huge increase in resources, though not fully up to Auchinleck's desired level, put a powerful British and Commonwealth force in the field with 175,000 men and 756 tanks. There were 259 tanks in reserve and another 96 still en route from Britain. In addition to these forces, 32nd Army Tank Brigade with Matildas was landed by sea at Tobruk in September, and the Australian forces there were withdrawn to Egypt and replaced by British, South African and Polish formations.

There were changes, too, on the German side. Rommel and his DAK were nominally answerable to the Italian C-in-C in Cyrenaica, General Gariboldi, whose staff actually gave Rommel a free hand. Back in Germany the Army Command (OKH) was still extremely nervous of Rommel and his activities. So General Halder had the idea of sending a senior staff officer, Generalmajor Alfred Gause, and a big team of staff officers to be attached to General Gariboldi and his Comando Supremo HQ. They arrived almost without warning on 11 June to be the official liaison team between OKH and the Italian C-in-C. The Italians regarded this as an insult and an intrusion, and Rommel could see it was clearly intended to clip his wings. He outsmarted OKH by putting up a much better, and ultimately very logical alternative, accepted by Army C-in-C von Brauchitsch, that the new Panzergruppe Afrika be formed (effective 31 July 1941) commanded by Rommel with Gause as his chief of staff and Gause's team as the Gruppe staff. In this new arrangement Panzergruppe Afrika would have under command the original DAK (5th Light and 15th Panzer), strengthened by a new German infantry division and the Italian Savona infantry division. The Italian forces would form XXI Italian Corps (with Trente, Brescia, Pavia and Bologna divisions) and XX Mobile Corps (with the Ariete Armoured Division and Trieste Motorised Division). General Gariboldi was replaced by General Bastico, who commanded the Italian forces and on paper was still the C-in-C.

Effectively what this achieved was to give Rommel his head—the opposite to the original OKH intention. In the process it tidied up the problem of assorted Italian units which had previously only had a vague chain of command. Generalmajor Ludwig Crüwell then came out from Germany to replace Rommel as DAK commander.

5TH LIGHT TO 21ST PANZER

Panzergruppe Afrika was officially instituted on 31 July 1941, and a benefit in kind came the way of 5th Light, too, for on the following day, 1 August 1941, it was renamed 21st Panzer Division, reflecting the new DAK status as a true corps of two divisions and support troops. Much of the change was on paper, though there were new staff officers. The 1a was Major von Heuduck, the 1b Hauptmann Böhles and the 1c Oberleutnant Rickert.

Additional units came under command to enlarge the division to something closer to the theoretical establishment of a panzer division. Most important was 15th Motorcycle Battalion, which was transferred from 15th Panzer Division, though the unit had been operating under 5th Light command in any case, right from its arrival as vanguard unit of 15th Panzer. Also from 15th Panzer came 104th Rifle (Schützen) Regiment. Newly formed was 155th Artillery Regiment, which was made up from three existing battalions, the first two with motorised 105mm field howitzer batteries while the third had heavy batteries of 150mm and 100mm K18 guns. 2nd Machine Gun Battalion transferred to 15th Panzer Division on this reorganisation date, and the attached 33rd Flak Regiment who operated the key 88s left the division to become corps troops. During August many of the support companies were reorganised and 'streamlined', and extra service and support units joined including a mobile bakery, butcher, maintenance, supply and repair companies. Divisional HQ was set up at Bardia. As noted earlier, 90th Light (Africa) Division was also formed and came under DAK command during this period.

Below: Crew of a Model 34 8cm mortar in action from a sangar.

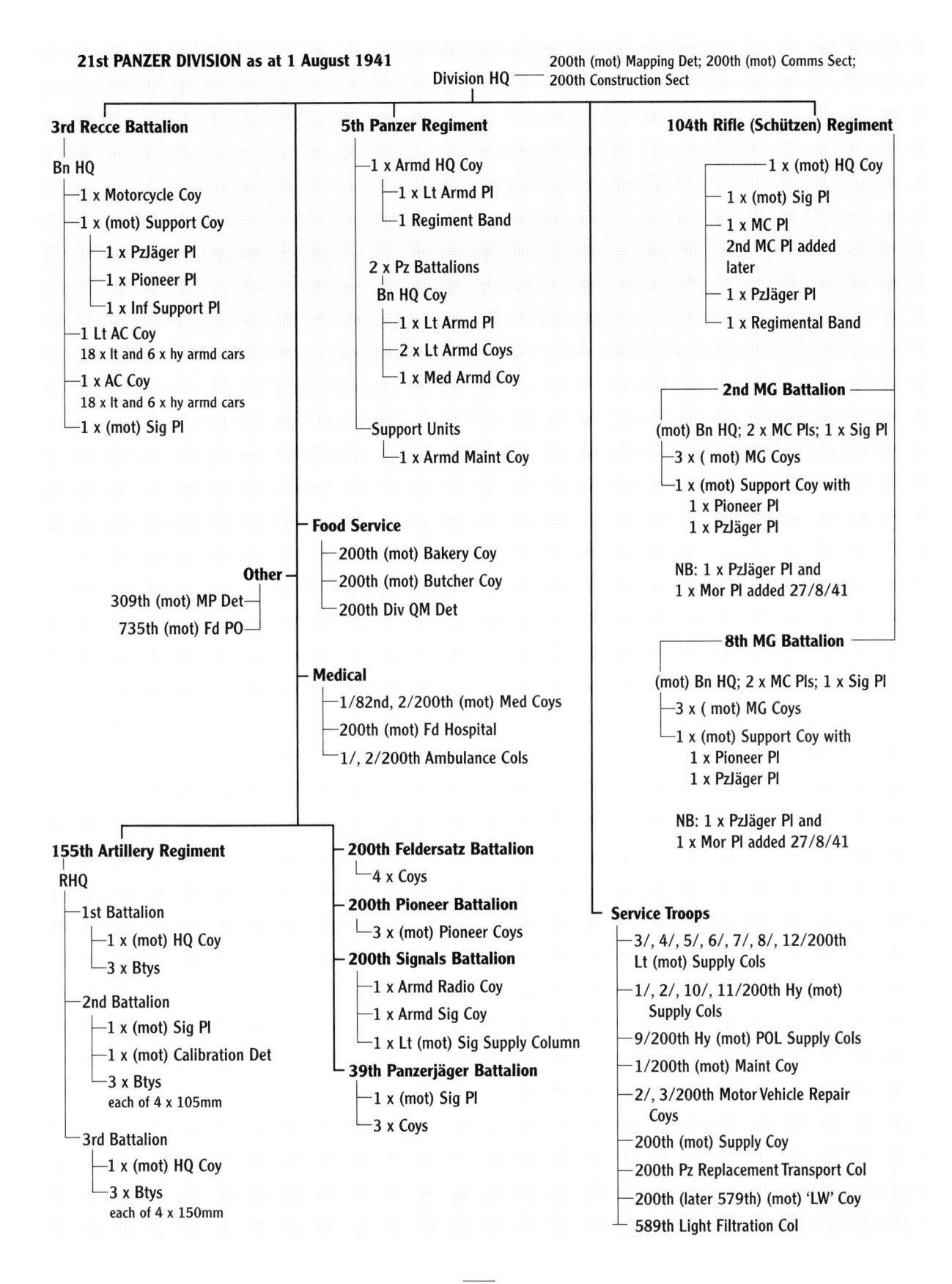

21st PANZER DIVISION as at 1 August 1941

Division HQ — 200th (mot) Mapping Det; 200th (mot) Comms Sect; 200th Construction Sect

3rd Recce Battalion
- Bn HQ
- 1 x Motorcycle Coy
- 1 x (mot) Support Coy
  - 1 x PzJäger Pl
  - 1 x Pioneer Pl
  - 1 x Inf Support Pl
- 1 Lt AC Coy
  - 18 x lt and 6 x hy armd cars
- 1 x AC Coy
  - 18 x lt and 6 x hy armd cars
- 1 x (mot) Sig Pl

5th Panzer Regiment
- 1 x Armd HQ Coy
  - 1 x Lt Armd Pl
  - 1 Regiment Band
- 2 x Pz Battalions
  - Bn HQ Coy
  - 1 x Lt Armd Pl
  - 2 x Lt Armd Coys
  - 1 x Med Armd Coy
- Support Units
  - 1 x Armd Maint Coy

Food Service
- 200th (mot) Bakery Coy
- 200th (mot) Butcher Coy
- 200th Div QM Det

Medical
- 1/82nd, 2/200th (mot) Med Coys
- 200th (mot) Fd Hospital
- 1/, 2/200th Ambulance Cols

200th Feldersatz Battalion
- 4 x Coys

200th Pioneer Battalion
- 3 x (mot) Pioneer Coys

200th Signals Battalion
- 1 x Armd Radio Coy
- 1 x Armd Sig Coy
- 1 x Lt (mot) Sig Supply Column

39th Panzerjäger Battalion
- 1 x (mot) Sig Pl
- 3 x Coys

104th Rifle (Schützen) Regiment
- 1 x (mot) HQ Coy
- 1 x (mot) Sig Pl
- 1 x MC Pl
  - 2nd MC Pl added later
- 1 x PzJäger Pl
- 1 x Regimental Band

2nd MG Battalion
- (mot) Bn HQ; 2 x MC Pls; 1 x Sig Pl
- 3 x (mot) MG Coys
- 1 x (mot) Support Coy with
  - 1 x Pioneer Pl
  - 1 x PzJäger Pl

NB: 1 x PzJäger Pl and 1 x Mor Pl added 27/8/41

8th MG Battalion
- (mot) Bn HQ; 2 x MC Pls; 1 x Sig Pl
- 3 x (mot) MG Coys
- 1 x (mot) Support Coy with
  - 1 x Pioneer Pl
  - 1 x PzJäger Pl

NB: 1 x PzJäger Pl and 1 x Mor Pl added 27/8/41

Service Troops
- 3/, 4/, 5/, 6/, 7/, 8/, 12/200th Lt (mot) Supply Cols
- 1/, 2/, 10/, 11/200th Hy (mot) Supply Cols
- 9/200th Hy (mot) POL Supply Cols
- 1/200th (mot) Maint Coy
- 2/, 3/200th Motor Vehicle Repair Coys
- 200th (mot) Supply Coy
- 200th Pz Replacement Transport Col
- 200th (later 579th) (mot) 'LW' Coy
- 589th Light Filtration Col

Other
- 309th (mot) MP Det
- 735th (mot) Fd PO

155th Artillery Regiment
- RHQ
- 1st Battalion
  - 1 x (mot) HQ Coy
  - 3 x Btys
- 2nd Battalion
  - 1 x (mot) Sig Pl
  - 1 x (mot) Calibration Det
  - 3 x Btys
    each of 4 x 105mm
- 3rd Battalion
  - 1 x (mot) HQ Coy
  - 3 x Btys
    each of 4 x 150mm

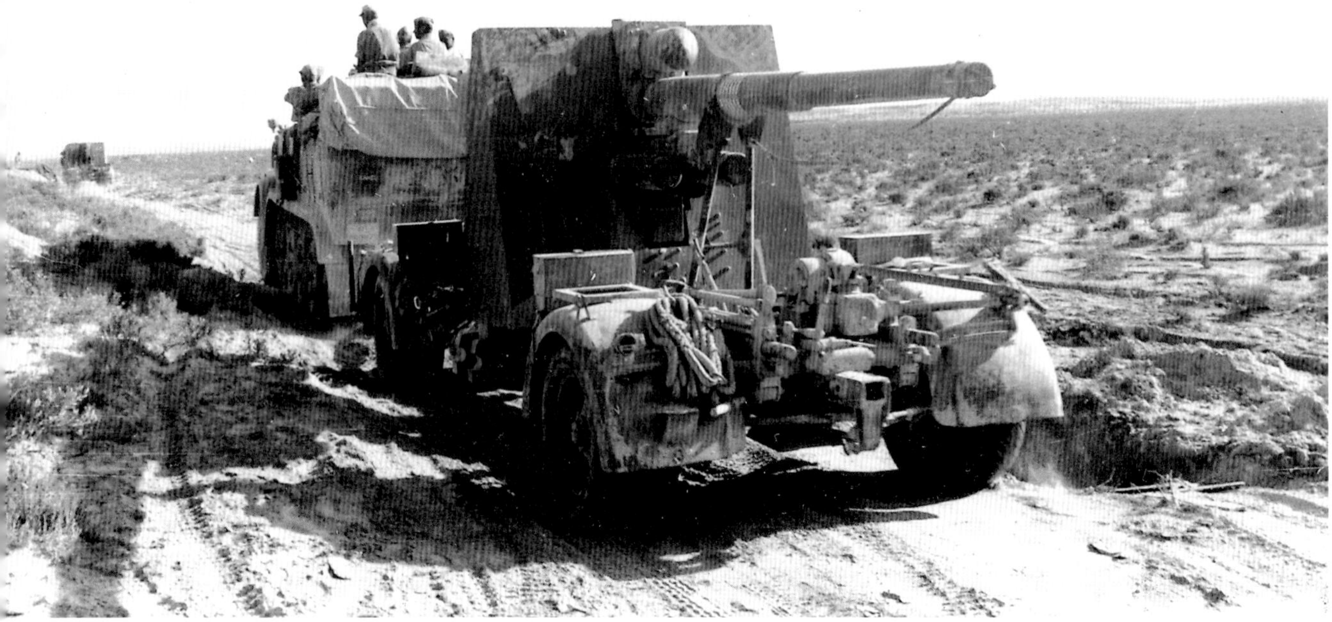

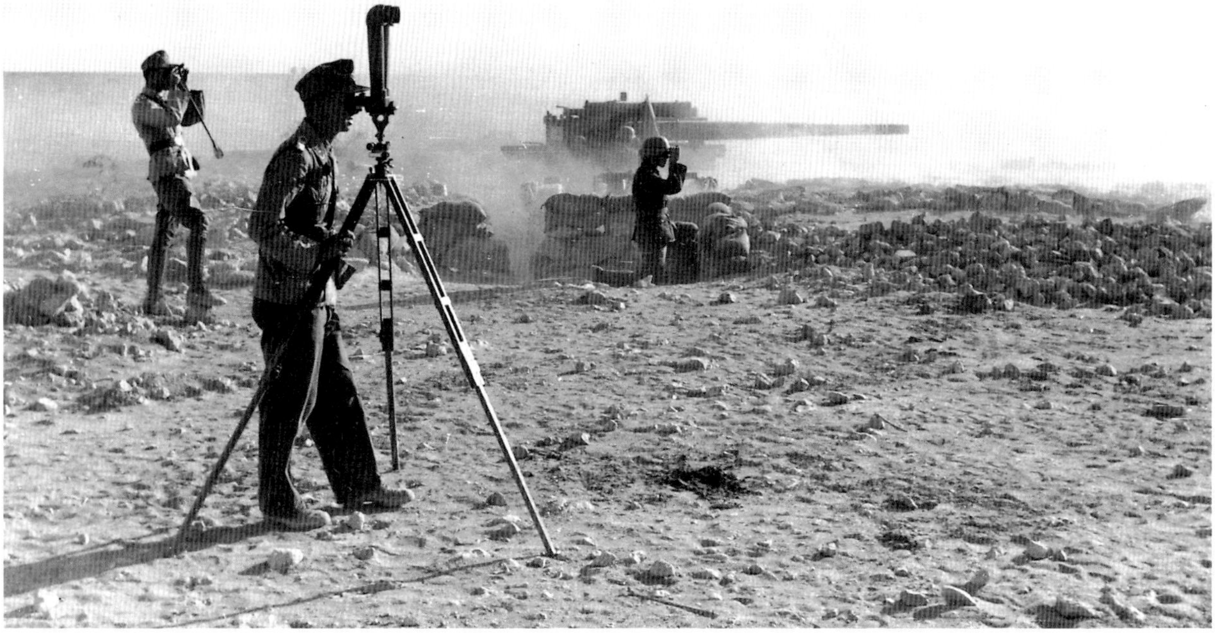

Opposite page, above: The most formidable German weapon in the desert fighting was the 88mm Flak 36, which became much more famous in the anti-tank role. Here is the gun on the move with its halftrack tractor.

Opposite page, below: A Flak 36 emplaced in a sangar going into action against approaching British tanks.

Above: The 88 was highly mobile thanks to its halftrack tractor, and could be moved quickly across the battlefield.

Left: One of the 88s emplaced at Halfaya Pass, with a ring painted on the barrel for every enemy tank destroyed.

Below left: The 88 was at its most effective when fired direct from its wheeled chassis, a technique developed by 21st Panzer Division in the desert fighting.

During the summer months Rommel moved both 21st and 15th Panzer Divisions to the area between Tobruk and the frontier, and ordered extensive exercises to perfect tank attack, support and anti-tank techniques. Most important of these was the idea of firing the 88 direct from its cruciform towing platform without stopping to emplace it. At Halfaya and other defence points, the 88s had been emplaced conventionally, on the ground and off their mobile towing trolleys, though well concealed in sangars. One battery had remained with the tank battalions, however, for possible deployment elsewhere. But in the famous running fire fight with 7th Armoured Division in the Sidi Omar area on 16 June, these mobile 88s had been fired straight from their wheeled towing trailers without being conventionally emplaced. This was done as an extemporised act in the heat of battle, simply because there just wasn't time to emplace the gun first in a running fight. The idea worked, however, and now it became the normal operational technique for using the 88 in the anti-tank role. It gave immense extra fire power and flexibility to the armoured units, particularly at the time when the most powerful tank-mounted gun with DAK was the 50mm in the PzKpfw III.

With its ability to fire straight from its trailer safely proven, the 88 batteries could now move mixed in among the tanks, a facility made possible by the reliable Sd Kfz 7 semi-track tractor, which also carried the crew and ammunition. The exercises tried various ways of deploying the towed 88 with tanks. They could travel inside the group and move to the front, sides or rear as required of a moving formation. If the tanks stopped to to exchange fire, the 88s could be moved out to protect the flanks, or they could move out to the front of the formation take well aimed long range shots at the enemy and swiftly retire again into the heart of the formation.

Skilfully deployed, they proved to have even greater value as an anti-tank weapon than the original deployment at Halfaya had suggested. The previous use of a battery of 88s in the field at the unsuccessful attempt to take Tobruk on 14 April was not in the anti-tank role but in the infantry support role, firing HE 'air bursts' though the results were negligible and the guns were too exposed and not mobile. Now Rommel and all the fighting units of DAK fully appreciated the true value of the 88 as a highly mobile anti-tank weapon of great power, and the 88 became legendary, intensely feared by opposing tankmen.

This flexibility of thought and imaginative and co-operative use of arms was a key factor of the German success in the desert war, and seems to have more than made up for total German lack of desert war experience before 1941. The British may have had a long tradition of service under desert conditions, but they had a much more compartmentalised style of thought. Infantry, tanks and artillery all had their own ways of doing things, and there was little inclination at all levels to integrate and co-operate. For example, the British had readily available much greater numbers of a gun that was similar—and in some ways superior—to the 88. This was the famous 3.7-inch AA gun. It could have been used in the anti-tank role just like the 88, but it was strictly limited to the AA use for which it had been designed. Only on a few unauthorised occasions was it used by the British against enemy tanks. Such was the orthodox thinking at British staff level that it was some months after the 'Battleaxe' debacle that the part played by the German 88s was appreciated. The British staff just hadn't seen that AA guns could be used for anything other than anti-aircraft defence.

Much the same was true when it came to armoured warfare. The Germans had fewer tanks than the British, and many were small PzKpfw Is and IIs. But in German armoured units there was no distinction between 'cruiser' tanks and dedicated

Below: Because of equipment shortages, the Afrika Korps had to be resourceful in repair and maintenance work. Here the engine is removed from an armoured car using a portable gantry.

'infantry' tanks, both of which existed in the British Army, each having different speed limitations. Artillery units were also handled differently. When they were available, artillery units were deployed in fully integrated measure by panzer units, but this was not always the case with British tank formations where artillery was often kept at arm's length.

The myth grew that German tanks were superior to British tanks in armour and firepower. In fact, the differences were not all that great, at least in 1941. The British 2pdr gun was, in fact, marginally superior to the equivalent German 37mm gun. The early versions of the PzKpfw III and IV were not as well armoured as they needed to be, though they were superior in reliability and build quality. But the Matilda tank, slow as it was, was actually feared by the DAK in 1941, for it was too well armoured for their tank guns to penetrate it. It took an 88 to smash a Matilda.

Above: A badly damaged Volkswagen Kfz 1 Kübelwagen is stripped down completely for rebuilding by DAK vehicle engineers.

Formation of Panzergruppe Afrika brought in the need for even more supplies to keep the bigger force going. As before, there were big losses in transit. Early in 1941 30,000 tons a month was the bare minimum just to keep going, but in July-October 1941, 72,000 tons, the average monthly arrival, was inadequate and in some subsequent months it was much lower than this.

Careful husbandry was the order of the day, and fullest use was made of all kinds of captured British stores, fuel and equipment, including lorries, tanks, guns and armoured cars. A well-stocked maintenance base was set up at Gambut in the summer of 1941, and here equipment was repaired, rebuilt, cannibalised and even fabricated. Wrecked tanks were carefully recovered from the battlefield, and by using all these ploys the limited arrival of new tanks and vehicles could be boosted. During that summer, these methods increased the tanks available to 15th and 21st Panzer Division up to around 250 each, with some limited reserve stock as well.

It is also worth noting that, in spite the value of the 88 in summer 1941, new arrivals of these weapons boosted the DAK numbers to only 35. Of these 12 were kept in mobile batteries to operate with the panzer divisions, the other 35 going to Halfaya and other frontier defence areas.

After all this training and preparation the first operation of 21st Panzer Division under von Ravenstein's command proved to be a near disaster. Rommel was planning a decisive assault on Tobruk for the autumn, but got wind of a British build up of forces near the frontier, suggesting than another big offensive was planned. His air reconnaissance showed signs of a big supply dump being built up 15 miles inside the frontier to support a large attacking force. In fact he was being duped by the British—the supply dump was a dummy, even though a real one was built at the same spot later. Rommel ordered 21st Panzer Division to mount a 'reconnaissance in force' to investigate the dump and attack any British forces found in the area. So, on 14 September, the division, accompanied by Rommel in his *Mammut*, swept round Sidi Omar and drove east across the border into Egypt. The border area was guarded by 7th Armoured Division Support Group who, acting

Official tank strength at 18 November 1941	
PzKpfw II	35
PzKpfw III	58
PzKpfw IV	17
Total	110

under orders, withdrew keeping just ahead of 21st Panzer's tanks and out of range. Eventually, 21st Panzer ran out of fuel near Sofafi, but not before discovering the dump to be a dummy and capturing a South African mobile office truck containing operational orders concerned with withdrawal and making no mention of any offensive plans. This, too, was a dupe which convinced Rommel that there was no immediate threat to his build up for the attack on Tobruk.

However, while 21st Panzer was still halted at Sofafi waiting for the supply column to arrive with fuel, they were heavily bombed by large RAF bomber forces, causing losses and a lot of discomfort. As soon as the fuel arrived, Rommel ordered a quick withdrawal, but even he almost got left behind because of a punctured tyre.

OPERATION 'CRUSADER'

British planning for an autumn offensive by the new Eighth Army had been extensive and ambitious, with the plans calling for a much grander version of 'Battleaxe' and with similar intentions—to relieve Tobruk and drive the enemy out of Cyrenaica. It would be on a big scale, using the greatly increased forces now available. Planned for 18 November, it would use XXX Corps to cross the frontier about 40 miles south of the most southerly German outpost at Sidi Omar. XXX Corps would strike northwest for Tobruk, engaging DAK armour which was positioned south and east of it. A force from Tobruk would break out to meet it. Meanwhile, XIII Corps was to engage the frontier defence line, mostly held by Italian divisions by then, outflank it and roll up behind it. Backing up XIII Corps was to be 4th Armoured Brigade now equipped with the fast (35mph top speed) M5 light tank—the Stuart or Honey—from America. 4th Armoured Brigade was to protect XIII Corps against counter-attack from the nearest German panzer division, the 21st, which was based east and west of Gambut at the time. It was hoped 4th Armoured Brigade would draw off 21st Panzer in the direction of XXX Corps' armour.

Below: Operation 'Crusader'—the attempt to break the siege of Tobruk.

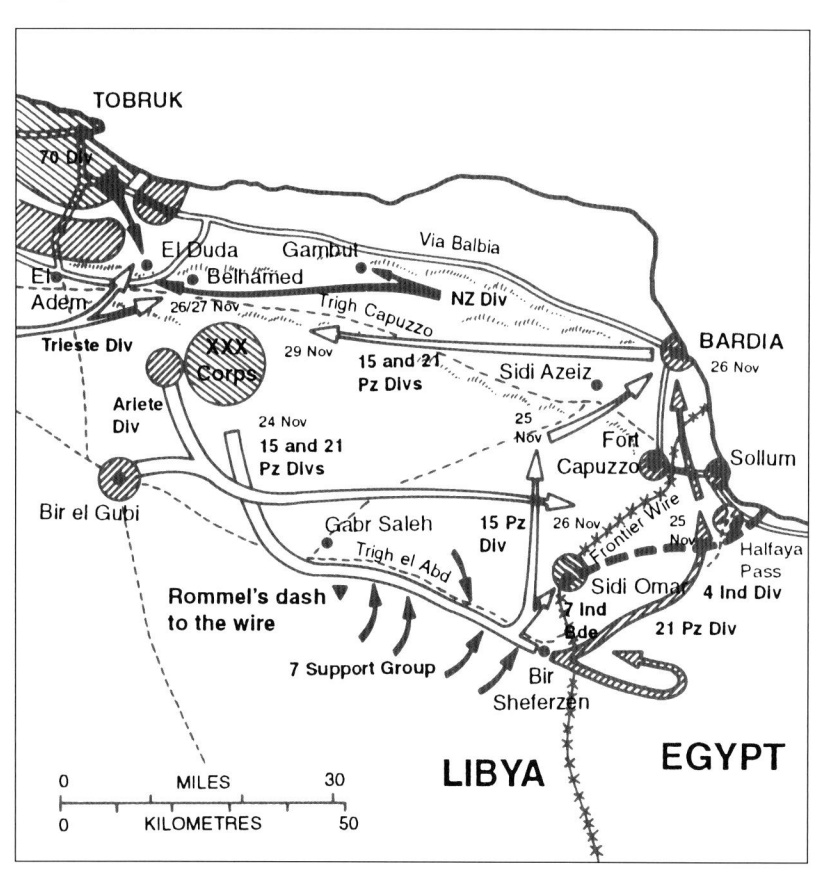

At the time 'Crusader' started, the British armoured units had the massive total of 724 tanks available, 201 of them infantry tanks, the rest cruisers. Additionally, there were some light tanks and armoured cars. By contrast DAK had only 174 effective comparable tanks (PzKpfw IIIs and IVs) since the rest were all PzKpfw I and II lights. The Italian divisions had 146 M13 tanks but by then these were even more of a liability than they had been before. If the Germans had an advantage at all, it was in the availability of 12 88s, in spite of the paucity of their numbers; they were backed up by 96 towed Pak 38 50mm anti-tank guns.

November 1941 was a bad month for the German forces in North Africa. Rommel's plans to retake Tobruk were negated when a resupply convoy from Sicily was completely wiped out on 9 November: nothing got through. In mid-November Rommel flew to Rome, partly to spend a brief leave with his family but also to meet Mussolini and Italian military leaders. Better ways of protecting convoys to Libya was high on the agenda. The assault on Tobruk was rescheduled for 20 November, and then put back to 3 December. A deciding factor was the exceptionally bad weather, a period of rain storms and floods which set in on 16 November along the coast and over the Gebel Akhbar area This prevented air reconnaissance so no British movements could be detected, and the British also kept strict radio silence.

Rommel arrived back from Rome on 17 November and got on with detailed planning for the taking of Tobruk, which included an attack by 21st Panzer from its eastern base near Gambut. Rommel had also sited his HQ there. Because of Ultra intercepts Eighth Army knew of Rommel's intentions and the positions of key formations. So Operation 'Crusader' was brought forward to 18 November, when at dawn, deep in the desert, the armour of XXX Corps moved in the direction of Tobruk. It was spread over a broad front of over 20 miles and 7th Armoured Division alone was spread over an area of 100 square miles. The 7th Armoured Division armoured cars were in the van of this big formation, acting as a reconnaissance force.

None of this was spotted or expected by the Germans. When first seen by an armoured car patrol of 15th Panzer west of Sidi Omar at about 10.30hrs, the forward British units were reported to Rommel as a 'reconnaissance in force' and he was still noting it as that two days later on 20 November after considerable fighting had already taken place. The XXX Corps' columns pressed on, still unchallenged. However, as they crossed the area west of Sidi Omar, they started to slow up as they ran into the nasty rain and mud of the coastal area weather system.

Against 'Crusader', it was 3rd Recce Battalion of 21st Panzer who were first in action. The Stuarts of 4th Armoured Brigade, which had covered the southern flank of XIII Corps, pulled into their leaguer between Sidi Omar and Gabr Saleh at 17.00hrs, and in the dusk clashed with an armoured car patrol of 3rd Recce. Some of the Stuarts pursued the patrol towards Derna, and the armoured cars reported '200 tanks attacking'. When von Ravenstein first heard the morning report of tanks being spotted by 3rd Recce Battalion, he sent a tank company and artillery battery

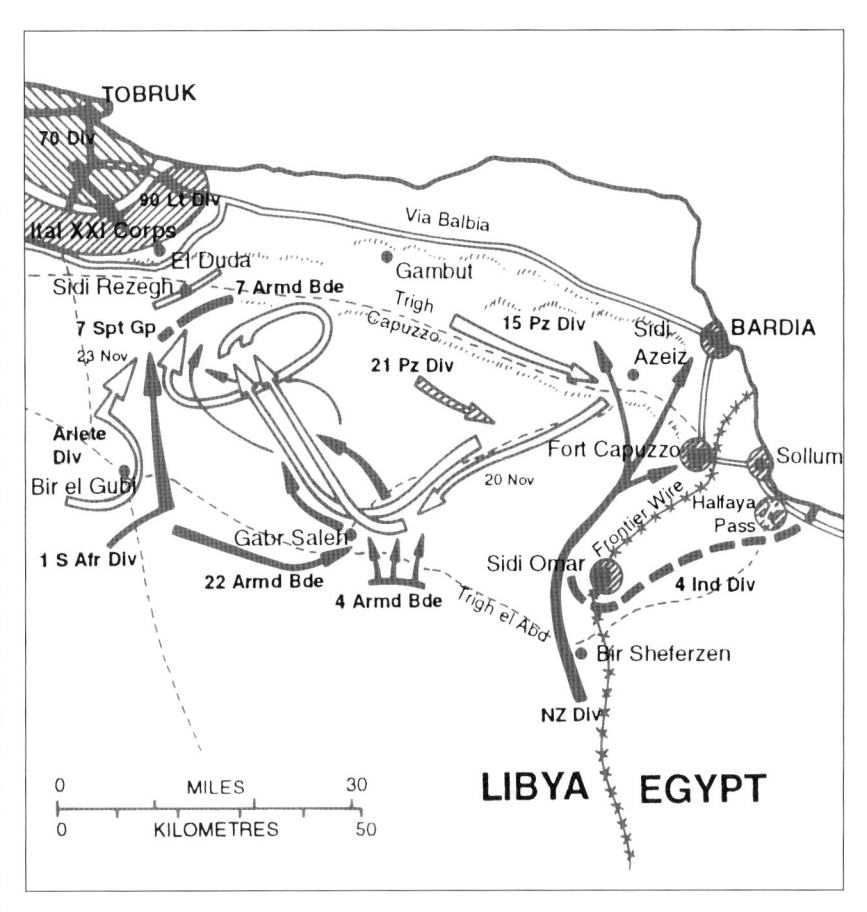

Above: Operation 'Crusader'—Rommel counter-attacks, but he would be forced to pull back his troops to El Agheila by the end of 1941.

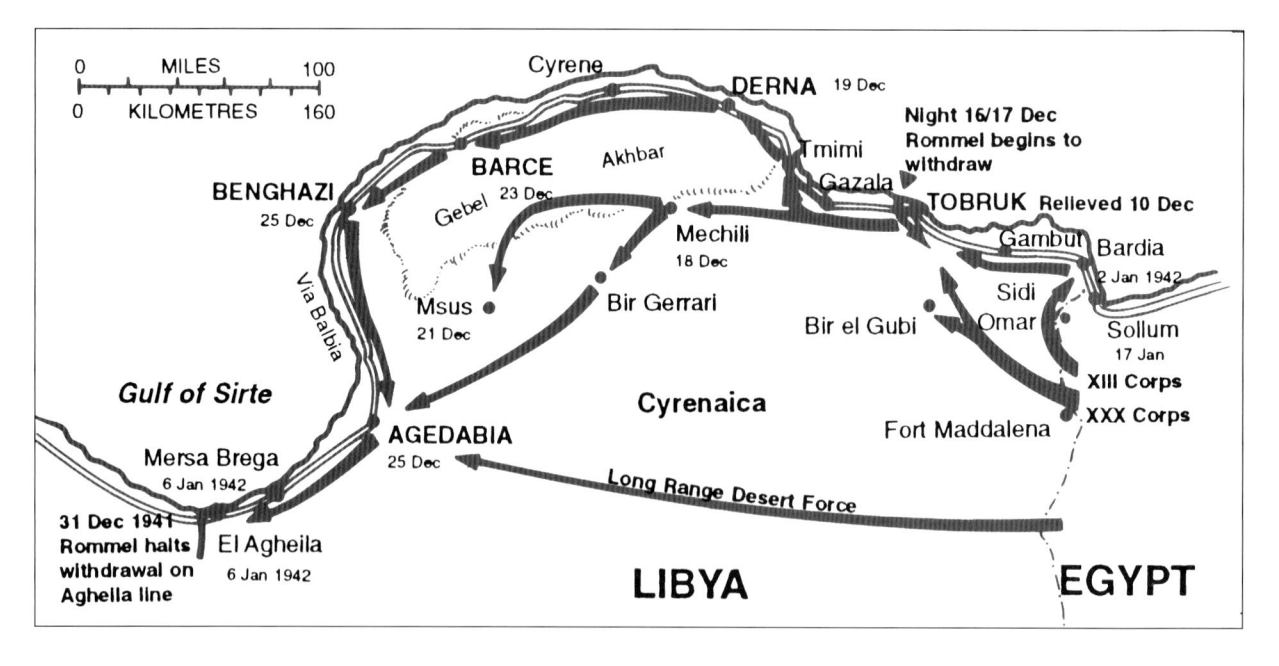

Above: The aftermath of Operation 'Crusader'—Rommel is forced to withdraw.

south to back up the armoured cars, and when he received the 3rd Recce Battalion's signal in the evening he planned to send 5th Panzer Regiment south overnight to attack the 4th Armoured Brigade Stuarts at Gabr Saleh.

However, Rommel countermanded this order and still maintained there was no threat. He thought it a feint or, at best, a diversion to dissuade him from attacking Tobruk. Even detailed movement information gleaned from XIII Corps prisoners taken at the border by the Italians failed to convince him. Hence, there were no German counter-attacks on 19 November, but there were limited British forays in the west including the capture of Sidi Rezegh airfield and the movement of 7th Armoured Brigade up to Sidi Rezegh, just south of Tobruk.

General Crüwell interpreted the attack on 3rd Recce, and a second clash with them, as an indication of the British line of attack. He ordered von Ravenstein to form a special force—5th Panzer Regiment with 12 105mm howitzers and four of the 88s—to move south from Gambut to Gabr Saleh and attack 4th Armoured Brigade there. This force was called Battle Group Stephan after its commander. Rommel watched the group depart that afternoon.

Chasing 3rd Recce's armoured cars and carrying out recce sweeps themselves had split up the 4th Armoured Brigade units. Battle Group Stephan encountered 8th Hussars late in the afternoon northeast of Gabr Saleh. In the vicious fire fight that followed, 20 Stuarts were knocked out, many by 88s using the new tactic of firing from their carriages. 5RTR was called up to aid the Hussars and lost another three Stuarts—though 12 of the knocked out tanks were later recovered. Battle Group Stephan lost only three tanks, with four more damaged but recoverable. The two sides withdrew for the night, but Battle Group Stephan, who had planned to move to Sidi Omar, was now stuck awaiting fuel from its supply column.

Crüwell assumed that 4th Armoured Brigade was the main British force and moved 15th Panzer and the rest of 21st Panzer south to attack. At dawn on 20 November the elements of 4th Armoured Brigade continued to engage Battle Group Stephan in what became a running fight. Eight more Stuarts were knocked out and four German tanks, two of them PzKpfw IIs. After two hours Battle Group Stephan moved off to the northwest to rendezvous with the rest of the division, now advancing southwards. The British thought they were withdrawing, beaten. By now 21st Panzer needed to refuel, so the rest of the day's fighting was done by 15th Panzer alone, leading to more heavy tank losses for 4th Armoured Brigade.

By now Rommel had belatedly realised the full British intention and ordered the DAK to move west at dawn to strike at 7th Armoured Brigade and other units drawn up at Sidi Rezegh. 15th and 21st Panzer Divisions did this so successfully in the dark, that when dawn broke 4th Armoured Brigade (and 22nd who had by now arrived in support) were surprised to find them gone, with the last units just disappearing west. A limited pursuit was called off and not resumed until that afternoon, when it then ran into rain and deep mud which slowed progress.

By the time 4th and 22nd Armoured Brigades arrived at Sidi Rezegh at dusk on 21 November, it was too late to help 7th Armoured Brigade which had been all but wiped out that morning. The day had started with 7th Armoured being ordered to move north to meet the Tobruk breakout force at El Duda. The British assumed that the apparent withdrawal of Battle Group Stephan the previous day meant the end of the German threat. However, just before the attack was about to begin, two big German tank groups were seen coming in on the right flank. These were 21st and 15th Panzer Divisions in full cry. 7th Armoured Brigade was, therefore, forced to split its resources; 7th Hussars and 2RTR moved east to meet and hold the approaching Germans while 6RTR alone led the charge for Tobruk. This was a fatal move. 6RTR lost 39 tanks in a futile charge. To the east, 7th Hussars were virtually wiped out by 21st Panzer in a brutal running fight marked by the bold use of 88mm and 50mm anti-tank guns often shielded behind lorries, and with the 88s firing on the move. By the end of the day, only 12 7th Hussars tanks, some damaged, were left running. Meanwhile, 16 tanks of 21st Panzer attacked 7th Armoured's Support Group, but here, in a static fight near Sidi Rezegh airfield, they had less success for they met their old bogey, 25pdrs firing over open sights. Manned by 60th Field Regiment, RA the 25pdrs succeeded in holding 21st Panzer off.

The Germans called for a Stuka attack on the guns, but this failed due to inaccurate bombing. A counter-attack made by five support and HQ company Crusaders was unsuccessful as all were hit. Further fire by the 25 pdrs held off the 21st Panzers tanks, but ammunition was running low on both sides. As the German tanks closed in, 22nd Armoured Brigade arrived from Gabr Saleh and the Germans withdrew. 2RTR was engaged by 15th Panzer Division and met a similar fate to the 7th Hussars, making it a black day indeed for 7th Armoured Brigade. While all this was going on, Rommel himself had got together a scratch force of reserves from Gambut and used them to repulse the British breakout from Tobruk.

At this stage in the operations, XXX Corps had taken such a pasting in its attempt to relieve Tobruk and bring DAK's tanks into a set-piece battle that a more prudent commander might have been inclined to call it a day and withdraw gracefully. Unfortunately, the Eighth Army commander did not have the full story. He had received optimistic reports of many German tanks destroyed and enemy movements westwards, but the full story of high British losses was still unknown thanks to scattered units and poor communications. The failure to link up with the Tobruk Garrison displeased him, and he suggested bringing up the 1st South African Division from Bir Gubi to help in another attempt on the morrow.

DAK's leaders decided to move away and reposition overnight. Crüwell wanted to move 21st Panzer and 15th Panzer back near their base at Gambut where their supplies were, but Rommel had now seen what was going on and had other ideas. He ordered them to form a defence line facing south along the escarpment from El Duda to Belhamed, so putting themselves between Tobruk and the British. Crüwell

Above: Motorcycle troops performed admirably in the reconnaissance role for the Afrika Korps. This photograph shows the 8th Machine Gun Battalion arriving in Tripoli. Note tactical numbers on sidecars.

modified this idea by placing only 21st Panzer there, and positioning 15th Panzer to the east of the British and south of Gambut. On 22 November the tail end of these movements was spotted by the British tanks and a few even exchanged fire as the Germans pulled away. The movements were interpreted by the British as a withdrawal, so the British tanks remained in the Sidi Rezegh area, mostly near the airport. They included 22nd Armoured Division, who had come late on the scene and had so far avoided major engagements. The chance was too good to miss. Rommel told von Ravenstein to attack 7th Armoured Support Group and other units at the airport that afternoon.

So, on the afternoon of 21 November, 21st Panzer's 155th Rifle Regiment put in a brisk infantry attack from the north, engaging the British infantry protecting the airport. Fire support came from Artillery Group Böttcher, an army artillery force Rommel had assembled to bombard Tobruk. Meanwhile, one tank battalion of 5th Panzer Regiment swept around Sidi Rezegh and charged the airport from the west. In the vigorous defence of the airfield that followed, 7th Armoured Support Group's commander, Brigadier Jock Campbell, won the VC. Tanks of 22nd Armoured Brigade tried counter-attacks but were ineffective in the smoke and confusion. Some of them fired at the approaching tanks of 4th Armoured Brigade by mistake as they, too, came in to counter-attack. Von Ravenstein's tanks were, of course, ably supported by his anti-tank guns in their flexible role. In the smoke, dust and carnage, the British units had little option but to withdraw, and they retreated

Right: A 15.5cm K419(f) in action bombarding Tobruk as part of Artillery Group Böttcher. This was a captured French type highly regarded by the Germans.

Left: A battery of 15cm K408(i) guns in action against Tobruk, again with Artillery Group Böttcher. These were Italian guns also used by DAK.

south of the airfield over a protecting ridge. As dusk fell, however, 15th Panzer arrived from the northeast and caused extra chaos. By the end of the action 22nd Armoured Brigade was down to 34 running tanks and 7th Armoured only had 15. German tank losses were very few. As a bonus, 15th Panzer also captured the HQ and staff of 4th Armoured Brigade in the night attack, but this was more than offset by the capture, on the 23rd, of the DAK's entire communication centre and staff (and valuable cyphers) from their base near Gambut as 6th New Zealand Division moved in from the XIII Corps front.

That day, 23 November, was a Sunday—*Totensonntag* (Remembrance Sunday) in the German calendar. It proved to be an apt name for it saw huge carnage and losses inflicted on both sides. Rommel ordered that the remaining 7th Armoured Division forces south of Sidi Rezegh be crushed by encirclement. Crüwell did this by charging 15th Panzer Division, plus 21st's 5th Panzer Regiment, down from the north, sweeping west, and joining up with the Italian Ariete Division coming up from the southwest.

British tanks and trucks were dotted everywhere and the shooting was wild on both sides. Crüwell did not have Rommel's instinct for wise commitment. He lined up his tanks, the Ariete Division and 15th Rifle Regiment in trucks and charged them northwards through the British forces. It was spectacular but wasteful, for it gave unnecessary exposure to his tanks. German casualties and losses were heavy, including 72 tanks out of the 162 that attacked. The British were decimated, too, but at heavy cost to the DAK. Rommel now took charge and decided to capitalise on the destruction and disarray of the British by making a dash to the border in a diversionary but spectacular sweep, with his command car leading 21st Panzer and 15th Panzer following along behind. The column at one time was 40 miles long. Back in the border area at the time things were quiet. Cunningham and his corps commanders were having a conference near the border and staff cars and trucks were parked everywhere. Suddenly, out of the blue, they found Rommel and his tanks bearing down on them and everyone scattered and ran east for Egypt, including the generals in what was later jokingly called the 'Matruh Stakes'!

However, the DAK was too depleted for Rommel's sweep to do much damage, but it had a good psychological effect. In military terms it was questionable—

spectacle for spectacle's sake. It was in the skirmish actions of this sweep (24–27 November) that the DAK finally found a way of tackling the 25pdrs that had given so much trouble by firing over open sights. They found the best technique was to give the batteries a plastering of HE from the short 75mm guns of the PzKpfw IV platoons, if necessary doing it over and over again until the crews were killed or cowed. Then the tanks would go in, aiming to crush the gun trails under their tracks.

The 'Crusader' offensive had been so clumsily handled that Auchinleck, the British C-in-C, was persuaded Cunningham was too demoralised to continue. He replaced him, therefore, with his own chief of staff, Maj-Gen Sir Neil Ritchie. The Sidi Rezegh battles had also exhausted and depleted the German side. Rommel's divisions on their border sweep had only shaky communications with Panzergruppe HQ due to the loss of the DAK signal centre. Faulty communications led to mistakes. Tobruk was now close to being relieved by the New Zealanders under General Bernard Freyberg coming up from the XIII Corps' front. In Rommel's absence, part of the Tobruk garrison managed a breakout. Elements of 21st Panzer on the border got the message and headed back to Tobruk. Rommel only got the message later and brought the rest of 21st Panzer, plus 15th Panzer, back with him. A further might battle, known as 2nd Sidi Rezegh, took place, yet again around the battered airfield area. This stretched over two days, 27–29 November, and was bloody indeed. The DAK tanks plus Ariete Division surrounded and pummelled the New Zealanders and the fighting was fierce.

During this, 21st Panzer suffered a setback on 29 November when von Ravenstein, en route for a meeting with Crüwell, lost his way and his car ran into an outpost of 25th NZ Battalion where he was captured. The wily British treated him well. He had lunch with Auchinleck's Director of Military Intelligence (during which his tent was 'bugged') and from all that he said it was deduced how hard pressed the DAK was, how bad communications were and how difficult Rommel could be to work for! Oberstleutnant G. G. Knabe took temporary command of 21st Panzer after von Ravenstein's capture, until Rommel appointed Generalleutnant Karl Böttcher commander the next day, switching him from command of the army

Below: The Sd Kfz 250/10 carried a 3.7cm Pak 36 gun and was issued to some motorised infantry company or platoon leaders to give fire support during an attack.

Above: A VW Kfz 1 Kübelwagen of a motorised infantry battalion on a scouting mission near Gazala in the summer of 1942.

artillery group. The British armoured brigades had had time to recover and had also received some new tanks. They attacked the DAK from the south on 30 November but not in a co-ordinated or effective way.

For the rest of 2nd Sidi Rezegh 21st Panzer was engaged from the east while 15th Panzer was sent by Rommel in a classic encircling punch that virtually crushed the brave New Zealanders and restored the Tobruk siege. But it was a Pyrrhic victory for Rommel. There was a lull in the fighting on 1 December and Panzergruppe Afrika sat tight to see what the British would do. Probing attacks to the border area on 3 December found they were still there. In fact, under Ritchie Eighth Army had found a new optimism, and more reinforcements were coming up from Egypt. Rommel realised that the Eighth Army was capable of mounting more attacks and so, on 4 December, he decided to cut his losses, abandon Tobruk and pull his forces back to El Adem. Eighth Army moved up only to find the Germans still withdrawing as Rommel now took his tanks back to the Gazala line. By 11 December all of Panzergruppe Afrika was back at Gazala, save stragglers and some isolated posts at Bardia and the frontier, and was now down to only 40 operational tanks.

Operation 'Crusader' had unexpectedly achieved its objective of driving the enemy out of Cyrenaica. The German defensive line, the Gazala Line, was shaky because it could be easily outflanked. This Eighth Army tried to do, but ineffectively, and weak attempts were repulsed by 15th Panzer. Gazala was clearly

Below and opposite: **The 'Cauldron'**
After the 'Crusader' battles, Eighth Army withdrew to a defence line comprising minefields and defended 'boxes' set up between Gazala on the coast and Bir Hacheim inland. Behind this line were further boxes, including 'Knightsbridge' and El Adem. Even though the armoured divisions were disposed to the rear, this defence line was extremely static. After three months of inactivity, during which DAK had received reinforcements and new tanks, Rommel launched an ambitious attack on the Gazala line on the night of 26/27 May, achieving considerable surprise as Ultra reports of DAK preparations had not been entirely believed by Eighth Army. While Italian forces engaged the Gazala line at the coast, 15th and 21st Panzer Divisions, with 90th Light, moved fast round the flank at Bir Hacheim and turned north. Eighth Army was unprepared for this and DAK took full advantage, 21st Panzer bypassing 'Knightsbridge' and reaching Point 209, only nine miles from the coast road. But this overstretched DAK's supply lines, and lack of fuel and late but determined Eighth Army resistance brought the advance to a halt. On 29 May Rommel personally led in a supply column from Bir el Harmat to refuel the tanks. DAK was too exposed, however, and withdrew too vulnerable, however, so on 16 December Rommel pulled all his forces back to Mersa Brega and El Agheila, which was an area easier to defend and nearer to his supply lines—and the original starting point back in February.

On 19 December, as the Germans pulled out, a convoy arrived at Benghazi with much needed new tanks. With these 15th Panzer clashed with 22nd Armoured Brigade at El Agheila in two sharp engagements on 28 and 30 December, destroying 60 British tanks in two battles and showing that even in retreat DAK still had very sharp teeth.

1942—YEAR OF THE CAULDRON

In the early months of 1942, the German supply situation improved. Malta was put under siege with heavy air attacks, and as the British concentrated on its defence more convoys of stores and equipment were able to reach Rommel's forces. While the British prepared Operation 'Acrobat' to drive the Germans back to Tripoli, Rommel launched a surprise lightning strike with DAK, including 21st Panzer, which took Cyrenaica again, so he was back in Derna by 3 February 1942. Meanwhile, 21st Panzer had a new commander, appointed on 30 January—Generalmajor Georg von Bismarck.

The British and Commonwealth troops were well established at Gazala and this was the scene of the next great battle on 27 May. Rommel used his famous outflanking tactics here, and 21st Panzer was in the centre of a three-division

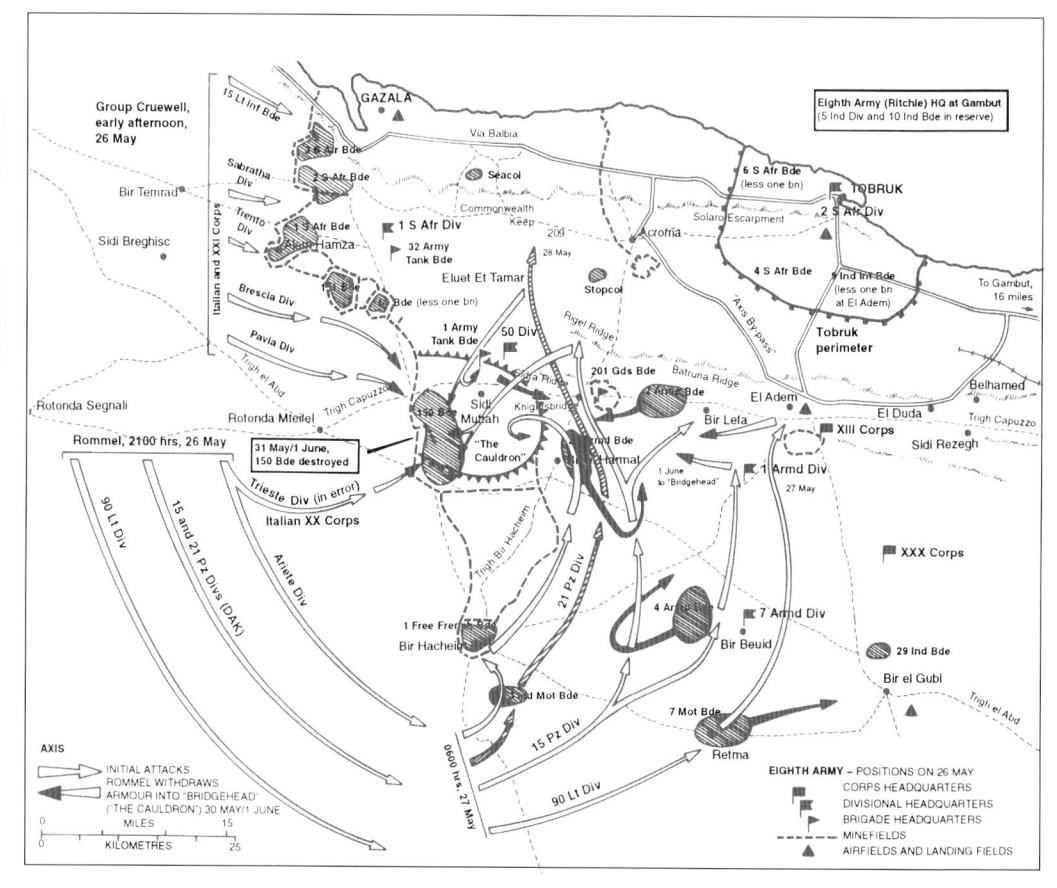

Official tank strength at 25 May 1942

PzKpfw II	29
PzKpfw III	122
PzKpfw IV	19
PzBefWg	4
Total	110

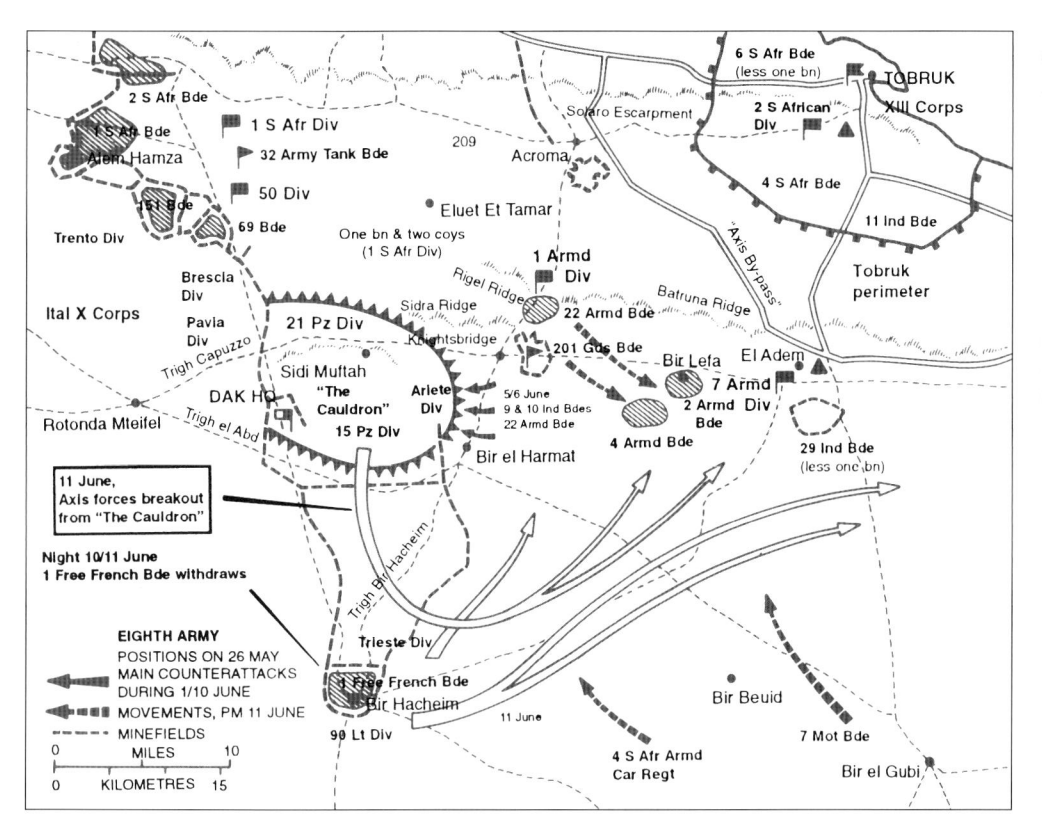

attack on 7th Armoured Division. This developed into a frantic fire fight. For the first time the British were using the Grant (M3 medium) tank from America with its useful, though limited, 75mm gun. In this battle 21st Panzer nearly succeeded in taking the key 'Knightsbridge' box, but lost too many tanks due to the unexpected encounter with the Grants. By 5 June the bloody Gazala fighting had reached the stage known as 'The Cauldron'. During the battle, 21st Panzer secured the key Sidra Ridge from which counter-attacks could be staged. While 21st Panzer held this feature Rommel, used his other divisions to 'roll up' the British forces and win the day. British tank losses were huge, German much lighter.

As the British withdrew, Rommel finally took Tobruk in another three-pronged divisional attack. For this, on 20–21 June, 21st Panzer formed the spearhead between 15th Panzer and 90th Light. In an attack from the southeast, 21st Panzer ran straight through to seize the town and the seaport, the brisk action ending with their tanks on the seafront. The flank divisions, meanwhile, took on the dogged defenders inside the perimeter. Nearly 35,000 prisoners were taken in this attack. Demoralised, Eighth Army fell back. But Rommel's forces were weak, too, dependent on British stores and vehicles to keep going. 21st and 15th Panzer only had 44 tanks between them, and when the Germans crossed into Egypt they estimated that four-fifths of their transport was British.

The Eighth Army decided to fall back to a defence line at Mersa Matruh but they had hardly reached there when Rommel struck on 26–27 June. In this action 21st Panzer was again the spearhead of a three-pronged assault, sandwiched between 90th Light and 15th Panzer. They were key to rolling up the British rear (with Rommel riding with them) and Eighth Army now pulled back in some disarray, establishing a defence line at Alamein—at this stage no more than a series of loosely linked boxes. Rommel attacked on 1–3 July, but resolute British

back to a bridgehead between Sidi Muftah and Bir Hacheim. On 1 June Rommel attacked again while Eighth Army was still slowly organising a counter-attack. Bir Hacheim box was cut off, as was the Sidi Muftah box. The bridgehead around this box was called the 'Cauldron', and was the scene of the fiercest fighting. Rommel deployed 21st Panzer to the north holding the key Sidra Ridge, 15th Panzer to the south and Ariete Division in the centre. On 5 June Eighth Army counter-attacked in a frontal assault on the bridgehead. Rommel outflanked it from the south (with 15th Panzer and 90th Light); Bir Hacheim was taken, and on 11 June 21st Panzer moved east to attack the Eighth Army northern flank units. This pincer movement was a disaster for Eighth Army and cut off 'Knightsbridge'. 21st Panzer Division captured the key Rigel Ridge and on 13/14 June Eighth Army pulled back, eventually to Alamein. By this time it had only about 50 cruiser and 25 infantry tanks left.

Right: Alam Halfa

After the battle at Mersa Matruh, Eighth Army pulled back to Alamein where Auchinleck planned to make the decisive 'no retreat' stand which would prevent Axis forces taking all of Egypt. Forty miles inland from Alamein was the impassable Qattara Depression forming a natural boundary. It was neither possible nor desirable to build a continuous defence line, so the Alamein line was actually held by a series of four defended 'boxes' but with mobile divisional columns held back in the desert for flexible deployment. The southern flank of the line—about 30 miles inland—was open, though strongly mined. Rommel decided to attack the Alamein position on 1 July 1942, before Eighth Army had time to strengthen its defences. In what became known as the First Battle of Alamein, Rommel planned to cut-off and bypass the Alamein box on the coast with 90th Light, and then drive 15th and 21st Panzer Divisions south behind the British lines. However, sturdy defence by the Deir el Shein box and the arrival of mobile columns held up DAK. Next day Rommel changed plans and ordered 15th and 21st Panzer to head east along Ruweisat Ridge, then head for the coast. Superior numbers of British tanks foiled this by attacking DAK's southern flank. Skilful use of 88s knocked out many British tanks, but DAK suffered even more, and was down to to only 26 tanks when the advance was halted. The British flank attack was not pressed home with vigour, however, allowing DAK to pull back with 21st Panzer covering the retreat.

In July DAK received reinforcements, including more divisions and more tanks. Fighting continued in early July with British probes westwards from Alamein and a contest for Ruweisat Ridge involving 21st Panzer Division, but eventually this petered out. Rommel's last attempt to outflank and 'roll up' Eighth Army was at Alam Halfa, 30 August–1 September 1942. DAK now had 166 PzKpfw IIIs, 73 with the long 50mm gun, and 37 PzKpfw IVs, including 27 'Specials' with the 75mm gun. Rommel attacked by night through the minefield on the southern flank of the Alamein line with 15th and 21st Panzer on the right flank. The minefields were denser than expected, slowing the advance, and in a mortar attack von Bismarck, commander of 21st Panzer, was killed. Surprise was lost. DAK was held up by 22nd Armoured Brigade and harried by 7th Armoured Division.

Short of fuel and opposed by superior numbers, as well as being exposed to heavy RAF bombing, Rommel withdrew to six miles east of his original start line. The only good thing to come from the battle was confirmation of the superiority of the PzKpfw IV 'Specials'. In the tank battles Eighth Army lost 69 tanks against 49 for DAK.

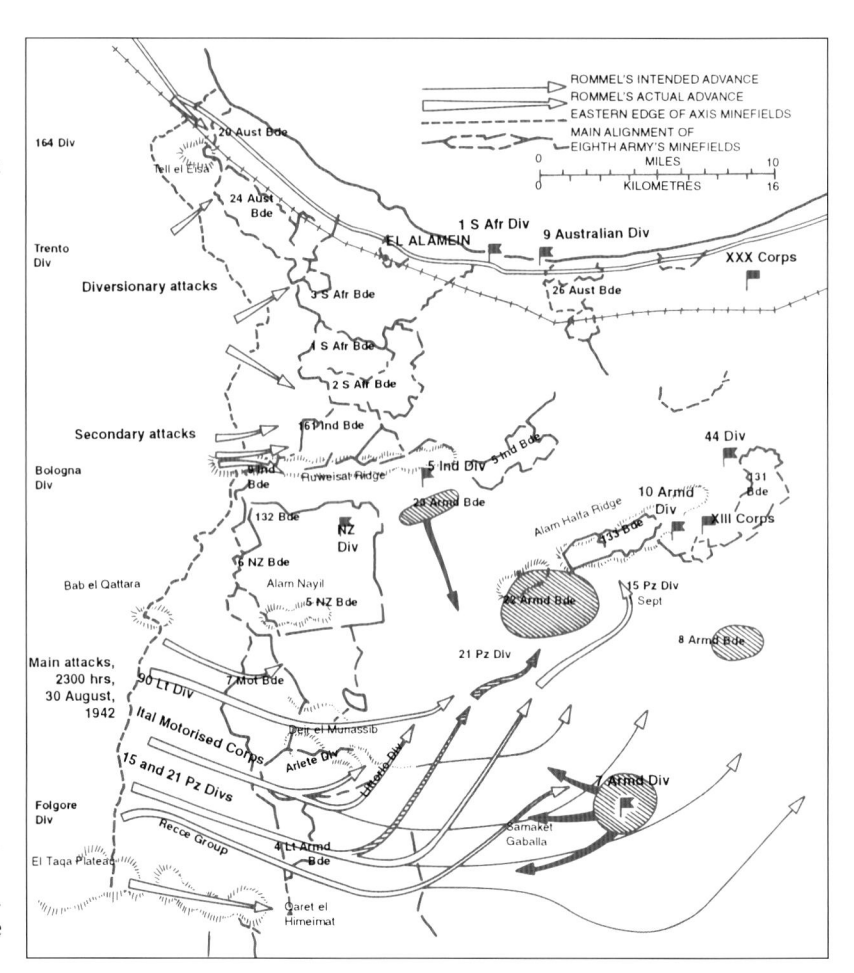

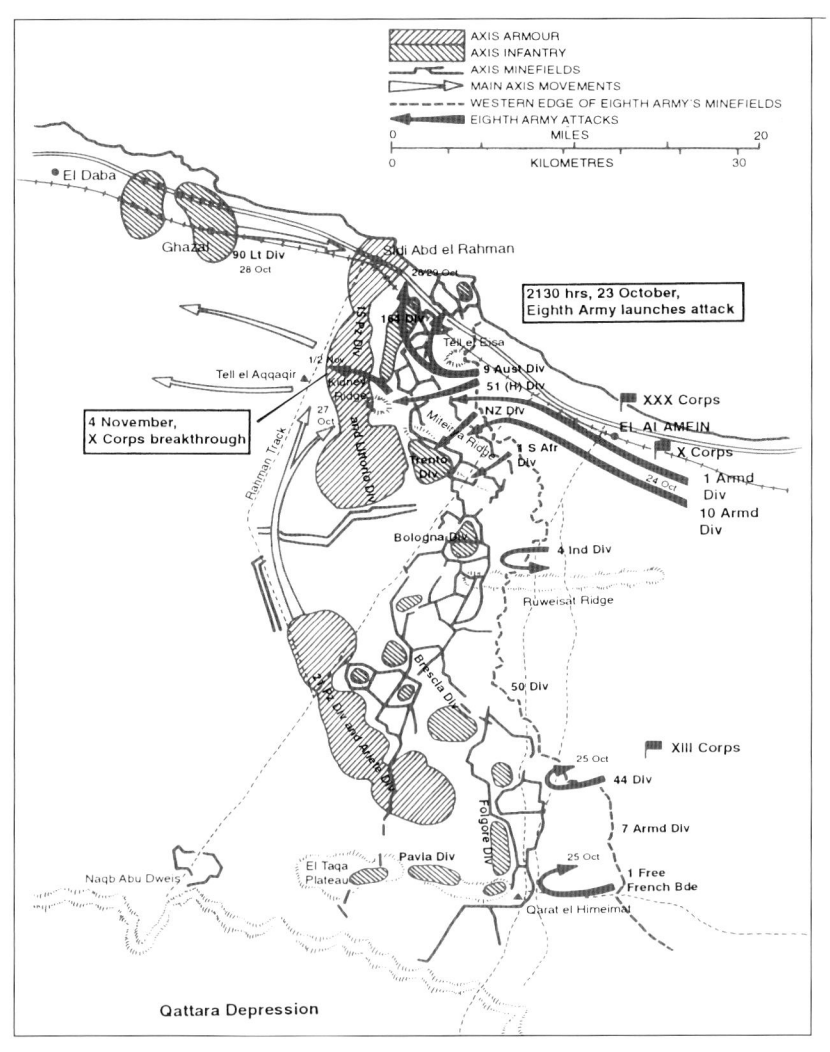

Left: **Alamein**

Under its new commander, General Montgomery, Eighth Army turned the Alamein line into a formidable defence in depth, with minefields and extensive barbed wire obstacles, strongpoints and a huge build up of forces, notably tanks and artillery, in readiness for a big offensive. The Axis forces, too, built up a defence line including minefields, but DAK was at some disadvantage both in strength and in being pinned to a static defence line when it was used to more fluid deployment. 21st Panzer Division was deployed on the southern flank, whereas the main British offensive opened (at 21.40hrs on 23 October 1942) with a massive barrage on the northern front which took the Axis forces by surprise. There was a much smaller opening barrage in the south. Rommel was on leave and his successor, Stumme, died of a heart attack at the start of the battle. Rommel returned on 25 October, but until he arrived there was an uncertain and slow Axis reaction. On 23 October, the British XXX Corps in the north and XIII Corps in the south began to advance. The latter's task was to engage and pin down 21st Panzer Division. In this they were unsuccessful, and in the opening fighting 21st Panzer lost only 15 tanks. Kidney Ridge and Point 29 to the north of it were considered key positions by Rommel and he ordered up forces, including part of 21st Panzer, to take these. But Kidney Ridge was well defended by the Rifle Brigade with well-sited anti-tank guns, and the attacks were repulsed. Many tanks and 88s were lost.

The first phase of the British attack—codenamed 'Lightfoot'—lost momentum and on 1 November a new offensive, Operation 'Supercharge', began. During this 21st and 15th Panzer Divisions made a spirited counter-attack on the Rahman track at Tel el Aqiqir but the new Sherman (M4 medium) tanks of 9th Armoured Brigade proved formidable, and DAK had only 35 tanks left after this battle. With their fighting strength so depleted, DAK had little option but to fall back, allowing Eighth Army to break out of the Alamein position in pursuit, as DAK made a fighting retreat back towards Cyrenaica.

defence finally brought his advance into Egypt to a halt. It was the end of a war of dashing movement for him, but he made one last attempt to outflank Eighth Army in the Battle of Alam Halfa on 31 July 1942. By now General Montgomery had become Eighth Army commander and both sides, but particularly the British, were starting to build up their defences and resources. Though Rommel tried to outflank his enemy here, his relatively feeble forces were easily repulsed by much stronger British armoured brigades. During the Alam Halfa action, 21st Panzer's commander, von Bismarck, was killed. Oberst C. H. Lungerhausen took over temporary command until Generalmajor Heinz von Randow arrived on 18 September.

Now started the well documented El Alamein period, the beginning of the end for German ambitions in North Africa. The desert war became a war of heavy attrition that the Germans could not win, thanks to the massive resources the British now enjoyed. Among these was new M4 medium (Sherman) tank from the United States. Its turret-mounted high-velocity 75mm gun made it superior to any tank the Germans then had in North Africa.

When the battle at Alamein took place, 21st Panzer was well inland next to the Italian Ariete Division. The disparity in numbers between the two sides was huge.

Far left: Well-known propaganda photo of British infantry 'capturing' a PzKpfw III.

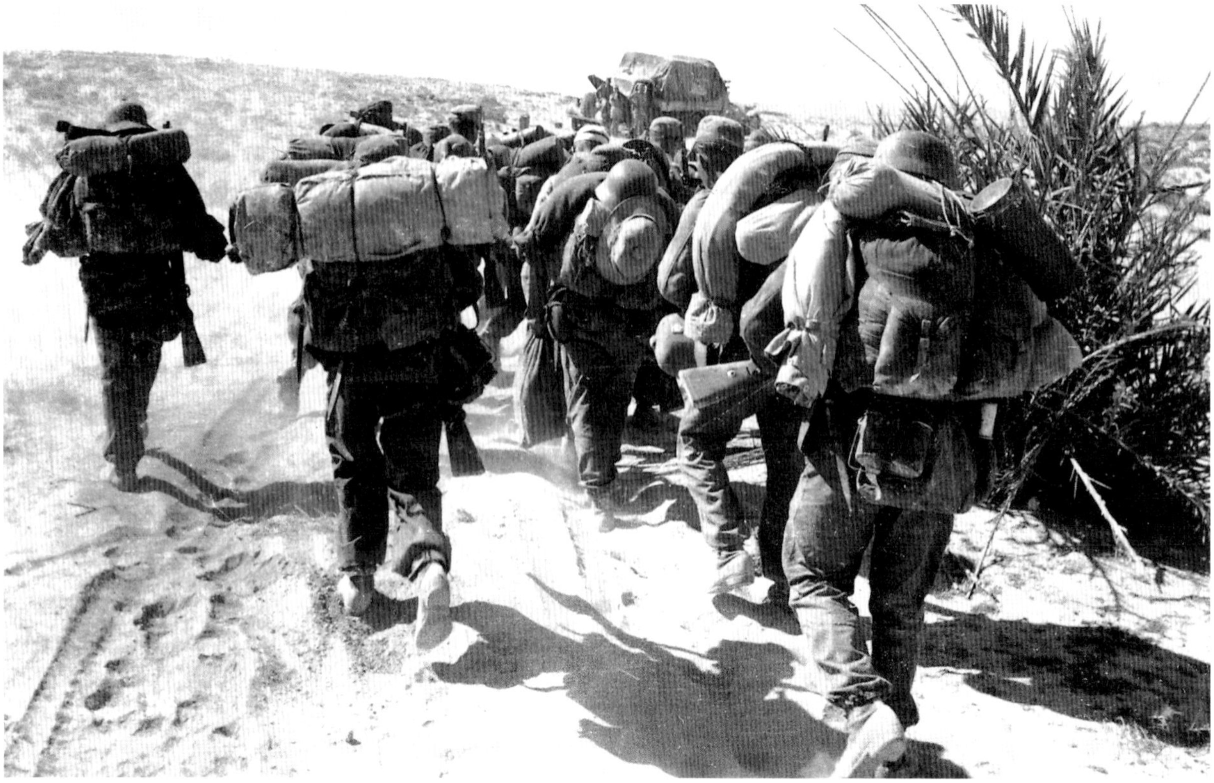

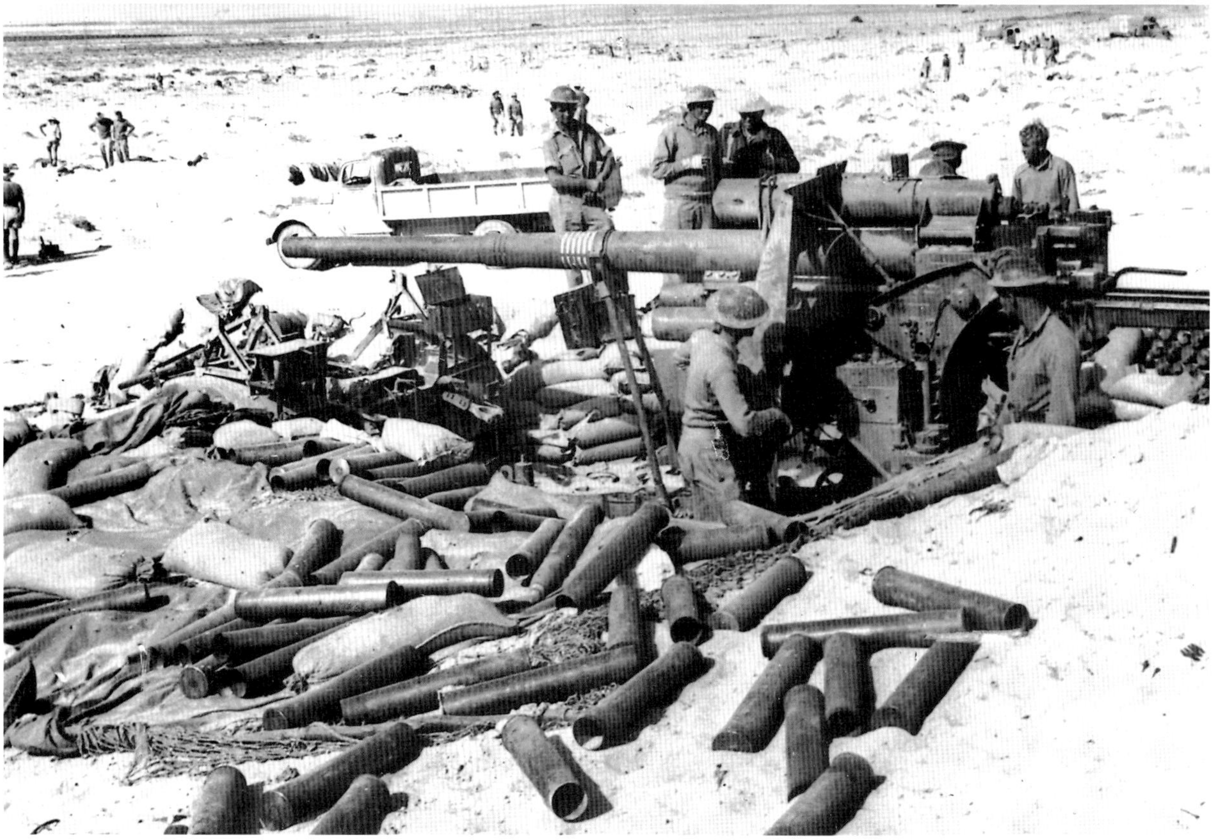

Opposite page, above: An infantry platoon on the march in the Alamein period, carrying full equipment and probably about to man a defence position.

Opposite page, below: Aftermath of Alamein. British troops examine an abandoned 88 after the German pull out. From the number of empty cartridge cases around the weapon, it appears to have seen hard action. Note the 'kill' bands painted round the barrel.

Above: A 2cm Flakvierling 38 is brought rapidly into action by its crew as enemy aircraft approach. A very effective weapon against low-flying aircraft, this one is probably operated by one of the light companies of 33rd Flak Regiment.

Left: Knocked out in the Alam Halfa battle is one of the formidable, and then new, PzKpfw IV 'Specials' with the long-barrel high-velocity 75mm gun.

Below left: One of the rarer vehicles used in the desert war was the Austrian-built Saurer RK7, Sd Kfz 254, which was a wheel-cum-track observation vehicle issued to some self-propelled artillery regiments.

Right: **Kasserine Pass**
During Rommel's last period of command in North Africa (he was commander of Panzergruppe Afrika until 21 January 1943, when it became Panzerarmee Afrika), 21st Panzer Division handed over its tanks to 15th Panzer Division in the Mareth Line and moved north to Sfax to re-equip with tanks held there. They were then deployed inland to Southern Tunisia to guard against an Allied drive to Gabes which would cut off the Mareth Line. 21st Panzer now came under control of Generaloberst Jürgen von Arnim, commanding west Tunisia. Using 10th and 21st Panzer Divisions, he carried out a bold offensive at the end of January/early February to seize the rugged Eastern Dorsal (roughly Bouarada to Gafsa). 21st Panzer took the southerly passes and at Faiad virtually destroyed a Free French/American force of II Corps which lost several battalions. Control of 21st Panzer now reverted to Rommel, who sought to take the next mountain range, the Western Dorsal, through Kasserine and Sbiba on 14 February. Sbiba was a sticking point (with minefields and good defences) so 21st Panzer was switched to Kasserine, backing up 10th and 15th Panzer Divisions. The week-long offensive alarmed the Allies, and 1st US Armored Division suffered severely before the Germans withdrew in good order.

Rommel's last offensive was at Medenine on 6 March 1943 against the British forces facing the Mareth Line. 10th, 15th, 21st Panzer and 90th Light were committed, but it was a massive failure against 460 well-sited British anti-tank guns and 300 tanks. DAK lost 50 tanks in a day's fighting and made no headway. Rommel, now very sick, handed over command to von Arnim and returned to Germany on 9 March.

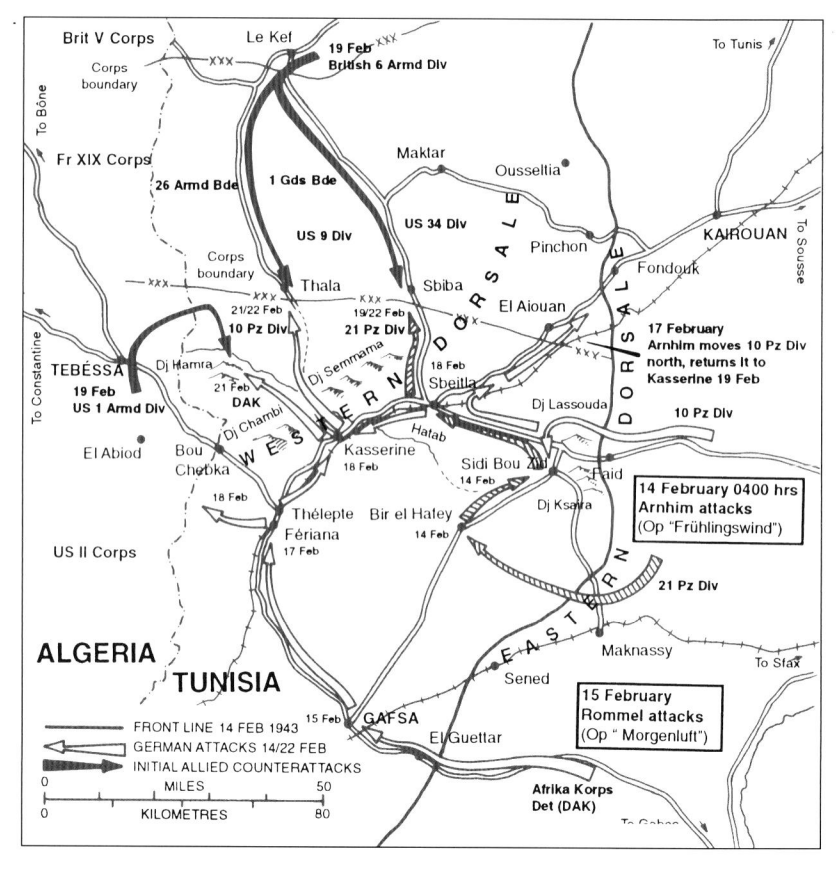

When the British offensive began on 23 October 1942, Eighth Army had 1,100 tanks against just under 200 available to DAK. In the 'Lightfoot' and 'Supercharge' phases of the battle, 21st Panzer suffered severely and were down to just four tanks by 7 November. In the long retreat that followed, as the renamed Panzerarmee Afrika fell back towards Tunis, 21st Panzer spent most of its time as a rearguard. In an action near Tripoli on 21 December, another divisional commander, von Randow, was killed. Attrition was so great and the fighting so desperate, that by the time it reached Tunis, 21st Panzer had ceased to operate as a unified formation but was split up in January 1943 into battle groups (*Kampfgruppen*)—in this case Battle Groups Pfeiffer and Gruen. In February 1943 these had changed (in

21st Panzer Division losses in North Africa

Division Staff
200th Mapping detachment
200th Print Shop

5th Panzer Regiment
   HQ Staff, Staff Coy
   2 x Battalions each of Staff,
   Staff Coy, 4 x Coys, 1 x Armd
      Repair Coy

192nd PzGr Regiment
   HQ Staff, Staff Coy
   4 x Bns and 13th Coy

21st Pz Recce Bn
   HQ Staff and 3 x Coys

39th Panzerjäger Bn
   HQ Staff and 3 x Coys

305th Army Flak Bn
   HQ Staff, Staff Bty,
   3 x Btys each with HQ Staff,
   Staff Bty, 3 x Btys, 1 x lt
      Supply Column

155th Pz Arty Regiment
   HQ Staff, Staff Bty
   3 x Bns each of HQ Staff,
   Staff Bty and total of 5 Btys

200th Pz Sig Bn
   2 x Coys, 1 x lt Supply
      Column

220th Pz Pioneer Bn
   3 x Coys, 1 x lt Supply
      Column

200th Feldersatz Bn
   4 x Coys

Left: British prisoners captured during the successful operations to secure the Eastern Dorsal area of Tunis in February 1943.

Below: The end of the fighting in Tunisia as thousands of German soldiers surrender and are taken into captivity.

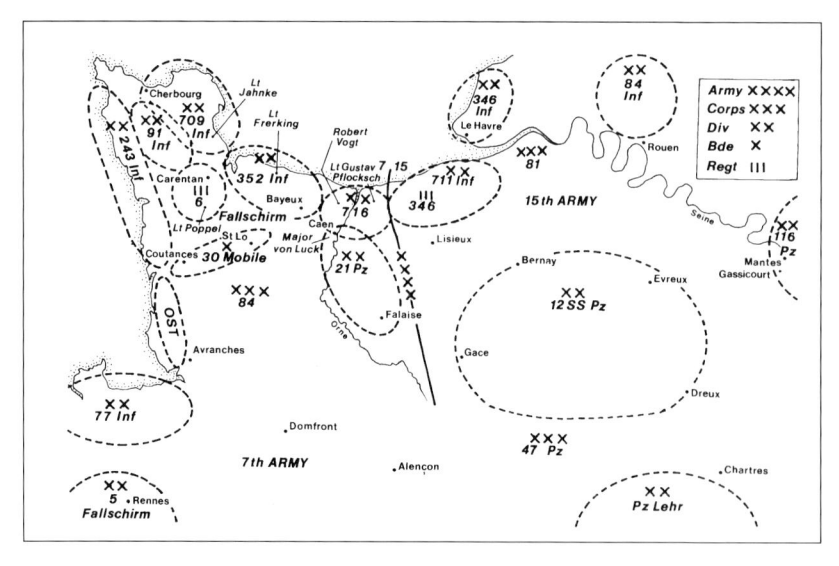

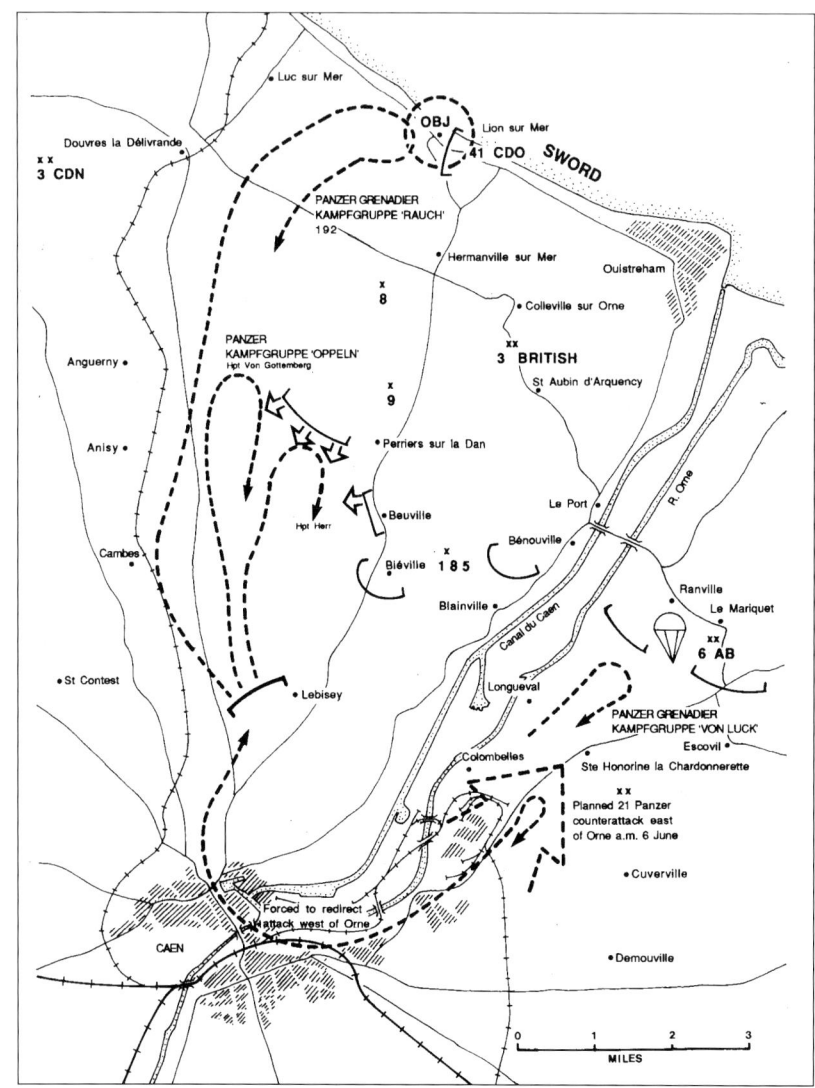

command and composition) to become Battle Groups Stenkhoff and Schuette.

The final operation as a complete division was for an attack on the Kasserine Pass on 19 February. This attack petered out, and for the confused last weeks in Tunis the division split again into battle groups, including a revived Battle Group Pfeiffer. This group surrendered on 11 May 1943, and the remaining forces did the same two days later.

The nominal divisional commanders in the last months of its existence were Oberst H. G. Hildebrandt, who went sick on 25 April 1943. He was replaced by Generalmajor H. G. von Hülsen, the man who finally surrendered the remnants of the division on 13 May.

AFTER THE DESERT

While the true spirit of the original 21st Panzer Division died in Tunis, the proud name came to life again within months as the designation for one of the new divisions that were being formed in France, largely from occupation troops, to face the threat of an expected invasion in Western Europe. Flexible, fast-moving divisions were seen as necessary for responding to a fast-moving invasion army, The type of division formed was known as a *Schnell Division West* (Fast Division West), and it was made fully mobile with tanks, halftracks, self-propelled (SP) artillery and trucks. There was a strong proportion of SP artillery, even if some of the equipment available was of older types. The 931st Fast Brigade (Schnell Brigade 931), an occupation unit, was used as the nucleus for the new division, and other occupation units and army troops were allocated and redesignated as required. One unit, however, 305th Army Flak Battalion, was specially formed for the division.

The new division's commander was Oberst Edgar Feuchtinger (promoted

IN ACTION

Generalmajor from 1 August 1943) and the division was officially formed at Rennes, Normandy, on 15 July 1943. The tank regiment was designated 100th Panzer Regiment, made up from various independent companies that were equipped with captured French Hotchkiss and Somua tanks forming two battalions. The infantry element was 125th and 192nd Panzergrenadier Regiments, each having one battalion with halftracks and one with lorries. The armoured artillery regiment was all self-propelled, the 1st Battalion having two batteries equipped with the 105mm Wespe and one battery with the 150mm Hummel. 2nd Battalion had three batteries equipped with the Wespe, and 3rd Battalion had three batteries of 150mm Hummels. Also of note was 200th Sturmgeschütz Battalion equipped with a a staff battery of four Nebelwerfer rocket launchers and four companies with light field howitzers and 75mm Pak 40 towed guns. The 305th Army Flak Battalion had three companies of four 88mm and two 20mm guns, all mounted on half-tracks. With comprehensive support companies (including 220th Panzer Pioneer Battalion with halftracks and a bridging column), the division was well equipped and hard punching for its anti-invasion role. The official listings for the division show that the old French tanks were supposed to be replaced by three companies per battalion each with 22 PzKpfw IIIs and one company with 22 PzKpfw IVs. This does not seem to have been done, however, for it was not until the invasion scare really set in that, on 20 May 1944, the 1st Battalion was told to re-equip with 17 PzKpfw IVs per company, and the 2nd Battalion with 14 PzKpfw IVs per company, all in place of the old French tanks.

As in North Africa, 21st Panzer Division was not long out of the limelight. For a start it was to come once again under command of Erwin Rommel, now a Generalfeldmarschall. With the Allied 'Second Front' expected soon, Rommel was asked by Hitler to carry out a detailed tour of the Atlantic Wall coastal defences—from Denmark to the Spanish border—to check their efficacy. This he did in November and December 1943, and found plenty to put right for there were critical weaknesses. This led to his appointment in late January 1944 as C-in-C of all the German armies from the Netherlands to the Loire.

Rommel believed that if the landing took place, the invaders needed to be pushed back into the sea quickly before they could get a foothold. Rommel's plans called for well-equipped armoured divisions all along the coast to do this. But because the coast was long and manpower was tight, the divisions had to be stretched out covering a big area each. Mobile divisions further inland were supposed to come up in support as required. As fate would have it, when D-Day came on 6 June 1944, it took place in 21st Panzer's area. The division had been based by Rommel near Caen, and it had to cover the entire coastal area where

Above: A German Marder III of 716th Infantry Division—operating with 21st Panzer—hurries to attack airborne troops on 6 June.

Opposite page, above: Disposition of German defence forces in Normandy, including 21st Panzer Division.

Opposite page, below: The 21st Panzer Division counter-attack on 6 June 1944.

Below: Rommel, as C-in-C in the Normandy area, inspects self-propelled gun crews, probably of 155th Panzer Artillery Regiment, 21st Panzer Division, during an inspection in May 1944.

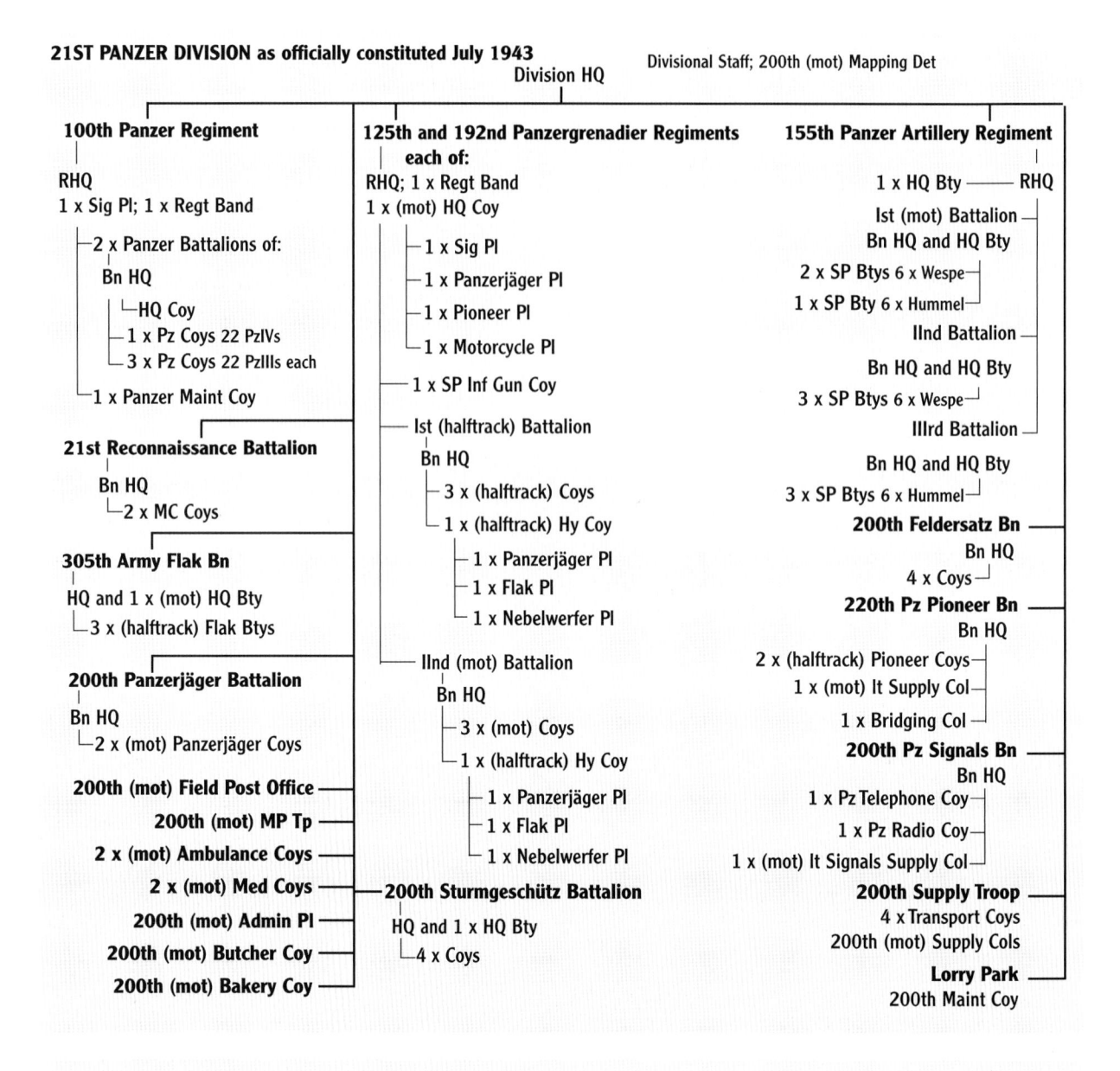

21ST PANZER DIVISION as officially constituted July 1943

Division HQ — Divisional Staff; 200th (mot) Mapping Det

100th Panzer Regiment
RHQ
1 x Sig Pl; 1 x Regt Band
- 2 x Panzer Battalions of:
  Bn HQ
  - HQ Coy
  - 1 x Pz Coys 22 PzIVs
  - 3 x Pz Coys 22 PzIIIs each
- 1 x Panzer Maint Coy

21st Reconnaissance Battalion
Bn HQ
- 2 x MC Coys

305th Army Flak Bn
HQ and 1 x (mot) HQ Bty
- 3 x (halftrack) Flak Btys

200th Panzerjäger Battalion
Bn HQ
- 2 x (mot) Panzerjäger Coys

200th (mot) Field Post Office
200th (mot) MP Tp
2 x (mot) Ambulance Coys
2 x (mot) Med Coys
200th (mot) Admin Pl
200th (mot) Butcher Coy
200th (mot) Bakery Coy

125th and 192nd Panzergrenadier Regiments
each of:
RHQ; 1 x Regt Band
1 x (mot) HQ Coy
- 1 x Sig Pl
- 1 x Panzerjäger Pl
- 1 x Pioneer Pl
- 1 x Motorcycle Pl
1 x SP Inf Gun Coy
- Ist (halftrack) Battalion
  Bn HQ
  - 3 x (halftrack) Coys
  - 1 x (halftrack) Hy Coy
    - 1 x Panzerjäger Pl
    - 1 x Flak Pl
    - 1 x Nebelwerfer Pl
- IInd (mot) Battalion
  Bn HQ
  - 3 x (mot) Coys
  - 1 x (halftrack) Hy Coy
    - 1 x Panzerjäger Pl
    - 1 x Flak Pl
    - 1 x Nebelwerfer Pl

200th Sturmgeschütz Battalion
HQ and 1 x HQ Bty
- 4 x Coys

155th Panzer Artillery Regiment
1 x HQ Bty — RHQ
Ist (mot) Battalion
Bn HQ and HQ Bty
2 x SP Btys 6 x Wespe
1 x SP Bty 6 x Hummel
IInd Battalion
Bn HQ and HQ Bty
3 x SP Btys 6 x Wespe
IIIrd Battalion
Bn HQ and HQ Bty
3 x SP Btys 6 x Hummel

200th Feldersatz Bn
Bn HQ
4 x Coys

220th Pz Pioneer Bn
Bn HQ
2 x (halftrack) Pioneer Coys
1 x (mot) lt Supply Col
1 x Bridging Col

200th Pz Signals Bn
Bn HQ
1 x Pz Telephone Coy
1 x Pz Radio Coy
1 x (mot) lt Signals Supply Col

200th Supply Troop
4 x Transport Coys
200th (mot) Supply Cols

Lorry Park
200th Maint Coy

21ST PANZER DIVISION on the Eastern Front early 1945

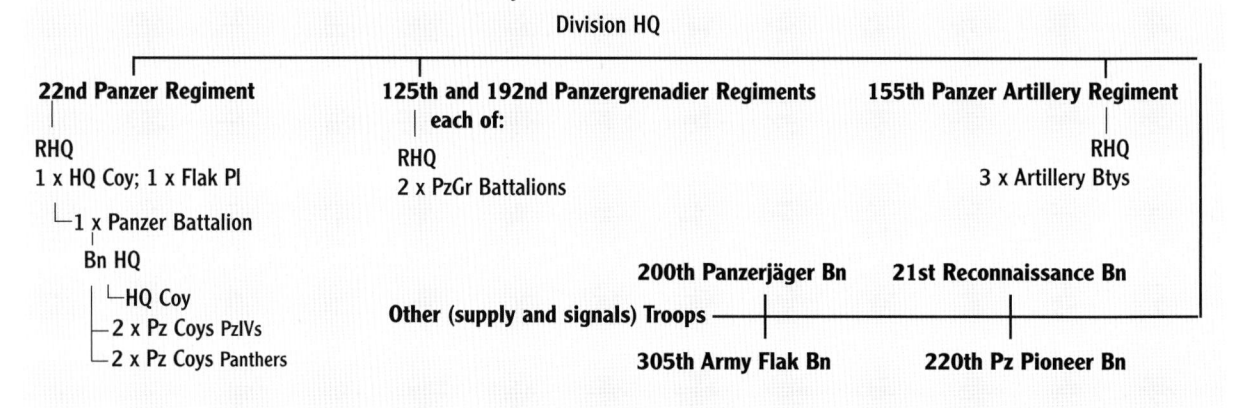

Division HQ

22nd Panzer Regiment
RHQ
1 x HQ Coy; 1 x Flak Pl
- 1 x Panzer Battalion
  Bn HQ
  - HQ Coy
  - 2 x Pz Coys PzIVs
  - 2 x Pz Coys Panthers

125th and 192nd Panzergrenadier Regiments
each of:
RHQ
2 x PzGr Battalions

200th Panzerjäger Bn
Other (supply and signals) Troops
305th Army Flak Bn

155th Panzer Artillery Regiment
RHQ
3 x Artillery Btys

21st Reconnaissance Bn
220th Pz Pioneer Bn

21ST PANZER DIVISION as at 1 March 1944

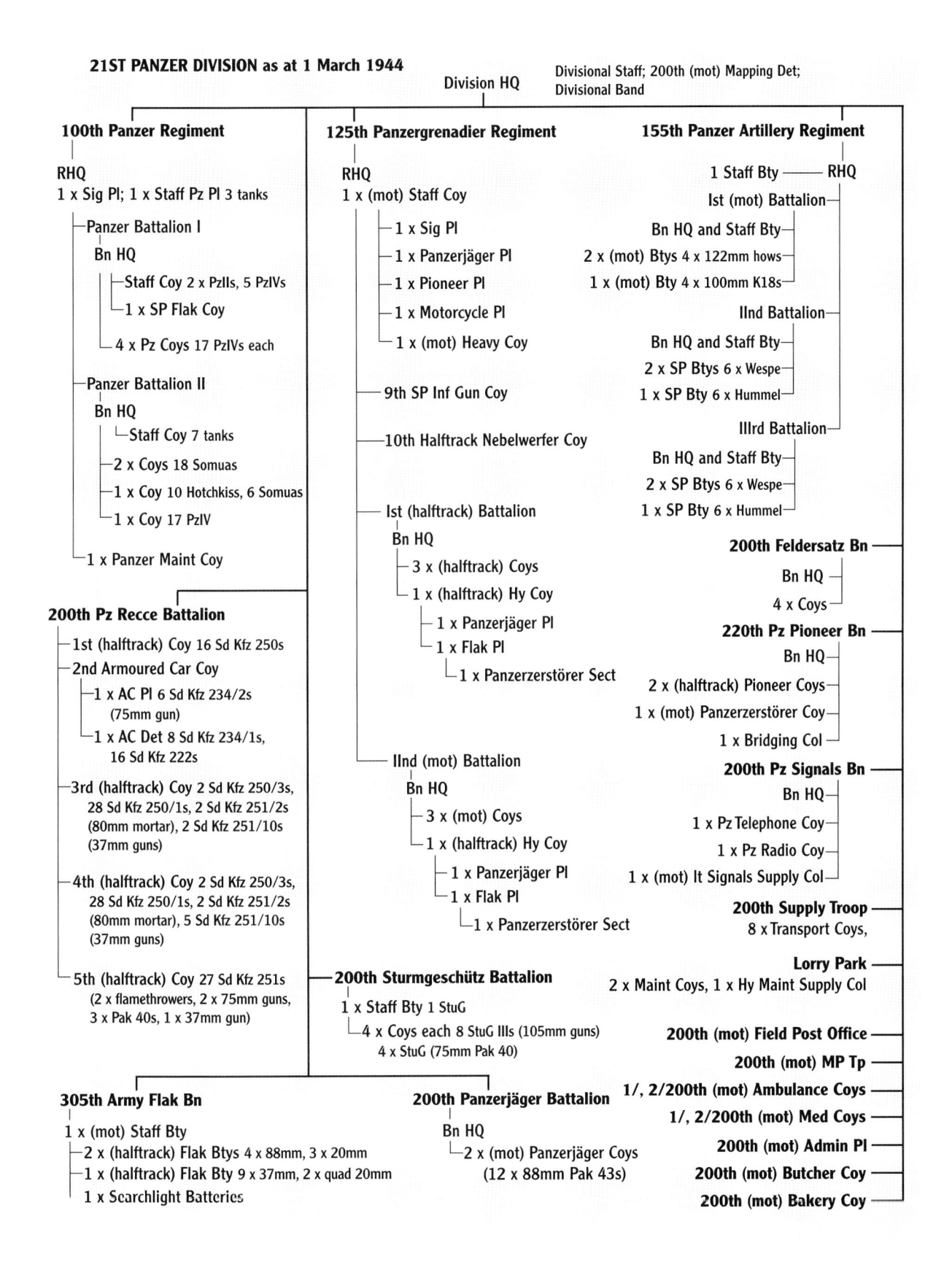

Division HQ — Divisional Staff; 200th (mot) Mapping Det; Divisional Band

100th Panzer Regiment
- RHQ
  - 1 x Sig Pl; 1 x Staff Pz Pl 3 tanks
- Panzer Battalion I
  - Bn HQ
    - Staff Coy 2 x PzIIs, 5 PzIVs
    - 1 x SP Flak Coy
  - 4 x Pz Coys 17 PzIVs each
- Panzer Battalion II
  - Bn HQ
    - Staff Coy 7 tanks
  - 2 x Coys 18 Somuas
  - 1 x Coy 10 Hotchkiss, 6 Somuas
  - 1 x Coy 17 PzIV
- 1 x Panzer Maint Coy

200th Pz Recce Battalion
- 1st (halftrack) Coy 16 Sd Kfz 250s
- 2nd Armoured Car Coy
  - 1 x AC Pl 6 Sd Kfz 234/2s (75mm gun)
  - 1 x AC Det 8 Sd Kfz 234/1s, 16 Sd Kfz 222s
- 3rd (halftrack) Coy 2 Sd Kfz 250/3s, 28 Sd Kfz 250/1s, 2 Sd Kfz 251/2s (80mm mortar), 2 Sd Kfz 251/10s (37mm guns)
- 4th (halftrack) Coy 2 Sd Kfz 250/3s, 28 Sd Kfz 250/1s, 2 Sd Kfz 251/2s (80mm mortar), 5 Sd Kfz 251/10s (37mm guns)
- 5th (halftrack) Coy 27 Sd Kfz 251s (2 x flamethrowers, 2 x 75mm guns, 3 x Pak 40s, 1 x 37mm gun)

305th Army Flak Bn
- 1 x (mot) Staff Bty
- 2 x (halftrack) Flak Btys 4 x 88mm, 3 x 20mm
- 1 x (halftrack) Flak Bty 9 x 37mm, 2 x quad 20mm
- 1 x Searchlight Batteries

125th Panzergrenadier Regiment
- RHQ
  - 1 x (mot) Staff Coy
    - 1 x Sig Pl
    - 1 x Panzerjäger Pl
    - 1 x Pioneer Pl
    - 1 x Motorcycle Pl
    - 1 x (mot) Heavy Coy
- 9th SP Inf Gun Coy
- 10th Halftrack Nebelwerfer Coy
- Ist (halftrack) Battalion
  - Bn HQ
    - 3 x (halftrack) Coys
    - 1 x (halftrack) Hy Coy
      - 1 x Panzerjäger Pl
      - 1 x Flak Pl
        - 1 x Panzerzerstörer Sect
- IInd (mot) Battalion
  - Bn HQ
    - 3 x (mot) Coys
    - 1 x (halftrack) Hy Coy
      - 1 x Panzerjäger Pl
      - 1 x Flak Pl
        - 1 x Panzerzerstörer Sect

200th Sturmgeschütz Battalion
- 1 x Staff Bty 1 StuG
  - 4 x Coys each 8 StuG IIIs (105mm guns) 4 x StuG (75mm Pak 40)

200th Panzerjäger Battalion
- Bn HQ
  - 2 x (mot) Panzerjäger Coys (12 x 88mm Pak 43s)

155th Panzer Artillery Regiment
- 1 Staff Bty — RHQ
- Ist (mot) Battalion
  - Bn HQ and Staff Bty
  - 2 x (mot) Btys 4 x 122mm hows
  - 1 x (mot) Bty 4 x 100mm K18s
- IInd Battalion
  - Bn HQ and Staff Bty
  - 2 x SP Btys 6 x Wespe
  - 1 x SP Bty 6 x Hummel
- IIIrd Battalion
  - Bn HQ and Staff Bty
  - 2 x SP Btys 6 x Wespe
  - 1 x SP Bty 6 x Hummel

200th Feldersatz Bn
- Bn HQ
- 4 x Coys

220th Pz Pioneer Bn
- Bn HQ
- 2 x (halftrack) Pioneer Coys
- 1 x (mot) Panzerzerstörer Coy
- 1 x Bridging Col

200th Pz Signals Bn
- Bn HQ
- 1 x Pz Telephone Coy
- 1 x Pz Radio Coy
- 1 x (mot) lt Signals Supply Col

200th Supply Troop
- 8 x Transport Coys,

Lorry Park
- 2 x Maint Coys, 1 x Hy Maint Supply Col

- 200th (mot) Field Post Office
- 200th (mot) MP Tp
- 1/, 2/200th (mot) Ambulance Coys
- 1/, 2/200th (mot) Med Coys
- 200th (mot) Admin Pl
- 200th (mot) Butcher Coy
- 200th (mot) Bakery Coy

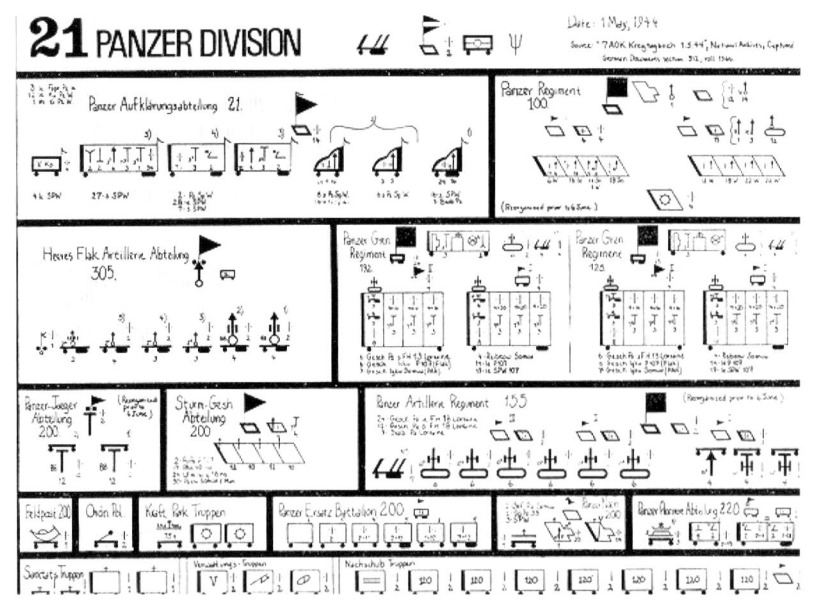

Above: German document showing order of battle of 21st Panzer Division on 1 May 1944 when covering the Normandy coast.

Above right: One of the self-propelled 20mm Flakpanzer 38s of either 100th Panzer Regiment or 22nd Panzer Regiment (as it was later redesignated) during exercises in the bocage country near the Normandy coast in May 1944. The flak platoon of the Ist Battalion had 12 of these vehicles.

Below right: Knocked-out in the fighting for Caen, this is one of the PzKpfw IV Ausf H tanks of 22nd Panzer Regiment, in July 1944. British troops in the foreground sort out mortar ammunition.

the landings too place. The problem was that Rommel was away from the area on the day of the invasion. The SS divisions which should have come up to assist were under Hitler's control, and nobody could get them released.

So for the first day of the Normandy landing 21st Panzer was operating alone. Muddled thinking by the area commanders delayed 21st Panzer's early entry into the fray, but the divisional commander himself ordered a 06.30hrs attack on the British paratroops who had landed at Ranville. They gave the Paras a tough time until withdrawn at 10.30hrs, with orders to counter-attack the British advance at Caen. They did well at this and for a time that evening they managed to reach the coast at Lion-sur-Mer and drive a wedge between the adjacent 3rd British and 3rd Canadian Divisions. But Allied air power and sheer numbers of opponents seriously restricted 21st Panzer's abilities. Notably, however, with 12th SS-Panzer Division, they blocked the scheduled early push inland to Villers-Bocage and Evrecy which stretched out I (BR) Corps considerably.

Rommel was back in charge on 9 June and he planned a counter-attack against both the British and American sectors. 21st Panzer was grouped with two SS divisions under Sepp Dietrich, and intended to push northwest to take Bayeux, but this bold plan came to nothing when corps headquarters and all the directing staff were blown away by Allied bombing. The division's final fling in Normandy was to put up a spirited resistance that gave the Guards Armoured Division a hard time and slowed their advance by a day during Operation 'Bluecoat', on 1 August 1944. After this, the battered survivors of 21st Panzer were largely destroyed in the Falaise Pocket during August 1944, but by this time it had merged with 16th Luftwaffe Field Division. The same commander and staff reformed the division in Lorraine in September 1944 by expanding 112th Panzer Brigade. At this time the tank component, 100th Panzer Regiment, may have been equipped with two companies of 17 Panther tanks and two of PzKpfw IVs. The much reduced division took part in the withdrawals through France and Germany, and fought in Epinel, Nancy, Metz and the Saar area. It ended up in Kaiserlautern.

Generalmajor Feuchtinger the originally appointed commander was temporarily replaced from January 15 until March 8 1944 by Generalmajor Oswin Grolig and he in turn was succeeded by Generalmajor Franz Westhoven until 8 May 1944, when Feuchtinger, now a Generalleutnant, again took command.

On 25 January 1945 the division was reformed as a 1944 type Panzer Division (ie much reduced). The commander was Oberst Helmut Zollenkopf. In this form the division contained a single combined battalion based on 22nd Panzer Regiment. It had a staff company, Flak platoon, two companies with Panther tanks and two companies with PzKpfw IV tanks. The last recorded issue of tanks was on 9 February 1945 when the division was directed to the defence of East Germany. It carried out defensive operations at Goerlitz, Slatsk, Cottbus and other areas and surrendered to the Soviet Army on 29 April 1945.

IN ACTION

INSIGNIA & MARKINGS

Below: Extensive use was made of motorcycles and motorcycle combinations in DAK. The tactical sign on the sidecar of this one shows it belongs to a towed artillery battery.

Right: A PzKpfw III Ausf E of 5th Panzer Regiment in Tripoli soon after arrival in North Africa. It is still in the European Panzer grey finish and carries the formation sign of 3rd Panzer Division on the front, the unit from which 5th Panzer Regiment's equipment was drawn.

COLOURS

The vehicles that first went to Libya in February-March 1941, and indeed most of the later replacement and reinforcement supplies, were all in the colours applied for Europe. In essence this was an overall 'Panzer grey' for tanks (a dark grey with a blueish tinge) and field grey (a greenish-grey) on other vehicles. Some of the tanks were also in field grey, particularly those shipped later. Because 5th Light went into immediate deployment, most vehicles in the early weeks of the Cyrenaica campaign were still in the dark grey or field grey colours.

To provide a better camouflage for desert conditions a dark yellow (*Dunkelgelb*) was supplied, and this was applied over the the dark original colours.

INSIGNIA & MARKINGS

Above: The DAK symbol.

Sometimes this was done neatly overall, but frequently it was only roughly applied, reflecting the pace of the campaign. Thus some vehicles could be seen part dark, part yellow, and often only upper surfaces were painted, leaving chassis, etc, still grey. Tactical signs were often painted roughly round, leaving them on a patch of the original dark colour. The sand yellow colour was sometimes referred to as ochre, and in the strong summer sun it often faded to a very pale yellow or stone shade. To give extra camouflage, a dark earth paste was supplied which could be thinned with water and applied with brush or spray gun in mottled or rough wavy effects, but there were no hard rules on this, so there was great variation.

When 21st Panzer Division was in Normandy in the summer of 1944, pictorial evidence suggests they stuck firmly to rules issued for vehicle painting by Rommel's HQ, confirmed by postwar interrogation of his staff. In 1943 the Germans adopted a basic sand-yellow for all tanks, and all units were issued with brown and green water-thinned paste to apply camouflage to suit the terrain. This was done universally in Europe, but the mighty Allied air superiority evident at the time of the Normandy invasion caused an overall dark earth to be ordered for tanks and vehicles in that theatre, and the brown and green camouflage colours could be applied over that. This gave much better concealment in the Normandy bocage country against marauding Allied Typhoons and P-47s seeking out tanks for rocket attack.

DAK MARKING

Universally applied, usually front and rear to the left side, but also sometimes showing to the sides, was the Deutsches Afrika Korps symbol, a stylised palm tree with a swastika superimposed. It was often shown in white only, but officially it was applied in white for 5th Light/21st Panzer, green for corps troops, and red for 15th Panzer Division. However, pictures show that the latter also sometimes used white for the symbol.

DIVISIONAL MARKINGS

No divisional sign was ever authorised for 5th Light Division, but many of their early vehicles were allocated from 3rd Panzer Division and the divisional sign on these vehicles was retained, sometimes for months. This sign was an inverted Y with two vertical strokes to the right and the sign was usually painted in yellow, sometimes white.

When 5th Light became 21st Panzer a runic symbol was authorised. Best described as a capital D with a horizontal bar in the centre, it could be seen applied in either rounded or elongated form, and was normally white. it was normally displayed on vehicles close to the DAK symbol, but it could also be seen on temporary roadside directional signs.

TACTICAL SIGNS

German Panzer troops had evolved an effective system before the war using callsigns whereby a tank's, armoured car's, or armoured halftrack's place in a unit could easily be identified, and unit commanders directing movement could instantly call up any vehicle by its tactical number. A three-digit number was used with the first digit indicating company, second digit the platoon (*Zug*), and third digit the individual vehicle. Before the war, on tanks, this number was usually

INSIGNIA & MARKINGS

Left: Not from 21st Panzer Division, but indicative of the use of tactical symbols, this staff car from Rommel's HQ in Tripoli displays the metal symbol for DAK Corps HQ.

Below left: PzKpfw II command tank showing DAK and 21st Panzer divisional sign.

Bottom left: Halftrack showing 21st Panzer Division and Afrika Korps markings on left front mudguard.

Right: This Sd Kfz 251/6 halftrack command vehicle displays the formation sign of 21st Panzer Division and a tactical sign of a towed artillery battery. Also visible is the *Wehrmacht Heer* numberplate (WH registration) painted on the nose.

Below: Use of the national flag as an air recognition sign is exemplified on the bonnet of a supply column truck waiting to replenish an armoured unit.

Opposite page, above left: Variations of the tropical uniform are shown by Rommel and his staff officers near Bardia in 1941. The reed-green uniform soon faded or washed out to shades between light green and stone.

Opposite, above right: The faded nature of the *Feldmütze* (cap) and shirt in use is shown by this NCO at an observation post.

Opposite, below left: The Panzer grey colour is shown on this PzKpfw III of 5th Panzer Regiment as it is landed in Tripoli, late February 1941. The three-digit callsign is seen on the turret rear.

Opposite, below right: The crew of an MG34 in a sangar show how the fading varied on uniform items. The sun helmets (discarded after the first few months as too cumbersome) started off with reed-green coverings, here faded to two different shades.

INSIGNIA & MARKINGS

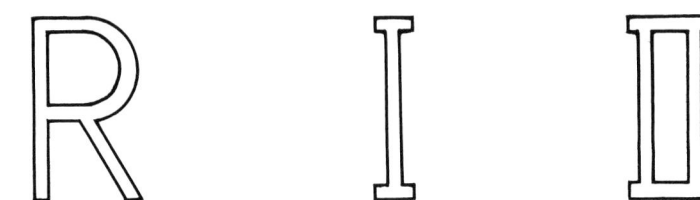

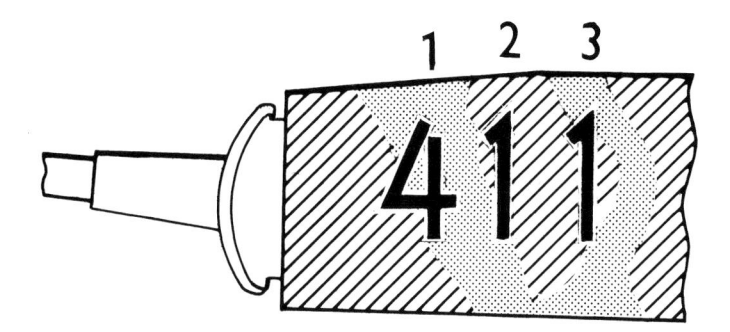

painted in small digits on a rhomboid metal plate (the rhomboid was the tactical symbol for a tank—see below) and this was affixed on superstructure or turret side and could be moved from vehicle to vehicle if desired. In the early part of the Cyrenaica campaign, some of the old tanks issued to 5th Panzer Regiment still carried this style of prewar marking.

However, most had the new style adopted when the war started. The same sort of three-digit numbering was used, but the numbers were now painted large on the turret or superstructure sides. These could be in plain white or yellow but were often red (or some other colour) outlined in white. Many tanks in 5th Panzer Regiment carried this style with the red number outlined in white.

Headquarters vehicles had a variation of this battalion (*Abteilung*) numbering system. Regimental command tanks had a prefix R in front of a two-digit number in the style:

R01	Regt commander
R02	Regt adjutant
R03	Regt ordnance or signal officer
R04-R08	other Regt officers

The medical officer's tank (when allocated) often had the medical serpent painted behind or interwoven with the number.

Battalion HQ tanks used the same system but with the Roman numeral I replacing the R for Ist Battalion staff vehicles, and the roman numeral II as the prefix for IInd Battalion staff vehicles. If there was a IIIrd Battalion, the roman III was used. Thus 'I01' indicated the battalion commander's tank of the first battalion and so on.

Companies were numbered through the regiment so the first company of the IInd Battalion had 5 as the first digit (assuming four companies in the Ist Battalion). In this system the company commander took the digits 01, so the company commander of the 1st Company in the IInd Battalion had 501 on his tank. The company sergeant major took 02, hence 502, and any other company staff tank would take 503, 504, etc. First tank in the first platoon would be 511, and so on.

TACTICAL SYMBOLS

The German army had a complex but logical system of small symbols indicating every type of unit in what amounted to 'pictogram' form. These symbols could be used on maps, organisation charts and even on directional signs if need be. They were also painted front and rear on vehicles. There were symbols for tank units (the rhomboid), wheeled artillery, recce units, SP artillery, supply columns, and so on. In the desert, at least, this method of marking tactical symbols was not applied thoroughly, and many vehicles carried no tactical symbols, indicating perhaps the fluid nature of both the fighting and the organisation which often led to the creation of ad hoc units. Some tactical symbols, such as those of divisional commanders, were painted on metal plates and were displayed on vehicles and in locations when appropriate.

NATIONAL INSIGNIA

When the war started a plain white (sometimes yellow) Balkan cross was applied to vehicles used in the Polish campaign. For the French campaign of 1940 this was modified to a white outline on the dark grey base colour. Vehicles sent to Libya early in 1940 carried these earlier markings. For example, Rommel's map caravan (see photograph on page 22) still had the plain white cross of the Polish campaign. Against the dark sand colour the white cross did not show up sufficiently so the centre was painted in black in similar style to the cross on Luftwaffe aircraft. However, DAK made extensive use of captured British vehicles and to distinguish these for their own troops they applied oversize versions on sides and sometimes tops. In a few cases a big white or black swastika sign was applied instead. For normal air recognition the DAK used the national flag tied over engine covers or turret tops as a very good temporary sign when needed in the presence of Luftwaffe aircraft.

Opposite page, top: This 5th Panzer Regiment PzKpfw III's tactical number is painted in the prewar style on a metal plate next to the national marking. Note the vehicle is still in Panzer grey

Opposite page, centre: Lettering style for regimental and battalion staff identification; numeral styles.

Opposite page, below: Digit identification system.

Above: A knocked out PzKpfw III (with a British Dingo scout car alongside) carries the R02 callsign of a regimental adjutant.

Below: Another example of the use of the national flag for air recognition purposes, this time over the front and spare wheel of a VW Kübelwagen. One of the soldiers carries a Thompson sub-machine gun captured from the British.

Right: Panzer III Ausf G of 5th Panzer Regiment in 1941. It is painted overall in Desert Yellow over Panzer Grey. Note national marking (cross) and turret callsign.

Below right: Panzer III Ausf J of 21st Panzer Division as it would have appeared during the fighting around Bir Hakeim in May 1942.

Bottom right: Rear turret view of grey PzKpfw III Ausf F at Saumur Tank Museum, showing the rear turret callsign applied to German tanks. **Artwork and photo on this page courtesy Accion Press**

Opposite page, top: MG34 crew in a defence position sangar, showing again the great variety in shade and style of uniform worn by DAK men.

Opposite page, below left: On the beach at Sollum, a Panzer II shows off its turret markings.

Opposite page, below right: A Panzergrenadier *Unteroffizier* (NCO) and *Schütze* (private) in a slit trench at the time of Alamein. The bleached sandbag helmet covers worn in British fashion were not common.

INSIGNIA & MARKINGS

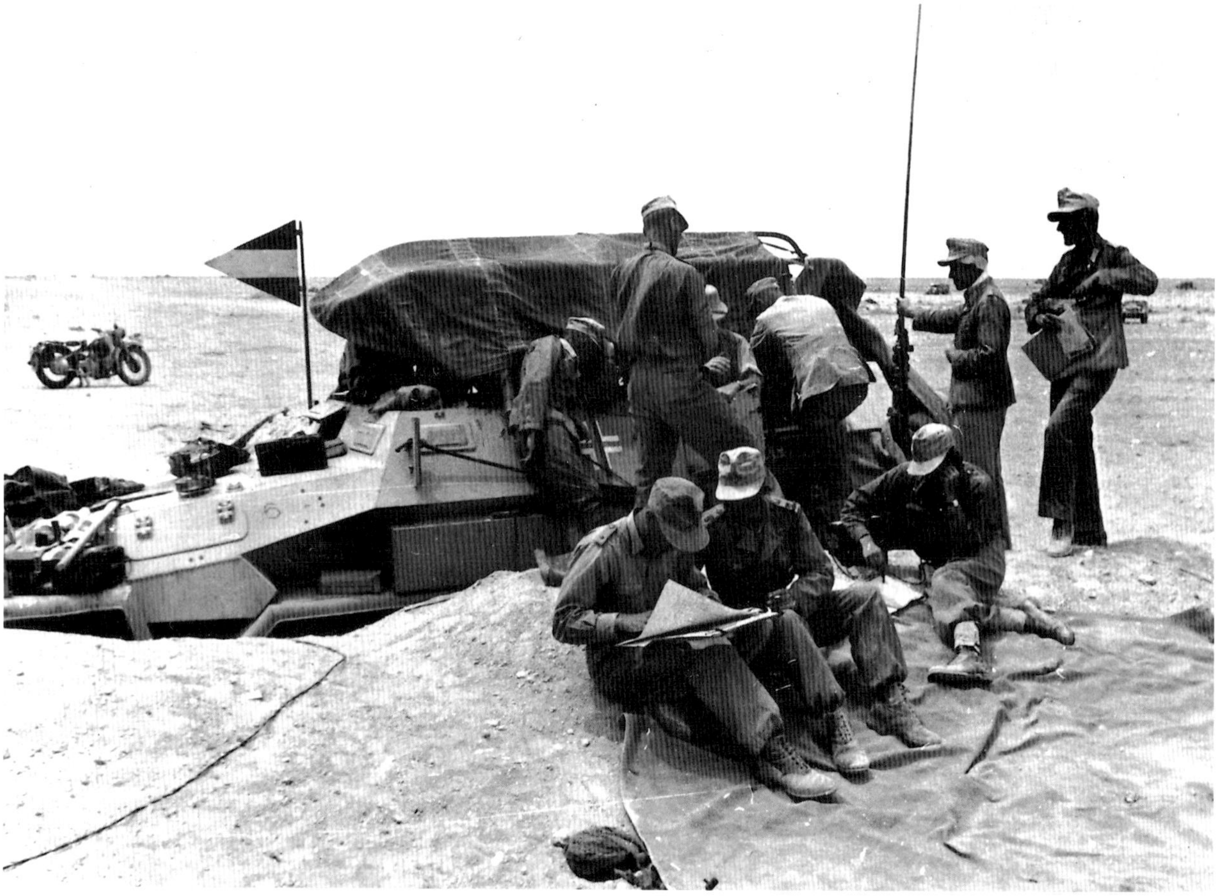

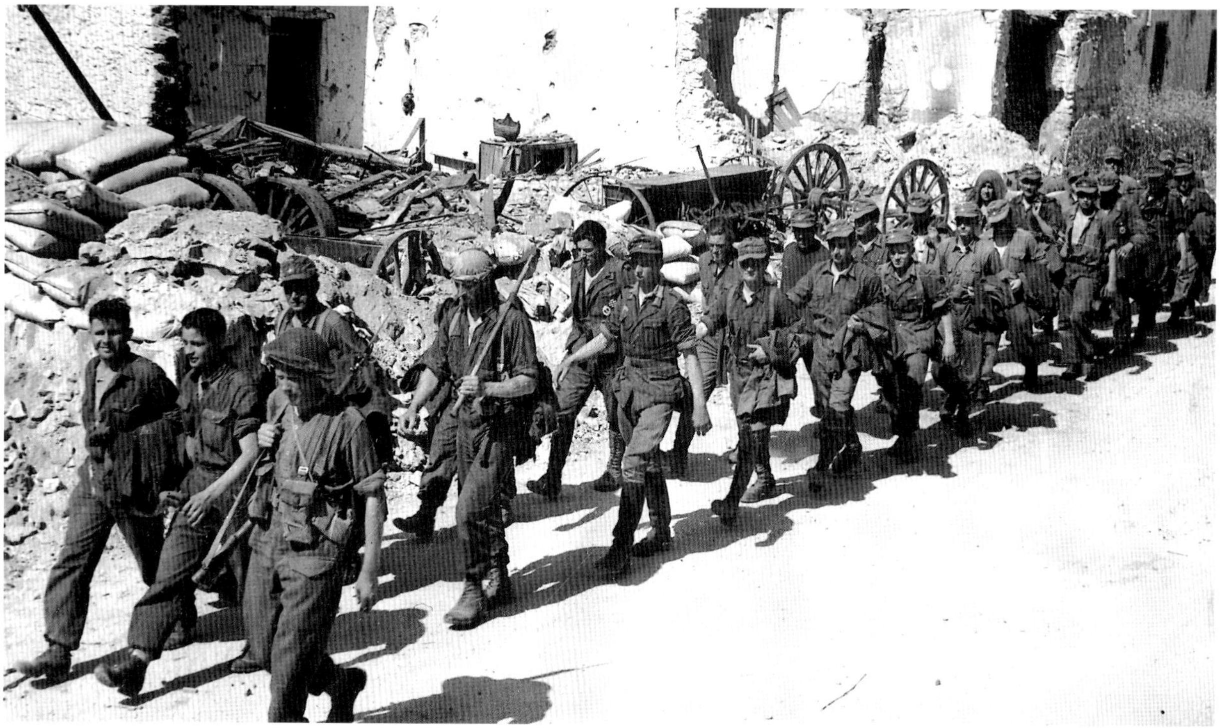

Opposite page, above: Divisional command post of 21st Panzer with Sd Kfz 251/6 command halftrack displaying the appropriate metal command pennant, pictured during the January–February 1942 offensive. The general (in sun helmet) is partly hidden by staff officers as he leans against the vehicle.

Opposite page, below: Afrika Korps men captured in Tunis are marched away by British troops. There is still a remarkable consistency in uniforms.

Above: A regimental command post set up near the coast road and near 'Marble Arch' at El Agheila just before the first Cyrenaica offensive.

Left: Staff officers of General Crüwell, then Afrika Korps commander, at a conference in summer 1942 near Alamein. Again there is great variety in uniform, including trousers, breeches, and shorts.

PEOPLE

ROMMEL

Erwin Rommel was born in Heidenheim, Württemberg, on 17 November 1891. He joined the army in March 1910, and that July entered the 124th Württemberg Infantry Regiment. Promotion came quickly and in 1911 he went to officer cadet school—the Kriegschule Danzig. Leutnant Rommel came back to his regiment in 1912.

At the start of World War I he was a platoon commander and saw his first action in August–September 1914 at Bleid, in the Meuse Valley. He was wounded during hand-to-hand fighting, and was subsequently awarded the Iron Cross, Second Class. Hospitalised, he went back to the front at Argonne, where on 29 January 1915 he was awarded the Iron Cross, First Class, for his part in a daring raid and in June he was wounded again. He was promoted Oberleutnant and company commander in September of the same year.

In November 1916 he married Lucie Maria Mollin in Danzig and transferred that same month to the Württemberg Mountain Battalion. He finished his spell on the Western Front at Hilsen Ridge and then transferred to the Eastern Front—to Romania where he fought at Gagesti and Mount Cosna—and then the Italian Front where he fought on Monte Majur. He won the Pour le Mérite in December 1917, returning to the Western Front where he ended the war a *Hauptmann* (captain) and a staff officer.

At the end of the war he returned to Württemberg. He survived the drastic reduction of German armed forces, ending up commanding an internal security company, No 32 IS Company at Friedrichshafen, where he quickly motivated a hostile unit. Appointed to command a company of Reichsheer Infanterie Regiment 13 based on Stuttgart in January 1921, he would spend the next eight years with the regiment before becoming an Instructor, at the Dresden Infantry School. During this time his only child, Manfred, was born.

Below: Rommel directs a tank battle on the horizon from his personal Sd Kfz 250/3 radio-fitted half-track 'Greif'. Visible (standing) is a Luftwaffe liaison officer to direct the air support.

In April 1932 he was promoted *Major*, and two years later, during 1934, he met Hitler for the first time, when his company formed an honour guard at a rally. This proximity to the Führer would see Rommel fall under the spell of the Nazi leader, and Rommel would be attached to Hitler's military escort for a party rally at Nuremberg in 1936 and command the *Führerbegleitbataillon* (escort battalion) at Hitler's field HQ during the occupation of the Sudetenland in 1938. During the 1930s, Rommel also did a three-year tour of duty as an instructor at Potsdam Infantry School, and in 1937 his book *Infanterie greift an!* (*Infantry attacks!*) was published.

He was promoted *Oberst* (colonel) in 1938 and became commandant of the Wiener Neustadt Kriegschule from November 1938 to August 1939. Twice during this period he was called on to command Hitler's field HQ. When the invasion of

Above left: Rommel discusses troop dispositions; at left, Streich with Schmidt, Rommel's ADC, at far right.

Left: The Desert Fox makes a point, cup in hand.

Poland began, he was once more given this duty with promotion to *Generalmajor*. Following Hitler's successful campaign, he decided he wanted an operational command and, thanks to Hitler's intervention, was able to plump for a tank unit rather than a mountain division.

On 6 February 1940 Rommel took charge of 7th Panzer Division—the 'Ghost' Division—on the Western Front. He handled the unit brilliantly, covering himself with personal glory: on 15 May 1940 he was awarded the Clasp to the Iron Cross and on 26 May the Knight's Cross to the Iron Cross. He exploited the tenets of Blitzkrieg and the mobility of his armoured units to the cost of the French and British forces ranged against him. 7th Panzer captured nearly 100,000 prisoners with losses of only 682 killed. Little did he know, when the armistice was signed with France, what awaited him on the shores of the Mediterranean.

In January 1941 Rommel was promoted *Generalleutnant* and in February he became Commander-in-Chief of German Troops in Libya, personally selected for the job by Hitler. His desert war has become legendary. Always short of men and equipment, frequently without sufficient air support, he would take the DAK almost to the Pyramids before being thrown back. On 21 January 1942 he was awarded Swords to the Oakleaves of the Knight's Cross. After the capture of Tobruk in 1942 he was promoted *Generalfeldmarschall*. It was the apogee of his success. While recovering from sickness in Germany in autumn 1942, the Battle of Alamein began and he was recalled to Africa where he presided over the long retreat back through Libya. In March 1943 Hitler presented him the Diamonds to his Iron Cross, only the sixth winner of this coveted award. He left Africa in summer 1943, becoming Commander-in-Chief Army Group B, Italy. In November 1943, Rommel left Italy, taking on special responsibilities for inspecting the defences on Northwest Europe. This he did and, subsequently, on 15 January 1944 Rommel's Army Group B took over control of the Atlantic and Channel coasts. Rommel did not have much time to improve the defences of the Atlantic Wall. On 6 June 1944 the invasion of Normandy took place and on 17 July, in the middle of the Battle of Normandy, Rommel was severely wounded when his car was strafed on his way to his HQ at La Roche Guyon. He was first hospitalised and then took sick leave. During this he was implicated in the bomb plot against Hitler and forced to commit suicide. He received a state funeral on 18 October 1944.

Commanders of 21st Panzer Division

Name	CO From	To	Comments
Generalmajor Johannes Streich	20/2/41	22/7/41	Dismissed by Rommel
Generalmajor Johann von Ravenstein	23/7/41	29/11/41	Captured by Commonwealth forces
Oberstleutnant Gustav-Georg Knabe	29/11/41	30/11/41	Retired due to ill health
Generalleutnant Karl Böttcher	30/11/41	30/1/42	Retired due to ill health
Generalmajor Georg von Bismarck	30/1/42	31/8/42	Killed in action
Oberst Carl-Hans Lungerhausen	31/8/42	18/9/42	Temporary commander
Generalmajor Heinz von Randow	18/9/42	21/12/42	Killed in action
Oberst Hans-Georg Hilderbrandt	1/1/43	25/4/43	Retired due to ill health
Generalmajor Heinrich-Hermann von Hülsen	25/4/43	13/5/43	Surrendered with DAK in Tunisia
Generalleutnant Edgar Feuchtinger	15/7/43	25/1/45	Commanded reformed division in Normandy
Generalmajor Oswin Grolig	15/1/44	8/3/44	Temporary replacement
Generalmajor Franz Westhoven	8/3/44	8/5/44	Temporary replacement
Oberst Helmut Zollenkopf	25/1/45	29/4/45	Surrendered to Russians

Rommel was a brilliant tactician, a courageous soldier and an inspiring leader of men. Respected by his foes as much as his friends, his desert campaigns showed him to be a consummate general with the knack of being in the right place at the right time, and the skill to make the right decisions when under extreme pressure.

GENERALMAJOR JOHANNES STREICH

Born 16 April 1891 at Augustenburg, East Prussia, Streich joined up in 1911 and fought throughout WW1, reaching the rank of *Leutnant*, commanding a company and winning the Iron Cross First and Second Class. Postwar he served in an MT company, then played an important part in the development of the PzKpfw I–IV, as a technical adviser in the Army Ordnance Office. In 1937 he took command of Panzer Regiment 15, promoted to *Oberst* in April 1938. He fell out with Rommel on two occasions, first in France in 1940 in the rush to the coast and later in Africa during the siege of Tobruk, where he was relieved of his command. Rommel criticised him, saying that he was far too concerned with the well-being of his troops, to which Streich replied: 'I can think of no greater words of praise for a divisional commander.' He was awarded the Knight's Cross for his bravery in France —his regiment had smashed through a blocking position at La Bassé, taking 20,000 prisoners and reaching the Atlantic coast. He was promoted to *Generalmajor* and given command of 5th Light Division before being sent to North Africa.

GENERALMAJOR JOHANN VON RAVENSTEIN

Lean, aristocratic and good looking, Johann von Ravenstein was born in 1889, in Strehlen, Silesia. He joined the army in 1909 and was commissioned as a *Leutnant* into the 7th Grenadier Regiment. He served in WW1 and was wounded several times in four years on the Western Front. He was awarded Germany's highest decoration, the Pour le Mérite, on 25 June 1918 for conspicuous bravery during the Battle of the Marne. He left the army at the end of the war, but rejoined in

Left: Von Ravenstein after his capture by the New Zealanders is seen with his escort officer.

1934 as CO 2nd Battalion 60th Infantry Regiment, which later became 4th Cavalry Rifle Regiment and which he led into action in 1940. He was then promoted to *Generalmajor* and on 20 May 1941 assigned command of 21st Panzer Regiment, taking it to North Africa. He took over command of 21st Panzer Division when Rommel dismissed Streich, holding the position for six months. He was captured by New Zealanders on 29 November 1941, while on his way to DAK HQ during the Crusader battles, when he mistakenly drove into their positions.

OBERSTLEUTNANT GUSTAV-GEORG KNABE

Born 8 July 1897 at Wichmannsdorf, near Templin, Gustav-Georg Knabe left school at 17 in order to volunteer for war service, joining the 8th Brandenburg Infantry Regiment. He saw action on the Western Front and was promoted up through the ranks to end the war as *Leutnant*. After WW1 he remained in the *Reichswehr*, spending a time at Kriegschule before serving with 1st Panzer Division. Promoted *Major*, after a spell of sickness he joined 66th Infantry Regiment. He saw action on the Western Front in 1940 as CO 2nd Battalion, 93rd Motorised Infantry Regiment, before being sent to Africa with the 15th Motorcycle Battalion. By now an *Oberstleutnant*, he was in the advanced elements of this unit when he took both Sollum and Capuzzo, for which he was awarded the Knight's Cross. He then commanded 104th Panzergrenadier Regiment until given charge of 21st Panzer Division in November 1941. His tenure was only nominal, for immediately ill health forced his return to Germany. Following his recovery, he was promoted to *Oberst* and served with Panzergruppe West. After a severe car accident while serving as a training and staff officer with Romanian forces he was invalided out of the army.

GENERALLEUTNANT KARL BÖTTCHER

Rommel's artillery commander, Böttcher was born in Thorn, East Prussia in 1891. He joined the army as an officer candidate in March 1909, becoming a *Leutnant* in the 5th Foot Artillery Regiment. He served in WW1, the interwar *Reichswehr* and began WW2 as commander of the 1st Artillery Regiment. Promoted to *Generalmajor* in March 1940, in November 1941 he was appointed CO of 21st Panzer Division when Knabe went home ill. He was awarded the Knight's Cross in December 1941 for preventing far superior enemy forces from breaking through to relieve Tobruk. After two months in charge of the division he, too, fell ill and was evacuated to Germany, where he was promoted to *Generalleutnant* on 1 March 1942. He subsequently served on the OKH reserve and commanded various infantry and artillery divisions.

GENERALMAJOR GEORG VON BISMARCK

Born in Neumühl, near Küstrin in 1891, Georg von Bismarck joined the army in 1911 as a young officer in the 6th Light Infantry Battalion. He served throughout WW1, winning the Royal House Order of Hohenzollern with Swords for bravery. In 1939–40 he commanded 7th Rifle Regiment in Poland and France, where he was awarded the Knight's Cross for his part in 7th Panzer Division's meteoric push to the Atlantic coast. On 5 January 1942 he was posted to Africa, where Rommel gave

Above: Rommel with von Bismarck.

him command of 21st Panzer Division. He then led it in a sustained advance from Cyrenaica to El Alamein. On 1 August 1942 he was promoted to *Generalleutnant*. He was killed in a mortar attack while crossing the minefields at Alam Halfa at the end of that same month.

OBERST CARL-HANS LUNGERHAUSEN

Born on 20 July 1896 at Darmstadt, Lungerhausen joined the army in August 1914, as a *Leutnant* in the Dragoons. Postwar he commanded 1st Battalion 8th Cavalry Regiment in the *Reichswehr*. He was promoted to *Oberst* in February 1939 and later commanded the 164th Leichte Division in Africa from August till late November 1942. From 31 August to 18 September of the same year he temporarily filled in as commander of 21st Panzer Division following Bismarck's death. He was promoted *Generalleutnant* on 1 January 1943, and served later in Sardinia and Italy, being awarded the German Cross in Gold.

GENERALMAJOR HEINZ VON RANDOW

Born on 15 November 1890 at Grammau, von Randow joined the army on 18 June 1910 as a *Leutnant* in the 18th Dragoon Regiment. He was a cavalryman who witnessed the transfer of the unit to tanks. Postwar he served in the *Reichswehr*, commanding Cavalry Regiment 13. He was promoted *Oberst* on 1 February, 1939. He commanded 21st Panzer Division from 18 September 1942 until 21 December 1942, when he was killed near Tripoli during the DAK withdrawal, a few days after being promoted *Generalleutnant*. He was the holder of the German Cross in Gold.

OBERST HANS-GEORG HILDERBRANDT

Born on 15 June 1896 at Fraustadt, Hilderbrandt joined the army in August 1914 as *Leutnant* in the 36th Fusilier Regiment. Following the end of WW1 he remained in the *Reichswehr*. He was promoted *Oberst* in November 1940, finally reaching

Right: Generaloberst von Arnim (left), the last commander of German forces in Tunisia, is briefed by the last commander of 21st Panzer Division in North Africa, Generalmajor Heinrich-Hermann von Hülsen a month before the Axis surrender in May 1943.

the rank of *Generalleutnant* on 1 June 1944. He commanded 21st Panzer Division from 1 January 1943 to 15 March 1943, when he fell ill. After almost a year of sick leave, he then commanded 715th Infantry Division. He was the holder of the German Cross in Gold.

GENERALMAJOR HEINRICH-HERMANN VON HÜLSEN

Born on 8 July 1895 in Weimar, Hülsen joined the army on 28 April 1914 as a *Leutnant* in the Fusiliers. Following the end of WW1 he, too, remained in the *Reichswehr*, commanding Cavalry Regiment 11. He was promoted *Oberst* in December 1940, and *Generalmajor* in May 1943. Having commanded Schützenbrigade 9, he was then a staff officer with Panzerarmee Afrika before commanding 21st Panzer Division. He surrendered with the division to the Allies and was taken prisoner on 12 May 1943.

GENERALMAJOR EDGAR FEUCHTINGER

Edgar Feuchtinger was born in Metz on 9 November 1894 and joined the army on 7 August 1914. He was originally an artilleryman, serving in both WW1 and afterwards in the *Reichswehr*, being promoted to *Oberstleutnant* in 1938. He was a strong Nazi sympathiser who had helped organise the annual rallies at Nuremberg. He became an *Oberst* in 1941 and *Generalmajor* in 1943, commanding 21st Panzer Division when it was reformed in Normandy, with two short breaks during which it was commanded first by Generalmajor Oswin Grolig and then by Generalmajor Franz Westhoven. Feuchtinger was awarded the German Cross in Gold, and in August 1944 he was promoted *Generalleutnant*.

OBERST HELMUT ZOLLENKOPF

Taking command of the unit in spring 1945, Zollenkopf's 21st Panzer Division consisted of a single combined battalion based on 22nd Panzer Regiment. Directed to the defence of East Germany, Zollenkopf surrendered the division to the Soviet Army on 29 April 1945.

ASSESSMENT

The story of 21st Panzer Division, particularly in the 1941 period when it formed the bulk of Rommel's very much understrength DAK, is unusual in that it was free from the taint of Nazi political intervention in the sense that there was no involvement of the SS or political leaders. This is not to say that Rommel was antipathetic to Hitler—far from it—or that his command was free of attempted military interference. Rommel's strength was that he almost always ignored interference, took gambles and won. The desert war in particular is free of rumours of atrocities or cruelty outside the the usual horrors of warfare. Both sides treated prisoners as well as they could in the circumstances, cared for each other's wounded, and generally engaged in a chivalry of warfare that has been almost absent from the battlefield ever since.

It is well known that each side respected the other, and there are many records of surrendered troops on either side congratulating their opponents for a victory well and fairly won, and for the victors treating their captured foes with respect in the aftermath of battle. Not for nothing was Rommel respected by the British soldier who admired his skilful handling of his troops and the achievements of those troops with, usually, numerically inferior forces. In fact Rommel was held in such regard by the British troops that British military leaders in 1942 had to make a conscious effort to belittle him as a dangerous enemy.

Because the desert was a 'neutral' battleground, almost free from towns and with few inhabitants, the warfare was very 'pure', almost like a large game of chess on which the pieces of war could be freely manoeuvred. This attitude percolated through both sides, and in no other theatre of war did both sides hum the same sentimental tune—'Lili Marlene', a German song popular in DAK which was also taken up by the British and Commonwealth forces, so that it became a common theme for all who fought under desert skies.

As a fighting force 21st Panzer reflected throughout the skill and dedication of its commanders, and a professionalism typical of all German military formations of the first rank. Much initiative was shown at all levels in keeping with German military training, and there was all-arms co-ordination that often made up for inferior numbers. Even in the hopeless situation of Normandy, where for the first day or two 21st Panzer was the only substantial German formation in the field, it gave a good account of itself. But lacking back-up in the opening hours, it was limited in what it could achieve despite brave fighting by men of the division.

Excluding actions in NW Europe in 1944–45, when 21st Panzer Division was pitched into battle against impossible odds, it enjoyed an enviable reputation as a highly successful formation, invariably well commanded both at divisional and corps level. In the Western Desert it only came off worse when the numerical disadvantage was huge, but even then, because of a certain amount of muddle and indecision on

Below: Young Iron Cross recipient:

Above: The mainstays of the desert fighting—German infantry advancing with a PzKpfw III in close support.

the British side, the division escaped being severely bloodied even when it expected to be. For example, at First Alamein a flank attack on 21st Panzer, which could easily have cut off the divisions, was not pursued with vigour and the division was able to make a withdrawal when it might, instead, have been annihilated. Similarly, stranded without fuel in the early stages of the Gazala battles, it survived because the British forces, not appreciating the situation, held off.

Faulty staff work, timid tank handling and ill-thought out decisions on the British side were an undoubted aid to the DAK Panzer divisions and often compensated for their weakness in numbers. Allied with this was the bold, instinctive handling by the corps commander, Rommel, whose legendary exploits often had a psychological affect on British morale. German Panzer divisions, including the 21st, scored over the British very often because of the German military philosophy of all-arms co-operation and organisation which allowed even small organic groups to be self-contained as fighting units. All too often the British rigidity of operation meant that there was little or no true co-operation between infantry, artillery and armour. This was seen several times in the desert war when the British used defended 'boxes' largely occupied only by infantry formations with no close-by or integral armour support since the armour itself was located further back in the desert.

Even when the British used mobile formations they tended to be single arms, such as armour, with no accompanying infantry of any substance. The German mobile columns, by contrast, included infantry, artillery and armour all working together. The Germans used their limited resources to the full. This is well illustrated by the use of the Flak 88 gun, which had been tried on occasions (and unofficially) in the anti-tank role before 1941 but was used purposefully as an anti-tank gun once Rommel realised its range advantage and immense destructive power against British tanks. Even after it was proven from emplaced ground positions, notably at Halfaya Pass, the Germans did not leave it at that. Expediency during the early running tank battles showed that it could fire successfully from its wheeled carriage without being emplaced, and the tactical advantage of that, first discovered by 21st Panzer Division, soon became a standard practice throughout the German Army. Throughout the rest of the war the Allies never really found an effective answer to the 88, whether it was used as a wheeled anti-tank gun or, later, fitted in late-war tanks. By contrast, inflexible British thinking never allowed the German practice to be copied, even though the 3.7-inch AA gun, available in large numbers, was slightly better than the 88. To the British it was designed as an AA gun and that was how it stayed.

In qualitative terms German tanks were usually more reliable and better built than the British equivalents, but against this only rarely did the Panzer divisions field more tanks in a battle than the British. In the early days the difference in gun performance and armour penetration was not as great as the British often made out. The 50mm gun of the early models of the PzKpfw III was almost exactly equivalent to the British 2pdr in performance and armour penetration (about 39mm–40mm), and the PzKpfw IV—in use for most of the desert campaign—only had a low velocity 75mm short calibre gun which was only really good for firing HE in a support role. Yet British tank crews reported being penetrated by PzKpfw IVs at 3,000 yards' range, obviously assuming tank guns were firing at them when it was an 88 doing the damage. The PzKpfw IV did not really become effective in the tank-killing role until it was fitted with the long calibre high velocity 75mm gun (the so-called PzKpfw IV 'Special') and these were not available to Rommel until summer 1942.

The Germans quickly realised that superior anti-tank guns were the key to winning in a tank battle. The 88 was soon joined by the 50mm Pak 38 in the desert and these two towed guns, highly mobile, did most of the real damage to the British as they could outrange the British tank guns.

Where the British had superior armour thickness, as on the Matilda tank, they were able to field an effective weapon, but the British forces were weakened by the prewar policy of having two classes of combat tank—infantry and cruiser—both with different top speeds, in the case of infantry tanks a very slow one. The shrewd combination of tanks and anti-tank guns in tactical situations was the real key to the success of the Panzer divisions in the desert fighting, and because of the open nature of the battlefield the advantage could be exploited to the full. Given the tactical ingenuity so often demonstrated by the corps commander, Rommel, and the fortitude and professionalism of the commanders, officers and men of the DAK Panzer divisions, they emerged from the campaign with a high reputation and a much-respected record which has not been tarnished by time.

Below: The aftermath of battle—a Panzer burns.

REFERENCE

INTERNET SITES:

http://www.tankclub.agava.ru/sign/sign.shtml
Russian-language site with excellent illustrations of the tactical signs of the German army

http://www.generals.dk
This is an private project trying to provide biographical data on the army generals of World War II, including many German generals.

http://members.nbci.com/dicemanrick/gerpg/ger1.htm
Good general site that provides an orbat, information on equipment, some details of opponents and a history of 21st Panzer Division May-August 1944. Includes specific sections on: German Records for 21st Panzer Division and information on deciphering the tactical symbols; Weapons and Equipment of the 21st Panzer Division; 21st Panzer Division in 1:300 models.

http://members.nbci.com/dicemanrick/gerpg/shpics/index.htm
The site above is part of the excellent Spearhead: France 1944 site:
This features items for WWII miniature wargaming using the Spearhead rules by Arty Conliffe and other items concerning WWII history.

REFERENCE

http://www.geocities.com/MotorCity/8418/21pz.htm
Giving orbats and a brief history, this site is from Tracks and Armour's Armoured Formation Profiles, which include many more Axis and Allied units, including most of the Panzer divisions. It includes information on the armed troops of all WW2 armies and has a glossary on Panzer divisions.

http://pzfaust.tripod.com/home.htm
A re-enactors' website for German units and dealers in re-enactor equipments. The 21st Panzer Division re-enactment unit is based in Southern California and is an active member of the California Historical Group. Unit members come from all over the West to participate in public events and battle re-enactments.

http://www.panzer-modell.de/referenz/abzeichen/15bis22.htm
Webite of Panzer divisional and units signs and badges. This site comes from www.panzer-modell.de

http://www.panzermuseum.com/
Panzermuseum Munster has 40 Wehrmacht vehicles from the 1934–45 era including: Panzer I, II, III, IV, V Panther, VI Königstiger, Sturmgeschütze, Jagdpanzer, Schützenpanzer, Spähpanzer.

http://www.feldgrau.com/
Comprehensive listing and info on German armed forces from 1919 to 1945.

You are visitor number to drop by this web site since 1st February 1997

Last Updated on 21st June 1999

Revised:

BIBLIOGRAPHY

Barnet, Corelli: *The Desert Generals*; William Kimber, 1960.
This famous book gives succinct accounts and analysis of the sequence of desert battles, and assesses the performance (and often the failings) of the various British commanders over the whole period. It is very interesting reading, though there is very little coverage of 21st Panzer Division individually.

Bender, R. James, and Law, Richard D.: *Uniforms, Organisation and History of the Afrika Korps*; R. James Bender Publishing, 1973.
Bender, R. James, and Odegard, Warren W.: *Uniforms, Organisation and History of the Panzertruppe*; R. James Bender Publishing, 1973.
These volumes are in the very thorough style associated with this publisher/author in that they have highly detailed coverage of units involved in Afrika Korps and Panzer troop operations, with comprehensive orders of battle and information on minor or little-known units involved. 21st Panzer Division is covered in both books, though only as part of overall coverage. There are lists of bravery awards, commanders, staff officers and other key personalities, most of whom are pictured. There are also many rare photographs of interest.

Bennett, Ralph: *Ultra and Mediterranean Strategy 1941-45*; Hamish Hamilton 1989.
A good general history of how Ultra intercepts in the Mediterranean area were used or interpreted by British commanders (not always successfully) to aid the course of their campaigns. The desert war operations are only a segment of the book which does, of course, cover the course of World War 2 over the whole Mediterranean region.

Top and Above: The re-enactors of US-based 21st Panzer Division.

Carrell, Paul: *The Foxes of the Desert*; Dutton, 1961.
A good general account from the German point of view with personal experiences of DAK men and their viewpoint of battles and equipment.

Carver, Michael: *Tobruk*; Batsford, 1964.
A very comprehensive well written account of all the fighting for Tobruk and related battles in considerable detail, with well informed analysis by General Carver, who as a young officer, had personal experience of the desert campaign.

Ellis, Chris: *A Collector's Guide to the History and Uniforms of Das Heer: The German Army 1933-45*; Ian Allan Publishing, 1993.
Short, pocket-sized guide to the German Army.

Ellis, Chris, and Chamberlain, Peter: *Afrika Corps 1941-42*; Almark, 1971.
A useful soft cover book covering all Afrika Korps operations in the Western Desert in pictorial form with sketch maps of the battles and some colour illustrations.

Above: Chris Ellis' guide to the history and uniforms of the German Army has been reprinted.

Forty, George: *The Armies of Rommel*; Arms & Armour Press, 1997.
Excellent survey of the people and equipment of the forces Rommmel commanded throughout his career.

Forty, George: *Afrika Korps at War* (2 vols); Ian Allan Publishing, 1978.
Excellent photos and personal stories. Recently reprinted.

Heckmann, Wolf: *Rommel's War in Africa*
An excellent account by a German writer who interviewed veterans of the North African campaigns, both German and British, 25 years ago when many were still alive. Contains many first-hand accounts, many from the German troops including 21st Panzer Division/5th Light Division members. Also has succinct accounts and maps of the main battles, also as seen from the German side. This book gives excellent insights into the whole period and is worth reading to get an idea of what it was like to be a soldier on either side involved in the desert fighting.

Jewell, Derek (Ed): *Alamein and the Desert War*, Sphere, 1967.
This was a well-illustrated paperback actually produced as a spin off from a *Sunday Times* series of 1967 commemorating the 25th anniversary of Alamein. It has contributions from several key participants including Montgomery. Apart from covering the desert campaign in popular readable style it has some good coverage of more social aspects such as life in the desert, life at base, popular songs and entertainment, army newspapers, propaganda, and so on.

Lewin, Ronald: *The Life and Death of the Afrika Korps*; Batsford, 1977.
A comprehensive account of the organisation and operations of DAK from start to finish in North Africa, including, of course, the activities of 21st Panzer Division. This is essential reading for full understanding of the DAK and its achievements.

Liddell Hart, B. H.: *The Tanks*, Vol 2; Cassell, 1959.
Volume 2 of the history of the Royal Tank Regiment includes coverage of the Western Desert, Tunisian and Normandy campaigns that involved 21st Panzer Division, with excellent battle maps and comprehensive coverage of the progress of battles. There is much comparison of British and German tactical and armament policies, but the emphasis is from the British point of view and the involvement of RTR units.

Moorehead, Alan: *The Desert War*; Hamish Hamilton, 1965.
A general history of the North African war as seen through the eyes of a distinguished war reporter who followed events at first hand. It gives a good impression of what the war was like from the point of view of British and Commonwealth forces, though coverage of the enemy forces is more generalised.

Nafziger, George F.: *The German Order of Battle* (2 vols); Greenhill 1999.
Comprehensive book covering the entire German Army, division by division.

Phillips, C. E. Lucas: *Alamein*; Heinemann, 1962.
A highly detailed account of all aspects of the battle, with many personal accounts and detailed operational maps, as well as fully detailed orders of battle for both sides. This is probably the most comprehensive account available.

Young, Desmond: *Rommel*; Granada, 1950.
An early biography by a distinguished officer who fought against (and was captured by) Rommel in the desert war. Apart from good coverage of his DAK command and operations it includes interviews with former colleagues of Rommel, including Johannes Streich.

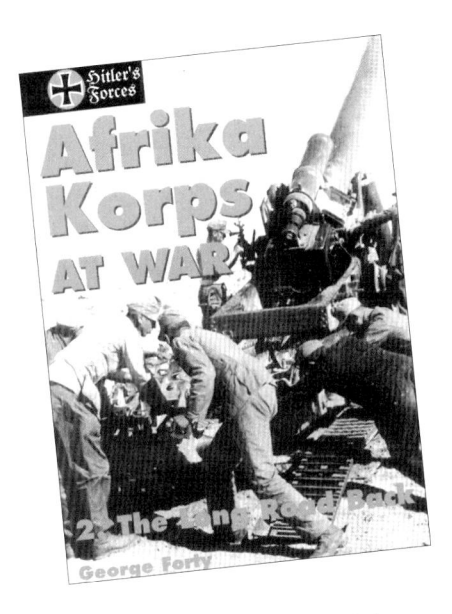

Above: George Forty's *The Afrika Korps at War* (Vols 1 and 2) provide a fascinating series of personal accounts and photos.

Above: One of Rommel's 21st Panzer Division adversaries in the North African desert was the Cruiser tank of the 7th Armoured Division. Here, one meets a Light Mk VI. Both would have shown the British red/white/red identification markings.

Right: The gun crew of a 40mm Bofors, part of the garrison at Bir Hacheim in 1942, supporting the French garrison there who kept Rommel at bay for many days during the fighting for the Gazala line.

7th ARMOURED DIVISION
The 'Desert Rats'
George Forty

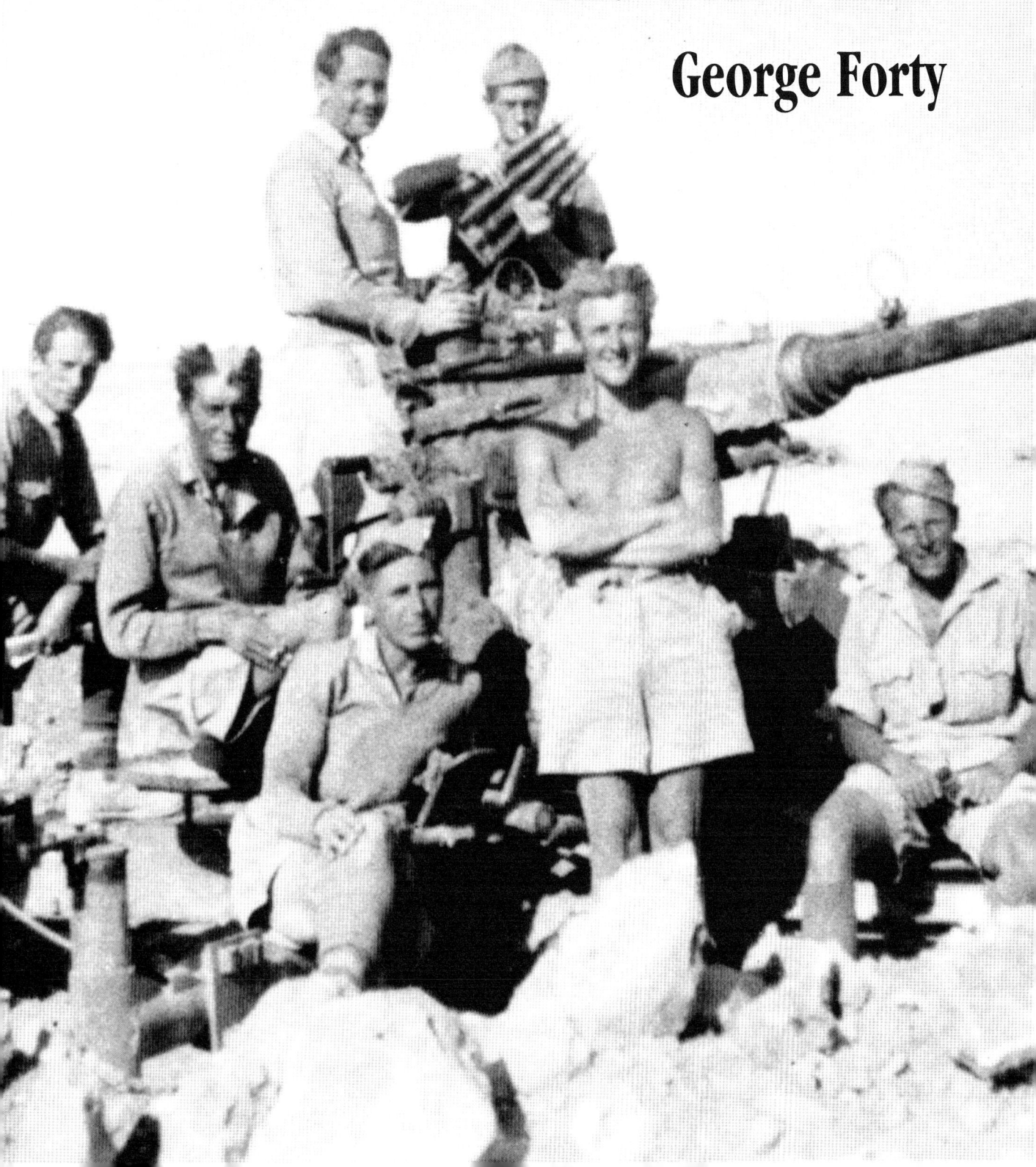

ORIGINS & HISTORY

Above: This is a woodcut of the original drawing by Mrs Peyton, wife of the division's first GSO3, from which the very first "Desert Rat" flash was produced in 1940 — see Equipment and Markings chapter for more details.

"CREATE AN ARMOURED DIVISION"

"In 1938, the year of the Munich crisis, an officer was flown from England to Egypt on an important mission: 'Create an Armoured Division' ... those were his orders." That extract from the *Egyptian Mail* for Wednesday, 10 February 1943, then goes on to outline how Maj-Gen Percy Cleghorn Stanley Hobart ("Hobo" as he was known — but never called — by everyone in the Royal Tank Corps) produced the first of the three great armoured divisions that he would be responsible for raising and training during World War II — namely, the 7th, 11th and 79th. He had to start with the "prehistoric" vehicles, weapons and equipment, which at that time made up the units of the Cairo Cavalry Brigade. As the threat of war became more and more apparent, the implications of the German-Italian Axis that had been forged in September 1936 became more and more evident, namely that the Italians might well take action to threaten the Suez Canal, that vital life-line of the British Empire. There were already large numbers of Italian troops in Cyrenaica, directly on the western border of Egypt, and Mussolini was already making bombastic noises. Therefore, to counter this potential threat, on 17 September 1938 the Cairo Cavalry Brigade was hurriedly ordered to Mersa Matruh, some 170 miles west of Alexandria, to form the "Matruh Mobile Force" under the command of Brig H. E. Russell. Its initial composition was:

HQ Cairo Cavalry Brigade & Signals
3rd Regiment Royal Horse Artillery (3 RHA), equipped with 3.7in howitzers, towed by Dragons.
7th Queen's Own Hussars (7 H), with two squadrons of light tanks, Mark III to Mark VIIB (but with no .5in ammunition for their heavy machine guns.
8th King's Royal Irish Hussars (8 H), with Ford 15cwt pick-up trucks, mounting Vickers-Berthier guns.
11th Hussars (Prince Albert's Own) (11 H), with 1920s-vintage Rolls-Royce armoured cars and a few Morrises.
1st Battalion Royal Tank Corps (1 RTC) (to be renamed 1st Royal Tank Regiment [1 RTR] after the creation of the Royal Armoured Corps [RAC] on 4 April 1939). It was newly-arrived from England, complete with 58 light tanks, but with little track mileage left and few new tracks available.
No 5 Company, Royal Army Service Corps (RASC).
2nd/3rd Field Ambulance, Royal Army Medical Corps (RAMC).

Left behind in Cairo, on internal security duties, was the 6th Battalion, Royal Tank Corps, equipped with obsolete old medium and light tanks, whilst already at Mersa Matruh was the 2nd Field Company, Royal Engineers (RE) with whom the brigade would co-operate.

Air support for this motley collection of outdated vehicles and weaponry was equally prehistoric, viz: No 108 (Army Co-operation) Squadron RAF, equipped with Hawker Audaxes; No 80 (Fighter) Squadron RAF, equipped with Gloster Gladiators and No 45 (Bomber) Squadron RAF, equipped with Hawker Harts. The arrival of a flight of Bristol Blenheims from Iraq caused great excitement!

So this was the "Mobile Force", sometimes also known rather unkindly as the "Immobile Farce", which Maj-Gen Hobart came out from England to change into an armoured division and to command. He had already shown himself to be a superlative armoured trainer on Salisbury Plain in the early 1930s, commanding the first (and only) Tank Brigade from 1931 to 1935. In 1937 he had been appointed Director of Military Training (DMT) at the War Office, an appointment about which he had grave misgivings because of the "bad attitude" towards tanks prevailing at that time in the British Army. His year as DMT had not been an easy one and he had made many enemies, especially among those who still held old fashioned views on mechanisation. These included even the Secretary of State for War (Duff Cooper), who had apologised to the Cavalry in 1936, when they had begun to mechanise, with the words: "It is like asking a great musical performer to throw away his violin and devote himself to the gramophone!" Such stupidity at so high a level would leave the British Army woefully short of tanks when war came. "Hobo", who was not one to suffer fools gladly, was naturally a passionate supporter of the tank and of armoured warfare, so he was bound to be at loggerheads with such views. He also detested the pomp and circumstance of prewar Army life. On his arrival in Cairo, the then GOC-in-C Lt-Gen Sir Robert Gordon-Finlayson had greeted him with the words: "I don't know what you've come here for, and I don't want you anyway!" Nevertheless, "Hobo" typically did not let this open hostility deter him and immediately set about transforming the Mobile Division into a formidable fighting force.

After carrying out a few exercises in the desert around Mersa Matruh, the Force returned to Cairo, where it was joined by its first infantry element, the 1st Battalion, the King's Royal Rifle Corps (1 KRRC). "Hobo" then set about the difficult task of organising from scratch the formation, training, equipment and administration of the "Mobile Division (Egypt) and Abbassia District", as the Force was now called. He wrote: "I decided to concentrate on dispersion, flexibility and mobility … to try to get the Division and formations well extended, really handy and under quick control. To units unused to speed and wide frontages made possible by mechanisation, these matters presented considerable difficulties." Throughout the summer the fledgling division held indoor exercises and hammered out in theory every aspect of the administration of an armoured force that would be so important in an inhospitable desert setting. Once the weather was cooler, the division went back to the desert again, learning how to live and fight in these difficult conditions. As always, it also had to suffer the strictures that affected peacetime soldiering — despite the fact that war was imminent — such as strictly limited track mileage for tanks, and a desperate shortage of wheeled vehicles.

"Hobo" had continually to fight against a great deal of obstruction, ignorance and

Below: Maj-Gen P. C. S. Hobart taking an early morning ride near Cairo, with his stepson Robin Chater, soon after their arrival in Egypt. "Hobo" was the best trainer of armoured units in the British Army and had just finished a tour as Director Military Training at the War Office. He was disliked and distrusted by the very conservatively minded senior officers in command in Egypt, as a result of which he was quite outrageously sacked.

Above: The original Mobile Division drawn up on parade near Mersa Matruh in 1939. Despite its outdated, obsolescent equipment, "Hobo" turned it into a highly effective, mobile force, which, as an integral part of the Western Desert Force, would do exceptionally well against the Italians.

even idleness, but his enthusiasm and determination never flagged. The difference between the Mobile Division of August 1939 and the "Immobile Farce" of just a year earlier was truly remarkable. However, he was still thwarted at every turn, especially by senior officers who simply did not understand modern war.

As well as gaining much-needed expertise in the art of mobile armoured warfare, the division also received some new equipment: 7th Hussars, for example, was now complete with three squadrons of light tanks, whilst 8th Hussars had begun to receive light tanks from 7th Hussars to replace its 15cwt pick-ups. 3rd RHA now had half 37mm anti-tank guns and half 25-pounders, and a 25-pounder battery of 4th RHA had been attached to the division to provide extra gunner support. 11th Hussars had received more Morris armoured cars and 6 RTR its first 10 A9 cruiser tanks. The order of battle now was:

Light Brigade (Commander: Brig H. E. Russell) — 7th, 8th and 11th Hussars
Heavy Brigade (Commander: Lt-Col H. R. B. Watkins) — 1st and 6th RTR
Pivot Group (Commander: Lt-Col W. H. B. Mirrles) — 3rd RHA, F Battery 4th RHA and 1st KRRC

Once war had broken out with Germany, the division went on another series of exercises under the watchful eye of "Hobo", returning to Cairo once again in November 1939. Gordon-Finlayson's place had now been taken by Gen "Jumbo" Wilson, with whom "Hobo" initially got on very amicably until one particular exercise, when a series of misunderstandings arose between them. These were mainly due to the fact that, like most successful armoured commanders, "Hobo" led from the front and was therefore never available at his HQ, where more orthodox commanders like Wilson expected to find him. This led to a personal row which resulted in Wilson writing to Gen Wavell (then C-in-C Middle East) saying that he no longer had any confidence in Hobart and asking for him to be relieved of his command. So "Hobo" left without further ado. It is interesting to note that Gen O'Connor who, as commander of the Western Desert Force, had worked closely with Gen Hobart on the desert exercises, had had no difficulties working with him and expressed the opinion that the Mobile Division was the best trained division he had ever seen. In his book about his wartime career (*Eight Years Overseas 1939-1947*) Wilson makes no mention of their disagreement, merely just stating that Hobart was relieved by Creagh during the winter. A measure of the high esteem in which he was held by the men of his division can be judged by the fact that without any orders being issued, the men of the Mobile Division lined the route as he left his headquarters to bid him farewell. "Hobo" went back to the temporary obscurity of retirement, exchanging his general's badges of rank for those of a lance corporal in his local Home Guard — fortunately, however, not for long, Winston Churchill personally going "into bat" for him. "I think highly of this officer," Churchill wrote to the CIGS on 19 October 1940, "and am not at all impressed by the prejudices against him in certain quarters. Such prejudices attach frequently to persons of strong personality and original view. In this case General Hobart's original views have been only too tragically borne out. The neglect by the General Staff even to devise proper patterns of tanks before the war has robbed us of all the fruits of this invention. These fruits have been reaped by the enemy with terrible consequences. We should therefore remember that this was an officer who had the root of the matter in him, and also the vision."

Maj-Gen Hobart's place was taken by Maj-Gen Michael O'Moore Creagh (late 15/19 H), but his influence remained long after his departure and many times his views were quoted — "'Hobo' used to say …". As Maj-Gen Verney said of him, in the prologue to his history of the division: "His departure came as a rude shock to the Division. To his country the General's services had been considerable, to the Division he formed and trained they were immeasurable and the long record of success in the years that followed stands as a tribute to their first commander."

Above: Light MkVI tanks of 1 RTR on manoeuvres near the Pyramids, 24 January 1939. Despite being of little use in battle, these tiny, light tanks were ideal as training vehicles for the Mobile Division, and, despite being restricted on track mileage, they enabled the division to acquire a great deal of desert experience.

REDESIGNATION

More changes followed the departure of "Hobo". The Heavy Brigade became 4th Armoured Brigade and the Light Brigade, the 7th Armoured Brigade; the Pivot Group became officially known as the Support Group and was enlarged with the arrival from Palestine of the 2nd Battalion the Rifle Brigade (2 RB). 3 RHA was converted into an anti-tank regiment and 4 RHA complete joined the division, together with 2 RTR and other units from the UK. Brig J. A. L. Caunter, late RTR, took command of 4th Armd Bde. On 16 February 1940, the Mobile Division was officially redesignated as the 7th Armoured Division. War against Italy now became a distinct possibility, so the division moved light forces up to the frontier wire.

AND ON TOWARDS WAR

When, towards the end of April 1940, it became obvious that Italy was going to enter the war the 11th Hussars and the Support Group moved out to Mersa Matruh. In the middle of May they were followed by divisional headquarters and 4th Armd Bde. For another month intensive training continued, together with surreptitious reconnaissance of the Italian frontier posts (undertaken only by the squadron commanders of 11th Hussars). These had to be very carefully done as they were under orders to do nothing that might be considered provocative. 11th Hussars also had to get used to maintaining its subunits on a very wide front — the distance between regimental headquarters and squadrons being some 60 to 80 miles. This necessitated reorganising its unit transport on a double echelon basis. Everyone was stretched to the limits, so the welcome arrival of some volunteers from Southern Rhodesia was much appreciated. Forty-five of these volunteers went to 11 H and were formed into Scout Troops in Ford cars.

READY FOR WAR

ITALY DECLARES WAR

At 7pm on the evening of 10 June 1940, Il Duce declared war on Great Britain and France. He had been agonising what to do for some days, trying to decide whether or not to throw his lot in with the Axis or to remain neutral. "If we have decided to face the risks and sacrifices of war, it is because the honour and interest of Italy requires it of us." What that really meant was that he could not wait any longer to share in the "spoils of war" which would begin to satisfy his thirst for glory. Once the British had been forced to retreat from Dunkirk and the German Blitzkrieg had swept through most of France, Mussolini made his decision and opted for the Axis camp. Clearly he had designs on "empire building" in North Africa, despite naming Egypt among the neighbours whom Italy did not intend to: "… drag into conflict". Indeed, when the Italian envoy HE Nobile Serafine dei Conti Mazzolini, Envoy Extraordinary and Minister Plenipotentiary of Italy in Egypt, had been given his marching orders when Egypt broke off diplomatic relations, Mazzolini had said, with a knowing look: "We shall be back in a fortnight," and had left his car and his entire wardrobe behind!

Below: Radio vehicles and their crews belonging to RHQ 1 RTR pause during an exercise in the desert during the late spring of 1939. The use of radio was very much in its infancy before war began and wirelesses were still not widely issued within the British Army, except within armoured units and other mobile troops. Even within a tank squadron, troop commanders invariably used hand signals to control their troops so as to reduce radio transmissions, but were in touch with their squadron commander via the radio.

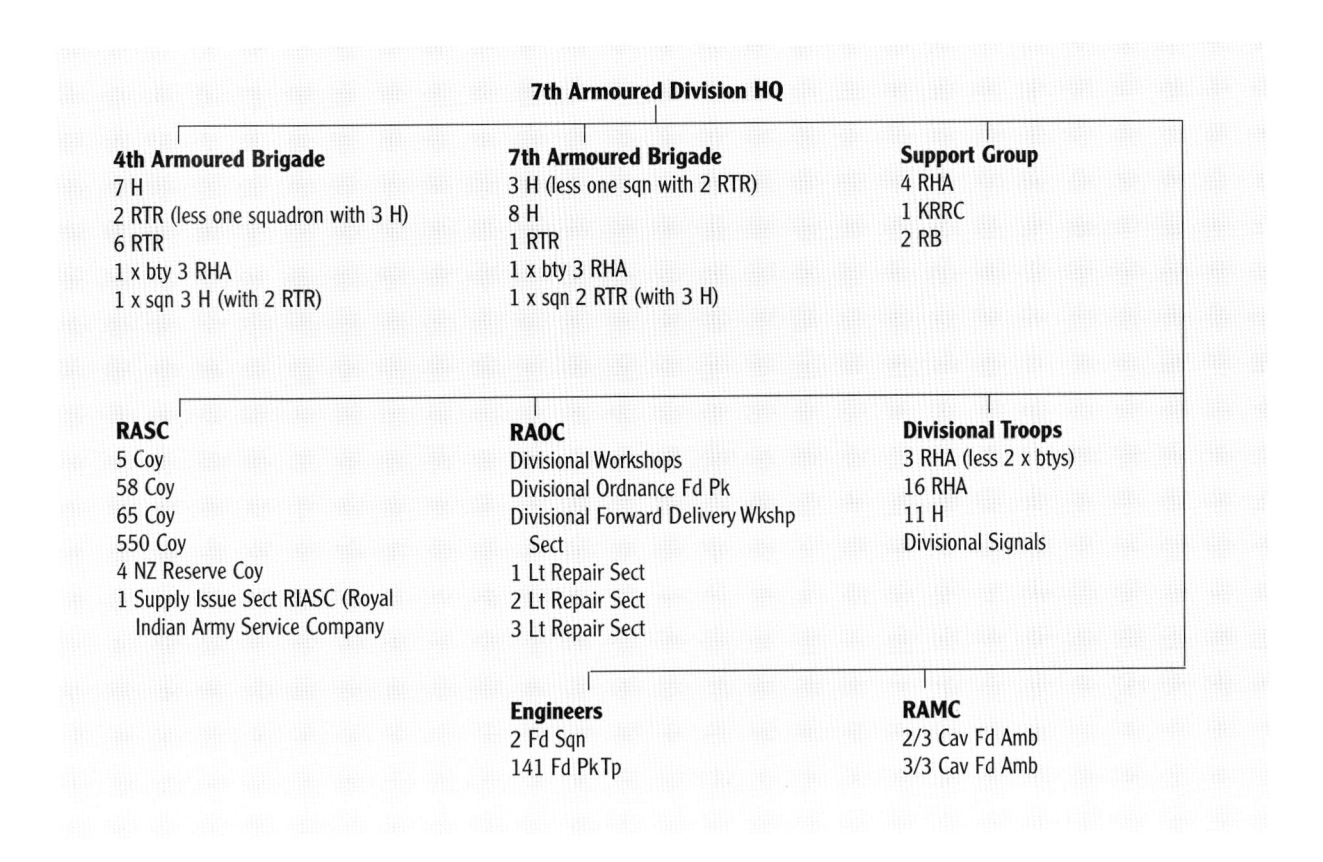

```
                        7th Armoured Division HQ
    ┌───────────────────────────┼───────────────────────────┐
4th Armoured Brigade        7th Armoured Brigade        Support Group
7 H                         3 H (less one sqn with 2 RTR)  4 RHA
2 RTR (less one squadron with 3 H)  8 H                 1 KRRC
6 RTR                       1 RTR                       2 RB
1 x bty 3 RHA               1 x bty 3 RHA
1 x sqn 3 H (with 2 RTR)    1 x sqn 2 RTR (with 3 H)


    ┌───────────────────────────┼───────────────────────────┐
RASC                        RAOC                        Divisional Troops
5 Coy                       Divisional Workshops        3 RHA (less 2 x btys)
58 Coy                      Divisional Ordnance Fd Pk   16 RHA
65 Coy                      Divisional Forward Delivery Wkshp  11 H
550 Coy                       Sect                      Divisional Signals
4 NZ Reserve Coy            1 Lt Repair Sect
1 Supply Issue Sect RIASC (Royal  2 Lt Repair Sect
   Indian Army Service Company)  3 Lt Repair Sect

                            ┌───────────────────────────┐
                        Engineers                   RAMC
                        2 Fd Sqn                    2/3 Cav Fd Amb
                        141 Fd Pk Tp                3/3 Cav Fd Amb
```

The following day the complete 7th Armoured Division moved up to the frontier. Between its first move up to the frontier on 11 June and the first major operation conducted by the Western Desert Force, of which the Division formed a major part, in early December, it received some reinforcements. For example, 2 RTR left the UK on 20 August and arrived in mid-October. Equipped with A13s, plus some A9s and A10s, the Second entrained immediately for the Western Desert, where it joined 4th Armd Bde. Thus the divisional order of battle at the start of Operation Compass is shown in the table above.

Above: Divisional organisation as at November 1940.

MAIN COMPONENTS

Divisional Headquarters In the early days, Div HQ was divided into two main groups or echelons — Advanced and Rear. Advanced HQ (later known as Main HQ) contained only those necessary for the control and command of the division during operations; in other words, the GOC, his "G" and "I" staffs, artillery and engineer advisers, together with the crews of the communications and protection vehicles. Before the Command vehicles were armoured, two armoured cars were also included in this group, so that a Battle HQ (later called Tactical HQ) could be formed and all unarmoured vehicles withdrawn when action was imminent.

Rear Division contained the rest of Div HQ, that is to say everything that was not required for immediate operational control. The Heads of the Services (CRASC, ADMS, SOME, etc) worked here under the AA & QMG. Their duties were mainly concerned with the control and direction of the administration of the division. Rear HQ was usually located some distance behind Advanced HQ, where it could work free from the risk of enemy ground interference.

ADVANCED HQ ON MOVE
3 x Cruiser Tanks — Protective Detachment
1 x Armoured Car — Navigator

Group "A"
ACV 1 — Command ACV (nerve centre of Div HQ)
Despatch rider on a motorcycle
ACV 2 — Intelligence ACV
ACV 3 — Rear Link
1 x Scout Car

Group "B" (160yd behind)
1 x Cruiser tank — GOC's Charger
Despatch rider on a motorcycle
1 x Cruiser tank — "G" Charger
1 x Armoured Car — "Q" Charger
1 x Scout Car

Group "C" (160yd behind)
ACV 4 — Spare ACV
1 x Scout Car
3 x Ford PU — Liaison Officers

Group "D" (160yd behind)
Office Truck — G Office
Office Truck — Signals Office
Despatch rider on a motorcycle
Ford PU — Frontier Force

When on the move, Advanced HQ moved in groups, as shown in the box at left. (When stationary it formed a scattered leaguer, closing into a tight box formation.)

Reconnaissance The Divisional Armoured Car Regiment (11 H) had the task of providing distant recce, anything up to 50 miles from the main body of the division. This difficult and dangerous work had to be undertaken in any direction — to the front, flanks, even, on some occasions, to the rear. There could never be any gaps of time or space in the recce screen, as a constant up-to-the-minute flow of information was essential. The regiment therefore had to be able to split into a large number of small independent patrols, each capable of operating on its own for extended periods. It was also necessary for a centrally held reserve to be maintained at squadron level to meet unexpected situations and allow time, in theory anyway, for vehicle maintenance.

To tackle this considerable task, the regiment consisted of three reconnaissance squadrons, each of five troops of three armoured cars, although on some occasions a fourth recce sqn was added. Armoured car troops acted as the eyes and ears of the recce screen, with the rest of the regiment in control and supporting roles. Radio communications were its lifeblood, so that the unceasing flow of vital information could be passed swiftly back to higher formation. Despite numerous changes of vehicles and terrain, the basic task remained unchanged throughout the war and the 11th Hussars remained the "eyes of the division" throughout hostilities.

Armour The most powerful tactical unit of the division was the armoured regiment. The organisation of these armoured regiments together with the numbers and types of tanks they contained varied considerably during the war years. For details of these see pages 72–3. Initially there were three types of tanks in vogue: small light tanks, generally only armed with machine guns, whose main task was reconnaissance; medium-sized, fast, lightly armoured cruiser tanks, whose main role was to exploit breakthroughs and spread havoc behind enemy lines; finally, heavily armoured, slow moving infantry tanks to support major assaults, in what was still basically an infantry-orientated army. As the war progressed, the role of light tanks was taken over almost entirely by armoured cars/light recce vehicles, whilst the heavy infantry tanks were taken out of armoured divisions and organised into independent tank brigades. This left the cruiser tank as the main equipment of the armoured division — an unhappy situation due to its poor firepower

Left: Light tanks of 1 RTR are seen here on yet another parade, possibly the Royal Review of 1939 for King Farouk of Egypt. He had ascended to the throne in 1936 and ruled Egypt until 1952 when his regime was overthrown by Gamal Abdel Nasser. During the war, Farouk tried unsuccessfully to maintain neutrality despite the presence of British troops.

Below left: Echelon vehicle crews of 1 RTR line up for a briefing. Note all wear their respirators in the ready position; also all wear steel helmets. The NCO doing the talking has his pistol slung low on a special webbing strap and tied around the thigh like a Wild West gunfighter. Until the Sten gun and Thompson submachine gun became more widely available, the .38 pistol was the most commonly issued weapon for tank crews.

and woefully thin armour. Fortunately, however, help was at hand, the USA generously supplying firstly better-armed, more reliable, light tanks (the M3 Light, known officially as the Stuart in British service, but nicknamed the "Honey" by the crews), then Mediums (M3 Lee/Grant and M4 Sherman) with their 75mm guns and thicker armour, their main gun having both anti-tank and anti-personnel capability — the first time that British tanks had been armed with such a large-calibre weapon in quantity since 1918! Eventually, the cruiser and the Medium tank lines became indistinguishable in firepower, protection and mobility, Comet and Centurion being the end of the cruiser line and the beginning of the medium gun/main battle tank line that has progressed through Chieftain and Challenger 1, to the modern-day Challenger 2, which has performed so well in the latest war in Iraq.

Below: Moving up to Mersa Matruh. This tank train, loaded with light tanks of 1 RTR, was photographed at Fuka, en route to Mersa Matruh. Using the railway saved on track mileage, which was very strictly limited (for monetary reasons) even when troops were preparing for war.

Above: Cruiser tanks of 2 RTR on their way "Up the Blue". 2 RTR arrived in Egypt from the UK in mid-October and entrained immediately for its move to Mersa Matruh, where it joined the 4th Armd Bde of 7th Armoured Division.

A FORMATION OF ALL ARMS

From the outset it must be appreciated that an armoured division is a formation of all arms. "Tanks by themselves cannot win battles, so the unarmoured units of the armoured division are just as indispensable as the armoured ones, whilst the administrative services play roles no less vital and equally dangerous in maintaining supplies of all kinds, and in dealing with casualties to men and vehicles. Each arm or branch of service is a member of a team and has its vital part to play. Mutual understanding and confidence, based on experience during training and during action, form the keystone to success." These down-to-earth words of wisdom appeared in a wartime Military Training Pamphlet and must have been well appreciated, understood and followed by every member of the 7th Armoured Division throughout its wartime existence. The tank would finish World War II in a pre-eminent place on the land battlefield and has lost none of its usefulness during the turbulent days of peace that have followed. However, what must never be forgotten is that it is teamwork by a force of all arms that wins battles — and this was the case from the very first minor engagement that took place "Up the Blue" in the trackless wastes of the Western Desert.

Infantry The infantry will always be a vital component of any properly balanced fighting force and this was certainly the case in 7th Armoured Division. Tanks can capture ground, then dominate it for limited periods, but need infantry support if they are to hold for long or sustain their attacks. Within the division there were two types of infantry — a motor battalion and a mounted infantry brigade. The former was an integral part of the armoured brigade and its soldiers were experts at working closely with tanks (cf German Panzergrenadiers) and invariably travelled into battle in half-tracks, but dismounted to fight. They also had a high proportion of armoured scout carriers, scout cars and SP or towed anti-tank guns, so they could and did, provide immediate infantry support. On the other hand, the mounted infantry brigade at best travelled in lorries (TCVs), which made their speed on roads and good tracks even faster than that of the AFVs they were supporting. However, they were not tactically mounted so had to be careful not to expose their lorries to direct enemy fire .

Artillery Within the armoured division all three types of artillery — field, anti-tank and light anti-aircraft — had to be able to move at the same speed as the armour. Therefore, unlike German artillery which was horse-drawn in many instances, British artillery was motorised (towed by a tractor in which the gun crew travelled) or self-propelled. Lighter guns were initially carried "portee" — that is to say, in the back of an open truck (eg 2pdr anti-tank). Medium and heavy artillery might well be used to support the division but was never an integral part of its basic organisation.

Engineers Whatever the phase of war — advance, attack, defence or withdrawal — the Engineers were constantly needed. Their primary role was to assist the division in maintaining its mobility, so they had to be able to deal with a wide variety of natural obstacles (by preparing diversions, building bridges, etc) as well as dealing with enemy demolitions, booby traps and minefields — in fact, anything that hampered the division's progress. Additionally they were responsible for many other engineering tasks, which in the desert included the vital supply of water. In defence, they carried out specialist engineer tasks, like laying and recording minefields, or building defences and strongpoints.

Signals Communications were the lifeblood of any mobile armoured force and it is no exaggeration to say that the successful operation of an armoured division — especially in the desert — depended upon reliable communications. The system had to be flexible enough to meet any situation that arose, especially since fighting a mobile battle over vast areas of trackless desert wastes produced new problems hourly. The Royal Signals were responsible for communications at divisonal and brigade headquarters and down to units. Within units it was the responsibility of regimental signallers. All types of communications were used — wireless, land line and message carriers (LOs, DRs etc). Wireless provided the fastest and most flexible means but was dependent upon the skill of operators, the range of the radio sets and on the amount of outside interference, both climatic and from enemy jamming. Codes and ciphers had to be used as the enemy could, and did, listen in.

The Services The armoured division was a formation of all arms, in which the administrative services played no less a vital and dangerous role as the "teeth" arms. So "A" and "Q" Services, which included supplies and transport, medical and dental, ordnance, EME repair and recovery, provost and field security, pay, postal, welfare (eg NAAFI), chaplains and all the rest, played their part in keeping the division fighting fit and able to fight efficiently no matter the circumstances.

IN ACTION

"A PLACE FIT ONLY FOR WAR"

That is how the Western Desert of North Africa has been somewhat cynically described, so it is well worth looking briefly at the geography of the area in which the campaigns of the ensuing two and half years took place. It consisted of a level inland desert plateau stepping down in steep escarpments to a narrow coastal plain approximately 30 miles in width. The endpoints of these escarpments (south of Sidi Barrani and west of Tobruk), and their main gaps (Alamein, Halfaya near Sollum and Sidi Rezegh just south of Tobruk), along with the (only metalled) vital coast road connecting the two opposing capitals (Cairo and Tripoli), were to become the main focus of the actions that took place.

The climate of the area spanned the extremes of heat and cold within each 24-hour period, while the inimical desert terrain harboured winds and dust storms, thinly crusted impassable sand seas and other hazards. Yet for all its harshness, few were left untouched by the desert's austere beauty.

For both sides the problems of maintenance, recovery and supply were paramount, with all *matériel* having to be transported into the battle area. Water, fuel, ammunition and spares were always critical, while rations were often minimal and rarely followed army norms. "Living off the land" was impossible, but to capture a portion of the other side's supplies could prove to be a fortunate, at times even a life-saving, bonus. The logistics of these operations were to accelerate the development of new arms of service organisations, that would include the formation of the Corps of Royal Electrical and Mechanical Engineers (formed under Army Order 70 of 1942) to provide specialist electrical and mechanical servicing and repairs for the increasingly mechanised Army.

Below: Light tanks exercising with infantry. The white "24" shows that these light Mark VIs belong to 1 RTR. They are exercising with men of the 1/6 Rajputana Rifles of 4th Indian Division, as they prepare for Operation Compass, Gen O'Connor's daring raid on the Italian forts. Unbeknown to all but the "top brass", O'Connor had caused dummy forts to be built in a similar layout to those constructed by the Italians, so that everyone knew precisely what to do when battle was joined. *IWM — E777*

THE FIRST OFFENSIVE — OPERATION COMPASS

C-in-C MELF, Gen Archibald Wavell, made the most of the strategic asset of the railway connecting Alexandria to Mersa Matruh and adopted a policy of defence in depth, with infantry based on the defended railhead and aggressive patrolling by 7th Armoured Division lying immediately

Above: "Piccadilly Circus." This well-known track junction, in the desert south of Sidi Barrani not only had its own signpost but also, as the photograph shows, its own statue of Eros! "Charing Cross" was the name given by the troops to another important cross tracks, whilst "Marble Arch" was the troops' name for the Italian triumphal arch (*Arco del Felini*) on the coast road.

behind the frontier wire. He was seeking to contain the massive Italian army on Egypt's western frontier (consisting of five divisions in Cyrenaica backed up by nine more in Tripolitania — a total of over 215,000 men), with a force less than a third its size.

In fact the excellent training and ethos of Gen Hobart, coupled with the attacking instincts of Gen O'Connor and his staff, enabled these hurriedly cobbled together elements now called the: "Western Desert Force (WDF)", to coalesce into a capable mixed force of all arms which went on to first dominate its larger enemy, then decimate and ultimately to destroy it.

The primarily unmechanised Italians chose to remain on their side of the frontier wire, in forts too far apart to cover each other properly, and to rely on their supposedly overwhelming air superiority. The moment war was declared on 11 June, the Support Group of the division and the 11th Hussars (its armoured car regiment) whipped through the border wire, into Libya and action, dominating the gaps between the Capuzzo and Maddalena forts, probing, raiding and taking ever increasing numbers of prisoners. On 14 June both forts were captured and partly destroyed. On 16 June the first tank-versus-tank encounter took place, with the Italian force being annihilated. These actions set the tempo of the whole campaign, kept the initiative with the British who through sheer aggression made the enemy think they were facing a much larger force.

For the next four months the Italians did little more than reoccupy their forts, but on 13 September Marshal Graziani finally ordered his army over the border — moving ponderously and stopping only halfway to the critical strategic objective of Mersa Matruh. Just south of Sidi Barrani on the escarpment they built some half dozen fortified camps, content to have symbolically occupied British territory.

For the next three months, with the Italians static, the WDF continued harassing and maintaining the initiative, using its mobile forces, such as 7th Armoured Division's armoured cars and "Jock Columns". The latter were named after the then Lt-Col "Jock" Campbell of 4 RHA who would go on to command 7th Armoured Division, be awarded the Victoria Cross and be killed in a car accident in the desert in February 1942. These columns consisted of a few field guns, some anti-tank guns carried "portee" in the backs of lorries, some armoured cars and up to a company of motorised infantry. They were used in a highly mobile role to penetrate behind enemy lines, disrupt and destroy his communications and supply lines, and to build up through excellent reconnaissance an in-depth knowledge of the enemy's defences and resources.

Operation Compass This pause also gave valuable time to the WDF, to improve its supply and service echelons and to plan and practice for Operation Compass, as Gen O'Connor's proposed five-day raid on the Italian positions was now called. Practice operations were carried out against exact replicas of the Italian forts which O'Connor had caused to be built in the desert in the utmost secrecy, so that the Italians would hear nothing, but the troops taking part would know exactly what to do when the time came. Gen O'Connor launched his surprise attack on the Italian camps on the night of 7/8

Left: This light tank crew is well wrapped up against the bitter cold of an early desert morning, as it brews up a reviving cuppa. Making a brew was very easy for tank crews as they always had the means of making a small fire and could carry billy cans, etc on their AFVs. *IWM — E1501*

Below: An A13 Mark II cruiser tank belonging to 2 RTR receives some maintenance from its crew after the successful capture of Sid Omar from the Italians. The A13 Mark II was essentially just an uparmoured version of the A13, bringing its armour thickness up to 20-30mm.

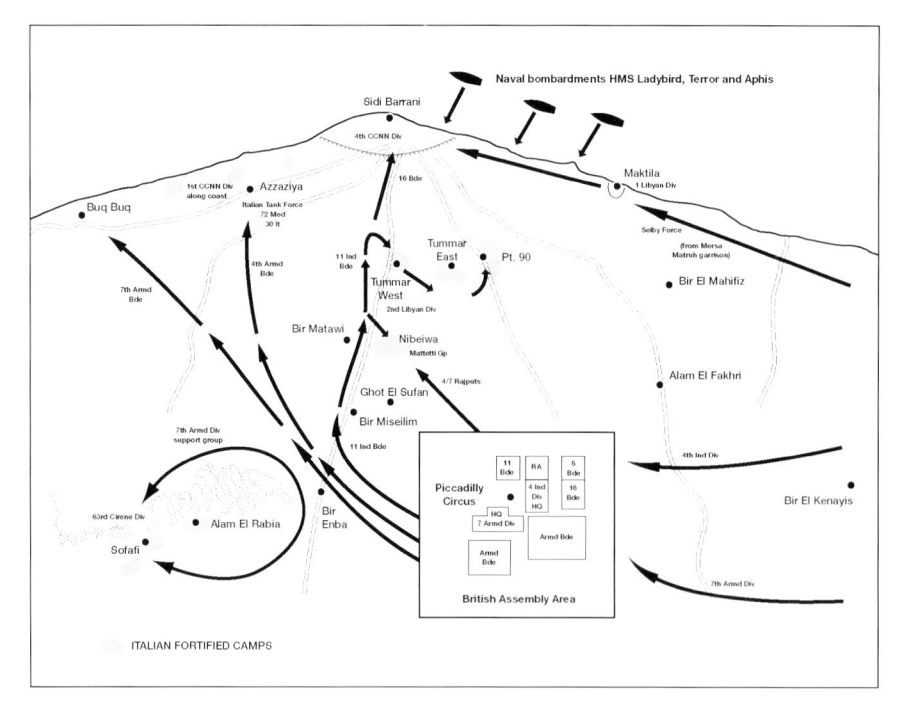

Above: Operation Compass — the capture of Sidi Barrani, 9–11 December 1940.

December 1940, moving to an Assembly Area (near "Piccadilly Circus" south of Sidi Barrani), then taking Nibeiwa and Tummar Forts with 4th Ind Div (Beresford-Pierse) supported by the Matilda MkIIs of 7 RTR, at dawn on 9 December 1940.

7th Armd Div's major roles in the operation were to cut the coast road to the west of Sidi Barrani, block the Italian escape routes from the forts and the town, and also prevent interference from other Italian forces to the west. It accomplished most of the missions without too many problems, however, one Italian formation made a stand to the west of Bug Bug, inflicting some damage with its dug-in artillery guns, before being broken and fleeing, leaving behind some four thousand prisoners. Now began an Italian retreat towards the border and back into Cyrenaica, pursued, despite the vagaries of supply, by the division followed by the rest of the WDF. To overcome salting of water sources by the enemy, fresh water and fuel was shipped in up the coast by sea.

A CHANGE OF DIVISIONS

The success of the WDF "five-day raid" led to its continuance, as first one then another of the coastal towns fell to O'Connor's forces. Progress was, however, not made any easier by the enforced removal of 4th Indian Division to East Africa. Fortunately, it was almost immediately replaced by 6th Australian Division, so the WDF — now called XIII Corps — was able to continue to maintain the pressure on the Italian garrisons as the enemy withdrew along the coast. Bardia was the next objective, with the 7th Armd Div being again used to cut the coast road and isolate the garrison from the west. It fell on 5 January 1941, yielding 45,000 prisoners. The division was then used in the same encircling movement westwards to isolate Tobruk, with the Support Group cutting the road west and the armoured brigades attacking in an arc ranged from the west to the south. Tobruk surrendered on 22 January, with another 30,000 prisoners and all their equipment taken.

It is easy to write that the division was used to encircle each of these towns, however, it is worthwhile remembering exactly what this meant to the tank crews involved, having to find their way across mainly uncharted desert wastes, over difficult, dangerous terrain, often by night and without proper maps. The wear and tear on engines, gearboxes, suspensions and all the rest of the mechanical "bits" was matched only by the pressure on the tank crews themselves to complete their vital task — otherwise the enemy would escape to live and fight another day! By now such wear and tear had reduced the division's tank strength considerably, so 8 H of 7th Armd Bde and 6 RTR of 4th Armd Bde were both temporarily dismounted and their tanks used to keep the other regiments of both brigades up to strength. The three Light Recovery Sections and a Field Supply Depot were brought forward in an attempt maximise declining resources for the next phase of the advance. As the WDF's supply line lengthened so too did the problems of maintaining its meagre resources.

Top: Ready for the great race to Beda Fomm. John March of 2 RTR, poses beside his well-laden A10 cruiser tank, before the long desert approach march to Beda Fomm. This daring manoeuvre by tanks of 7th Armoured Division cut off the Italian retreat and led to the surrender of the entire Italian Tenth Army.

Above: The advance to Benghazi and beyond, 12 December–8 February 1941. Inset, the Battle of Beda Fomm/Sidi Saleh 5–7 February 1941.

THE DESTRUCTION OF AN ARMY

By 22 January 1941, the British forces were within 20 miles of Derna, and it became clear that the Italians were preparing to leave Cyrenaica as quickly as possible, so O'Connor decided, with Wavell's blessing, upon a daring plan. He would order 7th Armoured to send a flying column through the desert to establish an armoured roadblock behind the retreating enemy, well southwest of Benghazi, in the Beda Fomm-Sidi Saleh area, whilst the rest of his force maintained pressure along the coastal route. "Combeforce" under the CO of the 11th Hussars was despatched and, despite the terrible going and several enemy air attacks en route, managed to reach the coast and cut off the Italian retreat on the morning of 5 February, at Sidi Saleh. The initial Combeforce was less than 2,000 men, mainly infantry with a few light guns and some armoured cars, but they were fortunately reinforced that afternoon by the leading elements of 4th Armd Bde (just 20 cruisers and 30 light tanks still motoring!), who established a second blocking position at nearby Beda Fomm, before the main body of the enemy arrived. The Italians were staggered to find their way blocked and, instead of trying to outflank the tiny British force, launched a series of uncoordinated frontal attacks, all of which were beaten off with heavy loss. The battle lasted until the early hours of 9 February, when the Italians surrendered. The tiny British force had by then captured 20,000 men, including six Italian generals, 216 guns, 112 tanks and 1,500 lorries, plus immense quantities of arms, equipment and stores of all kinds. The Tenth Italian Army was no more, whilst the cost to 7th Armd Div was just nine killed and 15 wounded! In less than 30 hours the "Desert Rats" had advanced across 150 miles on unmapped desert at high speed. Then, outnumbered, short of water, food, ammunition, petrol and without any prospect of reinforcement it had outfought and destroyed an army many times its strength — small wonder a leading historian called it: "one of the most daring ventures and breathless races in the annals of the British Army".

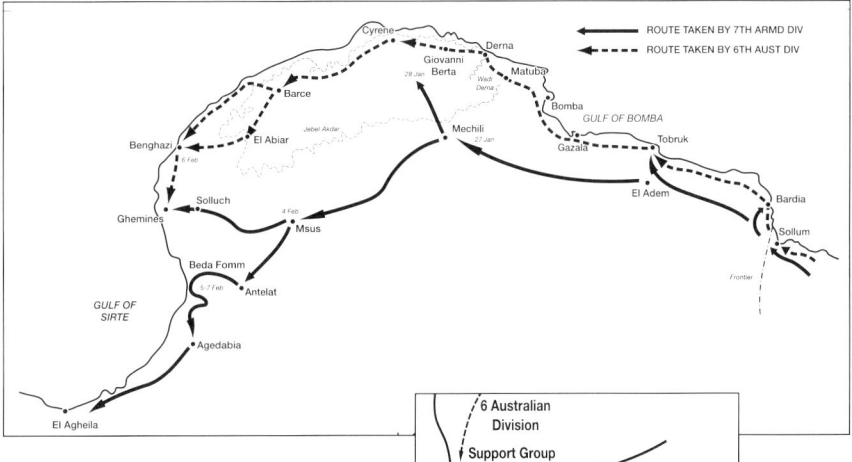

Thus ended the division's first campaign. Shortly after the victory at Beda Fomm/Sidi Saleh, it was withdrawn to refit and re-equip as its vehicles and equipment were now completely worn out.

THE DESERT 1941-2

With the surrender of the Tenth Italian Army, the whole of Cyrenaica was now in British hands and the road to Tripoli lay wide open. However, just two months later, the enemy was once again back on the Egyptian border, whilst the brilliant Gen O'Connor, plus two other senior commanders, were all "in the bag". What had caused this sudden reversal of fortunes? Undoubtedly a major shift in the strategic situation had been partly to blame, Wavell having to send considerable forces to help in the Balkans and Greece, where the Germans had once again stepped in to assist their inept Italian partners. Critical emphasis, attention and resources were switched there to counter the Axis assault. Nevertheless, Germany had not forgotten North Africa and still had ambitions to capture

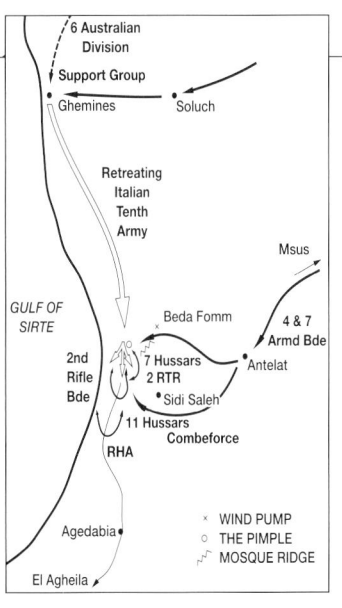

Above: A pair of 25-pounders in action. This gun's primary task was the destruction or neutralisation of enemy weapons, in particular anti-tank guns and field artillery. It was widely used by field artillery and had a maximum range of 13,400yd.

Below right: Spoils of war 1. An 11th Hussars armoured car towing a captured Italian CorroVeloce 3/33. The light tankette weighed only 3.2 tons and was used to support infantry with its twin machine guns.
IWM — E408

Egypt and cut Britain's vital Suez Canal lifeline to its empire. Early in 1941, therefore, the German High Command decided to create the *Deutsches Afrika Korps* (DAK), initially consisting of 5th leichte and 15th Panzer Divisions, and to send this force to help the Italians in Cyrenaica. To command them Hitler chose the charismatic *Generalleutnant* Erwin Rommel, who had recently sprung to fame as the GOC of the 7th (Ghost) Panzer Division in France. By the end of March 1941, Rommel, together with the leading elements of the DAK had arrived in Tripoli, where he immediately assumed overall control of the Axis forces, including two Italian divisions, the Ariete and the Brescia. True to his nature, Rommel lost no time in seizing the initiative and taking the fight to the British, his initial probing reconnaissance with 5 leichte swiftly turning into a daring assault. The "Desert Fox", as he was soon called by both sides, realised that he had caught his enemy "on the hop" and immediately turned the situation to his advantage. He began to attack on 1 April, with just skeleton forces, however, by the 3rd he had taken Benghazi and on 10 April began the first siege of Tobruk (which would last for 242 days). His advance was only finally halted after it had penetrated across the Egyptian frontier near Sollum.

7th Armoured Division did not play a major part in stemming this first German assault. Having left the desert in early 1941 for some well-earned rest, the division had found itself to all intents and purposes non-existent, due to a chronic shortage of tanks and other equipment. However, faced with this new threat that was "Blitzkrieging" its way through the untested troops then holding Cyrenaica (principally 2nd Armoured and 9th Australian Divisions, augmented by 3rd Hussars and 6th RTR, who had been left behind by 7th Armoured with the few serviceable light tanks and some captured Italian mediums), other elements of the division began hastily re-equipping and were then rushed to the front. Late March saw the 1st Battalion KRRC moved up to engage the enemy near Derna and then in early April the 11th Hussars, issued with South African Marmon-Herrington armoured cars, were back in action. On 13 April the Support Group HQ was moved to Mersa Matruh, with the 3rd Battalion Coldstream Guards temporarily attached, and engaged the enemy near Sollum. The following day Brig "Strafer" Gott arrived and took over command of all troops in the area.

Rommel had thus got off to a flying start and the Axis soon had the port of Benghazi in full working order. However there was now an inevitable pause whilst the tanks of 15th Panzer were landed and the Axis forces at the front were resupplied. Gen Wavell, with encouragement from Churchill, who had responded to the German attack by diverting a convoy of fresh armour through the risky Mediterranean rather than sending it on the longer route around the safer Cape, attempted to marshal his forces for an early counteroffensive, but it took time to prepare new equipment and to train the soldiers in desert warfare.

Above: "Fox killed in the open!" That was the message sent by O'Connor to C-in-C Middle East, Gen Wavell, after the victory at Beda Fomm. Here a KDG armoured car moves past groups of knocked-out Italian vehicles and artillery guns which stretched along the coast road to Tripoli as far as the eye could see.

In the forthcoming battles there was also the emerging question of comparative merits as regards to the equipment used by each side, as well as their organisation and tactics. German armour undoubtedly had the edge over the Allies, their tank guns having better penetrative power over longer ranges, whilst their thicker armour gave them increased protection. The Panzer division was also organised on a more balanced all-arms basis, with greater flexibility of manoeuvre. There was also an imbalance in anti-tank guns, the superlative German 88mm, encountered for the first time by the British in this campaign for example, showed itself to be a battle winner, with a performance that at the time the British could not match.

Right: Divisional organisation as at April 1942.

OPERATIONS BREVITY AND BATTLEAXE

Although preliminary attacks for the possession of Halfaya Pass and Fort Capuzzo (Operation Brevity, 15-17 May) had been repulsed by a strong German counterthrust, nevertheless Operation Battleaxe finally got underway on 15 June, with 7th Armoured Division consisting of two brigades, each of two regiments, and the Support Group. In 7th Armd Bde, 2 RTR still had the old cruisers (A9s, A10S and A13s), while 6 RTR was issued with the first new A15 Crusaders, as yet untried in battle. In the 4th Armd Bde, both 4 and 7 RTR were equipped with the heavy, slow Matilda MkII "I" tanks. The plan for the division was to move in tandem with the 4th Ind Div until such a time as the 4th Armd Bde was no longer needed and then for it to swing south/southwest to cut off the enemy forces near the frontier.

In the event this never happened, for the Germans had positioned 88mm guns and laid minefields in the Sollum area, placing the recently arrived 15th Panzer Division near Bardia, with 5 leichte near Tobruk. 4th Armd Bde lost heavily to the dug-in 88s and were held down by counter-attacks; the weakened 7th Armd Bde also could not break through the skilful German defence, and, lacking a third regiment, had great difficulty even in repulsing flank counterattacks from 5 leichte. After two days' fighting, Lt-Gen Beresford-Pierse, the corps commander, called off the operation, having decided he had lost too much for too little gain.

This aborted offensive was part of a learning curve. It showed the dangers of splitting up armour across too wide a front and highlighted various other operational mistakes. It also proved that the A15 Crusader MkI, with its tiny 2pdr gun, was rather a disappointment, as compared to its opposition, in particular the German "Specials". However, combat attrition had also affected the enemy and both sides were exhausted. Neither would do much for the next four months other than continue the siege of Tobruk, while both prepared for a fresh effort.

Below: Operation Battleaxe 15–19 June 1941.

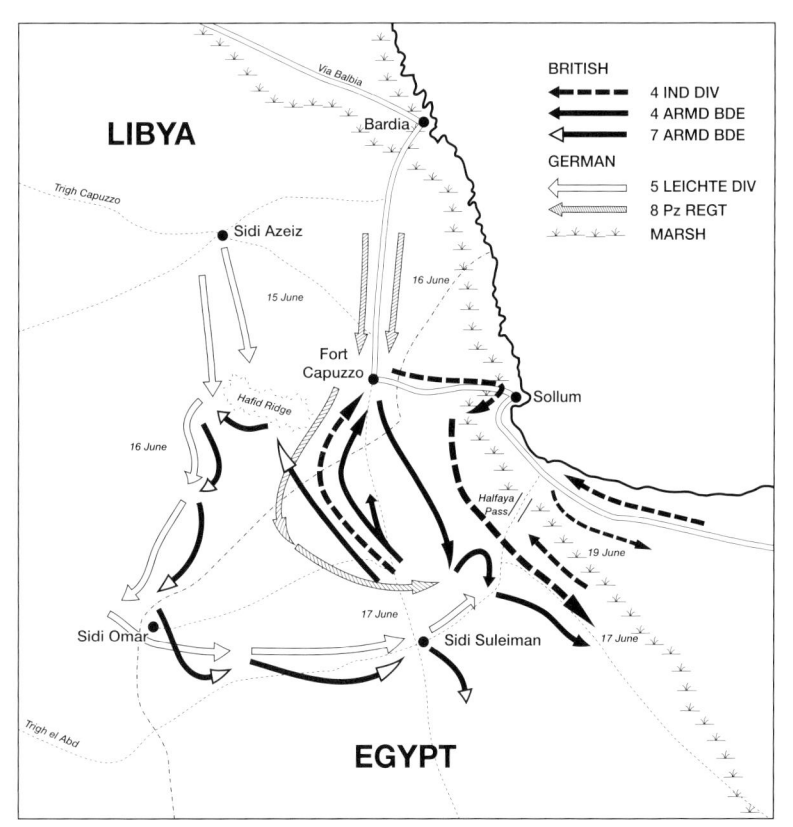

OPERATION CRUSADER

The Commander-in-Chief, Gen Wavell, was replaced by Gen Auchinleck in early July, while Maj-Gen "Strafer" Gott, an old desert hand, assumed command of 7th Armd Div, which was increased to three armoured brigades by the addition of the 22nd. Although on paper (see table) it now appeared larger than the enemy formations opposing it, in reality the variety and quality of the armour available belied this numerical advantage. Other organisational and tactical changes in the balance of elements within each brigade were also being tried, but the correct equation for an ideally balanced armoured division had yet to be attained.

By early November 1941, sufficient reinforcements had arrived in theatre for the Army of the Nile to become the new Eighth Army, commanded by Lt-Gen Sir Alan

```
                          7th Armoured Division HQ
                                    |
        ┌───────────────────────────┼───────────────────────────┐
4th Armoured Brigade         7th Armoured Brigade         22nd Armoured Brigade
8 H                          7 H                          2 RGH
3 RTR                        2 RTR                        3 CLY
5 RTR                        6 RTR                        4 CLY
2 RHA
2 SG

Support Group                Support Group                Divisional Troops
3 RHA                        11 H                         5, 30, 58, 65, 67 and 550 Coys, RASC
4 RHA                        KDG                          2, 13, 15 Fd Amb RAMC
60 Fd Regt, RA               4 SAAC Regt                  7 Lt Fd Hygiene Sect
1 x bty 51 Fd Regt, RA       102 RHA                      Div Wksp RAOC
1 KRRC                       1 LAA Regt                   Div OFP
2 RB                         Div Sigs Regt                LAA Regt Wksp
                             4 Fd and 143 Fd Pk Sqns RE
```

Note 1. Source — Maj-Gen G. L. Verney: *History of 7th Armoured Division 1938–45*.

Note 2. Also, in each Brigade and Support Group, one Light Repair Section, one Light Recovery Section and one Ordnance Field Park, RAOC.

Note 3. At this time, one company 1 KRRC with a troop of D Bty 3 RHA formed the garrison at Siwa Oasis and the Première Compagnie d'Infanterie de Marine, the vanguard of the Free French Forces of the Western Desert, was serving with the Support Group.

Cunningham. Operation Crusader would be launched on the 16th, with XXX Corps circumventing Rommel's forces, threatening his supply lines and forcing him to expend his armour in a high-attrition attack on the massed guns of 7th Armd Division in a preselected killing ground. Meanwhile, XIII Corps would move down the coast to relieve Tobruk.

Initially the plan went so well that Rommel had no idea he had been outflanked, but the British armour then divided itself in various directions, each brigade lacking the

Below left and Below: Operation Crusader, 16 November–15 December. 1 — the British advance toward Sidi Rezegh, outflanking Rommel on 18–21 November; 2 — the Tobruk Garrison joins the attack; 22–23 November. (See page 24 for map 3.)

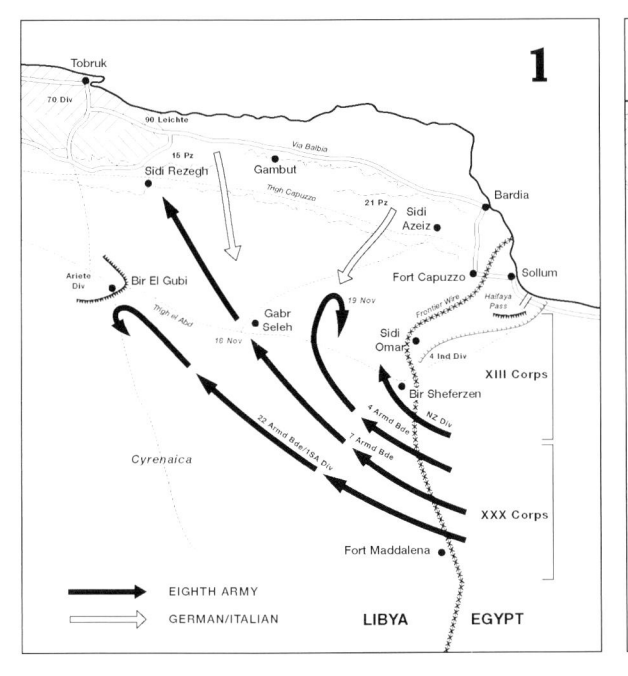

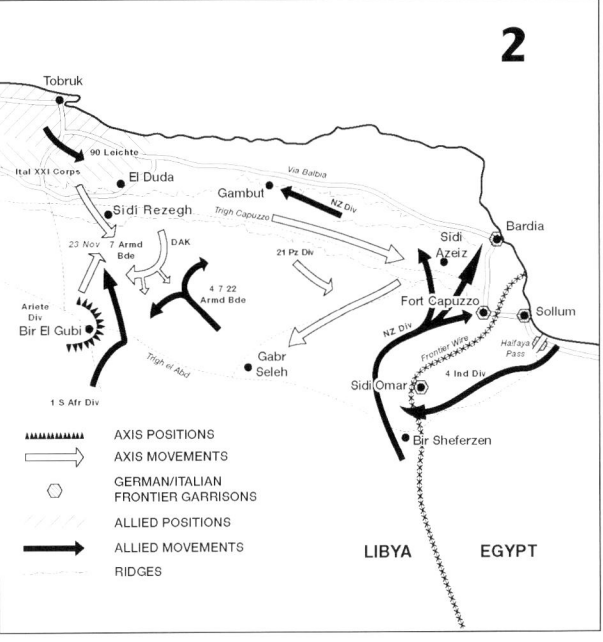

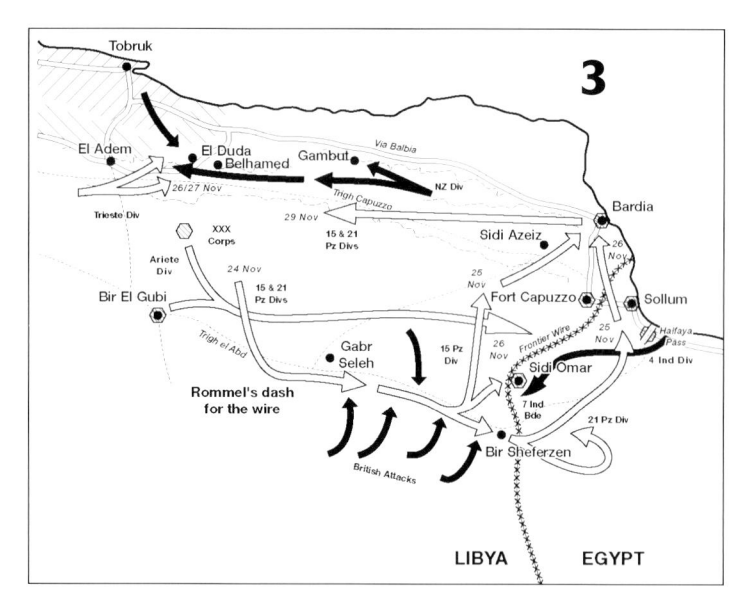

Above: Operation Crusader 16 November–15 December. 3 — the German attacks of 24 November onward.

Below: Spoils of war 2. Another "capture" by the Cherry Pickers armoured cars was this umbrella — possibly from the famous "Groppis" nightclub in Cairo. The Morris CS9/LAC was acting as regimental rear link at Bir Sheferzen, July 1940.

strength to accomplish its individual tasks. No wonder Rommel so often remarked: "What does it matter if you have two tanks to my one, when you spread them out and let me smash them in detail?"

4th Armd Bde, having drifted east to protect the flank of XIII Corps, was attacked by first one, and then by both, Panzer divisions, which then turned north together. 7th Armd Bde, followed by the Support Group, then went north to what was to become the main battle area, namely the airfield at Sidi Rezegh, just south of Tobruk. They occupied the town and airfield, but could not take the dominant surrounding hills. The two Panzer divisions then fell on the 7th Bde from the south, inflicting severe losses.

22nd Armd went west to attack the Italian Ariete Division, and had soon overrun the Italians at Gubi. However, owing to the lack of infantry support, it could not hold its gains and was then switched, initially to help the other two armoured brigades as the battle built up at Sidi Rezegh.

Despite its gallant efforts and those of the Tobruk garrison to break out, the division never managed to achieve sufficient decisive strength at the critical point of impact and on 22 November the Support Group was driven off the airfield by determined enemy counterattacks. During the two days of unceasing battle, in which it had stubbornly held out, the Support Group had been awarded no less than three Victoria Crosses (see pages 84–5 for full citations). Two were posthumous — Rifleman J. Beeley of the KRRC died while charging a machine-gun nest and Lt Ward Gunn, RHA, was killed while firing a 2pdr anti-tank gun from a burning portee. The third VC was awarded to Brig "Jock" Campbell, who organised and led many armoured counter-attacks in his open-topped, unarmoured staff car, holding the defence together by his stalwart example.

The Battle Damage Assessment for 24 November revealed the severity of the impact on the division — 4th Armd Bde's HQ and 8th Hussars had both been virtually wiped out, 22nd Armd Bde reduced to a single composite regiment and 7th Armd Bde had virtually ceased to exist. Rommel, thinking that XXX Corps was finished, raced eastwards towards the frontier to take on XIII Corps. However, despite having dominated Gen Cunningham (who was replaced by Auchinleck with Lt-Gen Ritchie), he had reacted too late. XIII Corps was progressing well down the coast and eventually recaptured Sidi Rezegh and even managed to link up briefly with the Tobruk garrison.

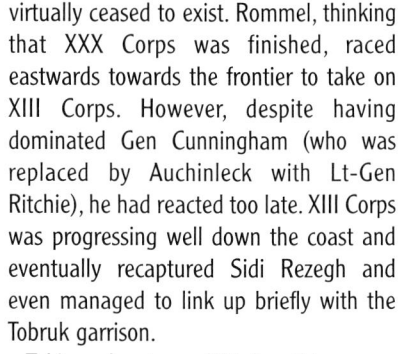

Taking advantage of this breathing space in the battle, 7 Armd Div was now able to reorganise and achieve some resupply of new tanks as well as salvage many others from the battlefield. When the Panzers returned to the west on 27 November to aid other Axis troops around Tobruk, 4th and 22nd Brigades had amassed 120 tanks between them and attacked a weakened 15th Panzer Division which they managed to catch on its own. However, its own intrinsic supporting arms of artillery and infantry enabled it to hold off the two brigades until nightfall, when it broke off contact.

XIII Corps was then forced to give up Sidi Rezegh as the Germans broke back through its positions and also cut the tenuous link established with Tobruk, while XXX Corps was held off to the south and prevented from coming to its aid.

By this time, however, attrition had also taken its toll on the Germans, who were forced to abandon their remaining frontier defences and pull back first to Gazala and finally by the end of the year to Agheila, the British taking Benghazi on 25 December.

Operation Crusader was the thus fastest moving, farthest ranging and most complex battle of the whole desert war. It was also perhaps 7 Armd Div's finest hour, when, despite inferior equipment and high attrition, it took a heavy toll of the *Afrika Korps* and won three VCs for outstanding bravery.

ACTION IN THE FAR EAST

Now action in other parts of the world would have its effect on the war in the desert. Japan's unprovoked attack on Pearl Harbor on 7 December 1941, coupled with Japanese assaults on Hong Kong, Singapore, Malaya and then Burma, meant that once again units destined for the Middle East Command, or already serving there, had to be transferred to the Far East. These included 7th Armoured Brigade, who, having changed its "Red Rat" symbol for a "Green Rat", carried out a masterly withdrawal through Burma, covering the retreating British forces safely back into India. In addition, the disastrous fall of Greece was followed swiftly by the successful German airborne assault on Crete, leaving the tiny but now vitally important island of Malta virtually unprotected. The brave population and its small garrison were subjected to the full weight of Axis air attacks, as they endeavoured to bomb the Maltese into submission. Fortunately they did not succeed. However, Axis resupply to North Africa was able to be stepped up, their convoys gaining increased protection from both U-boats and surface vessels as well as from the air. Axis influence in the Mediterranean was now at its height, enabling Rommel to receive replenishment and to plan, then launch, a fresh offensive.

Below: Getting to grips with their "Honeys". 5 RTR tank crewmen learning all about their new Light tanks, which they are just drawing up from Ordnance. They are looking carefully at the excellent .30 Browning light machine gun, the standard MG on American tanks throughout the war that is still in service worldwide.

After Operation Crusader, 7th Armoured Division had been taken out of the line to undergo another period of rest and refit, which included major changes to the divisional organisation. The division was reorganised into two armoured brigades and one lorried infantry brigade, with the main elements of the Support Group being divided between the three, so that all had, for example, integral artillery and Engineer support. In addition, the division received new tanks, generously provided by America — first the M3 Light Stuart, which, although only equipped with a 37mm main gun, was infinitely superior to the current British light tank in service. Next came the M3 Medium Grant with its thicker armour and 75mm gun, which was

Above: More newly issued "Honeys" are given a close examination by these 5 RTR officers. Note the "A" Squadron triangle on the turret and the 7th Armd Div "Desert Rat" on the nearest mudguard.

Above right: This replenishment point at Bir Sherferzen is a hive of activity as men of 1 RB replenish from cans — both the flimsy British 2-gallon can and the more durable German 4.5-gallon (20-litre) "Jerricans" are in evidence. Water was carried in much the same cans, so they had to be carefully marked to prevent mistakes — eg water cans were always black with "WATER" stencilled on them in white. Also, the 7th Armd Div sign is just visible on the tailboard of one of the 15cwt trucks.

Right: After the battle of Alam Halfa 30 August– 7 September 1942. The Germans seemed in control and Suez was threatened.

far superior to the British cruisers of the period and had a devastating effect on German armour when it first saw action. Each armoured regiment now had 24 Grants and 20 Stuarts. Also the 2pdr anti-tank gun began to be replaced by the far superior 6pdr, which went some way to restoring the balance against the German anti-tank guns, although none was comparable with the lethality of the 88mm. At this time the division tragically lost its newly appointed GOC, Maj-Gen "Jock" Campbell VC, killed in a freak driving accident. Campbell had just taken over from Gen "Strafer" Gott, who had himself been promoted to corps commander, then selected as the future Eighth Army commander, only to be killed when his aircraft was shot down whilst flying back to Cairo. Maj-Gen Frank Messervy of 4th Ind Div took over as divisional commander.

GAZALA

At the beginning of April 1942 the division returned to the desert as part of a defensive line, stretching from Gazala south to Bir Hacheim. It was made up of a series of fortified "boxes", protected by minefields. Churchill continually exhorted Gen Ritchie to go on the offensive, but, before he could do so, Rommel again seized the initiative and attacked first, retaking Agedabia. Originally planned as only another pre-emptive spoiling attack, his initial success spurred him on and on 26 May he launched Operation Venezia, skirting south of Bir Hacheim and then swinging north/northeast in a compact spearhead containing his main armoured formations. He caught 4th Armd Bde dispersed and vulnerable, overwhelming a major portion of its armour and throwing the rest into confusion. On 27 May Gen Messervy and his HQ were overrun and captured, although he later managed to disguise himself as a private soldier, then to escape and reassume command of his division.

The German assault was eventually checked by 1st Armd Div, whose Grants and 6pdr anti-tank guns came as a shock to Rommel, who now found himself in a critical position, virtually surrounded by minefields and "boxes". This phase of the battle, known as the "Cauldron", once again illustrates the superior enemy use of his all-arms organisation and equipment, for when the British attacked the "Cauldron" piecemeal they incurred heavy losses. Rommel then broke out and, clearing safe lanes through the minefields, took the critical 150th Brigade box. He then rolled up the line, taking box after box, the British having no choice but to fall back in a fighting withdrawal, with delaying actions near Sidi Rezegh and Mersa Matruh. They were pushed back to the Alamein-Ruweisat Ridge area. Tobruk had finally fallen on 21 June and Allied fortunes were at their lowest ebb — Rommel having been promoted to Field Marshal by Adolf Hitler for his successes. Cairo and the Suez Canal now appeared to be his for the taking.

However, the Germans were actually at the end of their tether. Behind them stretched mile upon mile of tortuous supply lines, whilst the British, despite having their "backs to the wall", were never closer to their own supply dumps. They also now had a new army commander, the charismatic Gen Bernard Law Montgomery, who would prove equal to the traumatic situation in which the Eighth Army now found itself. He ordered "No Withdrawal" and then made certain that his troops were in strong defensive positions at Alam al Halfa and had the wherewithal to defend themselves. In the July battles that followed, 7th Armoured met the enemy armour, checked it and destroyed many enemy tanks, forcing Rommel back on the defensive.

A rejuvenated Eighth Army now prepared for what would prove to be the most important battle of the Desert War. However, unlike his predecessors, "Monty" refused to be rushed into battle, carefully building up his supplies, manpower and weapons — which now included quantities of the even more powerful, reliable and manoeuvrable M4 Medium Sherman tank, the successor to the Grant. By the time it was ready for battle in mid-

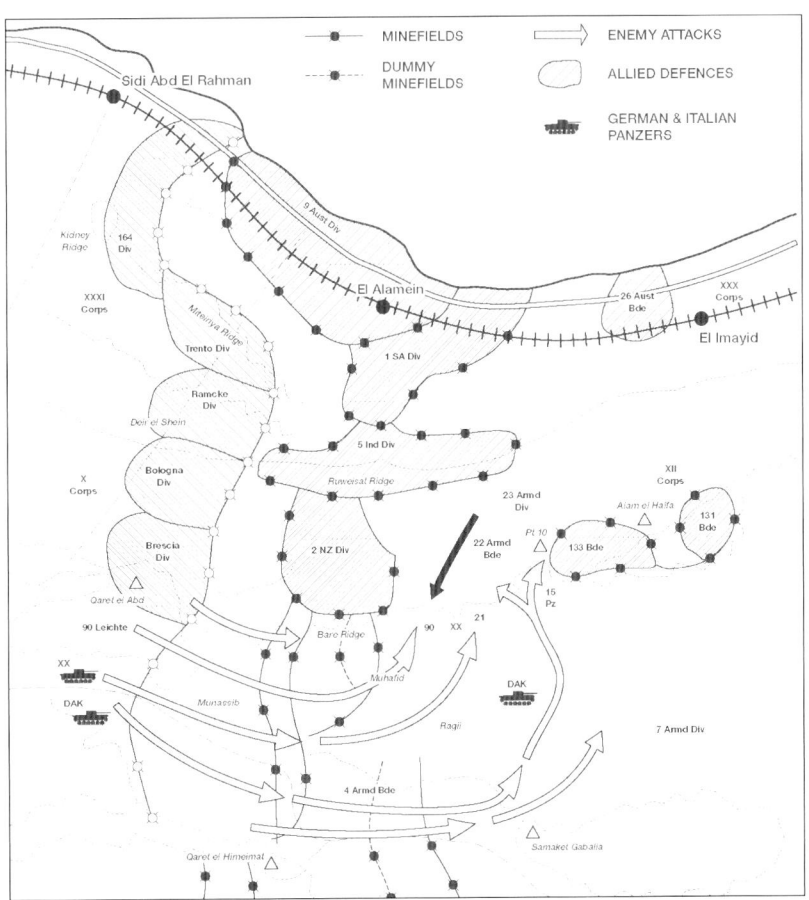

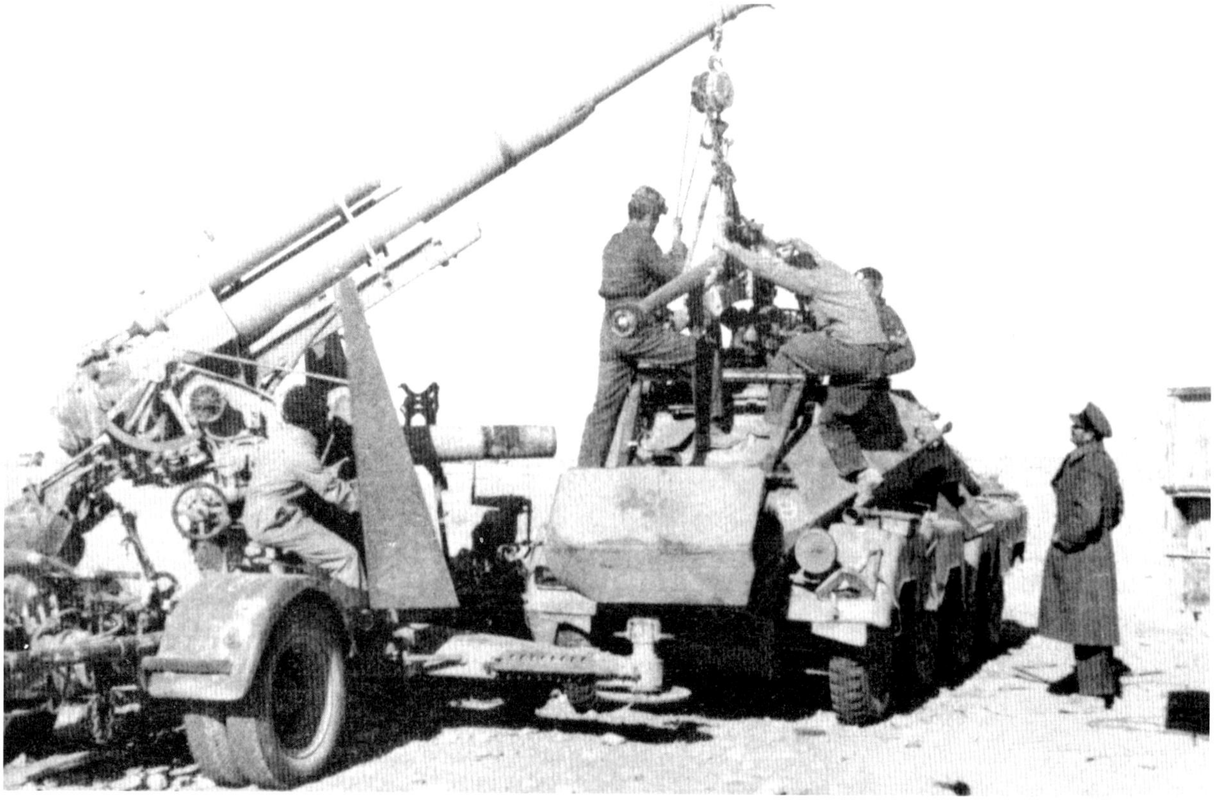

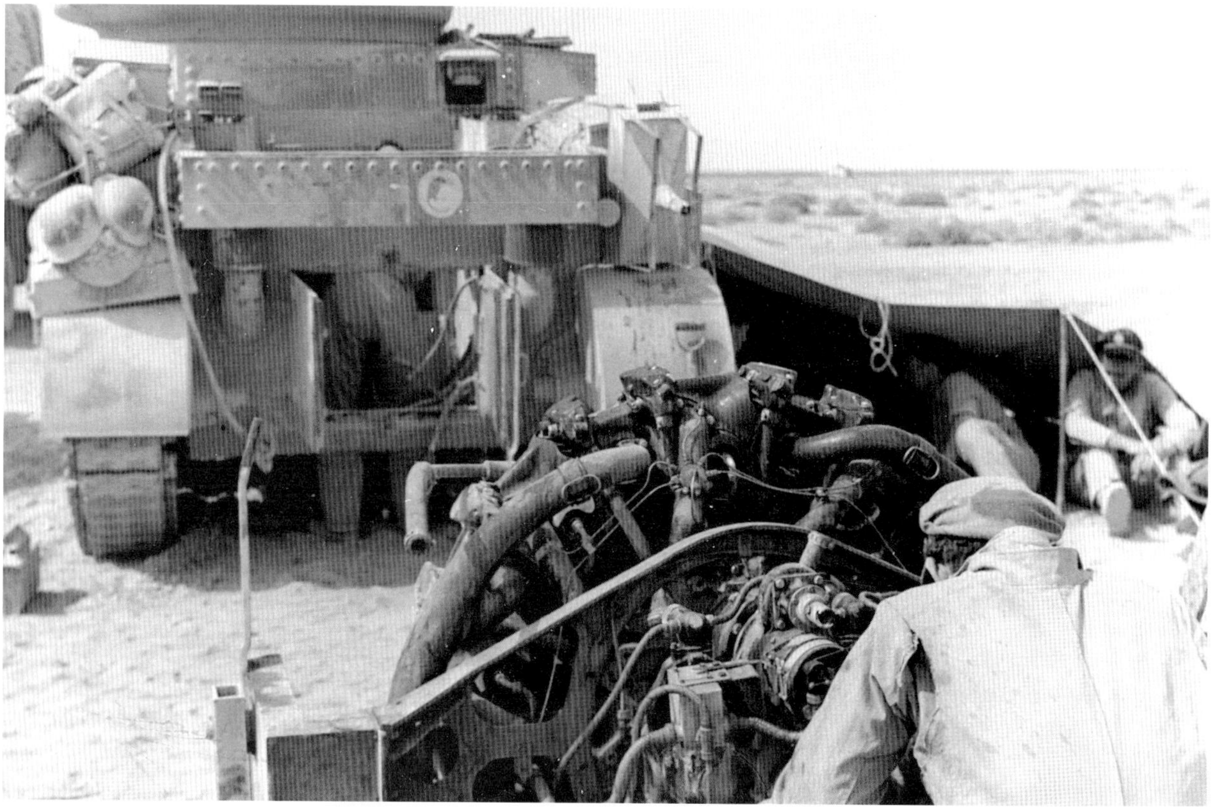

"Danger! Fitters at work!" It's amazing how innovative fitters can be. In the first picture (**Opposite, Above**) they are using a German 88mm AA/Anti-tank gun as a crane, to lift the gun out of what appears to be a German eight-wheeled armoured car. In the second (**Opposite, Below**) a fitter works on the radial engine of a Grant Medium tank (note the "Desert Rat" sign on the rear) whilst the crew members have a kip in their bivvie alongside the tank. The third shot (**Above**) shows a tank transporter crew, having loaded a cruiser tank, struggling to load one of the girders it has used to get the tank on board. Finally (**Left**), at the rear of what appears to be a tank open leaguer on either side of the coast road, another tank transporter, with a Sherman on its trailer, prepares to move off. Fitters on both sides did a marvellous job of keeping the tanks fit and ready for action.

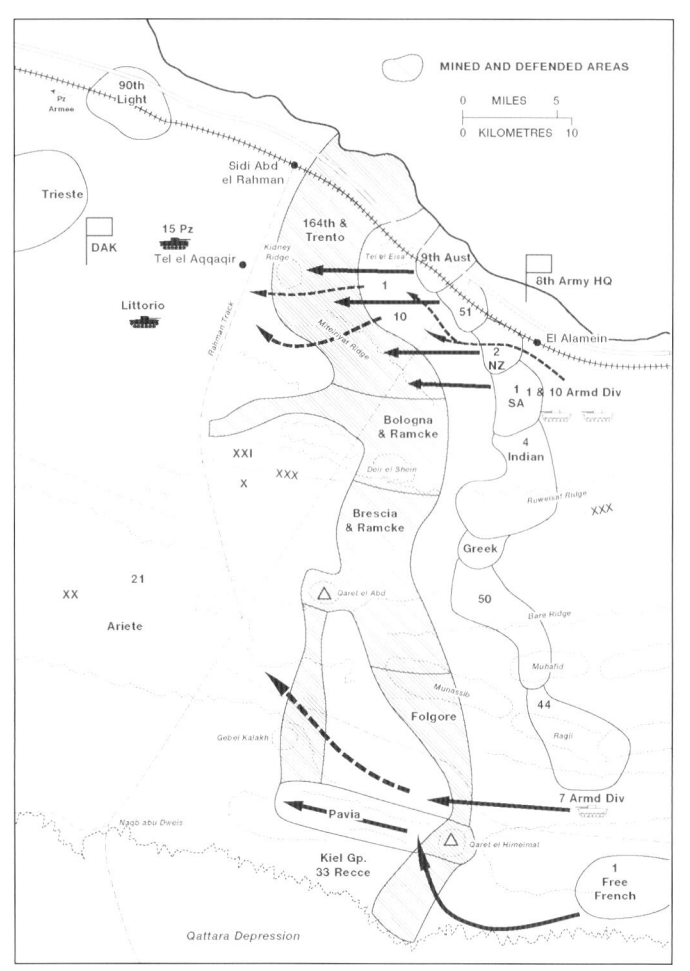

October, Montgomery's army easily outnumbered Rommel's, although the Axis forces were in a strong defensive position astride the El Alamein feature, protected by vast minefields (Rommel's "Devil's Gardens") and in-depth positions.

7th Armoured Division's initial task in the battle was to contain 21st Panzer Division in the south. It began by penetrating the first minefield, then forming a bridgehead, but progress was slow and by 27 October Montgomery had decided not to continue the main thrust there, but rather to look for an easier spot nearer the coast. 7th Armoured was accordingly moved north, then went into reserve as the infantry divisions pounded away. A few days later (2 November) it managed to make its way forward south of Tel el Eisa, ready to exploit any breakthrough. This took place shortly afterwards, the division being heavily engaged by enemy armour south of Tel el Aqqaqir. Here it destroyed 19 enemy tanks and forced the enemy to withdraw. This proved to be the beginning of the pursuit, although initially unexpectedly heavy rain saturated the ground and made the going virtually impossible, thus allowing the enemy to escape. Led by its armoured car regiment, the ubiquitous 11th Hussars, the division finally managed to break out through the remaining enemy positions to the west and after a short fight finished off the stubborn German and Italian rearguards, crossing the Egyptian frontier for a final time on the 9th. Further bad weather and petrol shortages continued to delay the advance, until the port facilities in Tobruk could be put back into service.

Above: The turn of the tide — the battle of El Alamein 22 October–4 November 1942.

Right: The divisional organisation as at October 1942.

Above right: Although radios were used for long-distance communications, land line was still laid on occasions, such as here at Agedabia, at a time when the battle was fairly static for a while.

Centre right: Despatch riders were also used to carry messages, such as this signalman (Jeff Orchard) on his beloved Norton motorcycle. Nortons were widely used, over 100,000 being produced during the war, the 16H being built in the greatest quantity.

Bottom right: The Afrike Korps retreats — El Alamein to Tunis, October 1942 to May 1943 — showing the route taken by 7th Armoured.

7th Armoured Division HQ

4th Light Armoured Brigade	22nd Armoured Brigade	131st (Queen's) Brigade
3 RHA	1 RTR	1/5 Queen's
R Scots Greys	5 RTR	1/6 Queen's
4 H + sqn 8 H	4 CLY	1/7 Queen's
2 Derbys Yeo	4 Fd Regt, RA	53 Fd Regt, RA
1 KRRC	97 Fd Regt, RA	2 x btys 57 Atk Regt, RA
	1 RB	11 Fd Coy RE

Divisional Troops
11 H
15 LAA Regt, RA
65 Atk Regt, RA
(Norfolk Yeo)
Div Sigs
4th and 21 Fd Sqn, RE
143 Fd Pk Sqn, RE
5, 10, 58, 67, 287, 432 and 507 Coys RASC
2, 7, 14 and 15 Lt Fd Amb RAMC
Div OFP and 15 LAA Wksp RAOC

Note 1. Also one OFP and one Wksp RAOC per Brigade

THE WITHDRAWAL

Slowly but surely, the Axis forces were pushed back until they reached strong positions astride the Tripoli road at Tarhuna. However, these did not hold for long and on 23 January 1943, the "Desert Rats" entered Tripoli unopposed. The ailing *Afrika Korps* fought on with its usual tenacity, causing numerous casualties through mines, boobytraps and rearguard ambushes. Just before reaching Tripoli, the Divisional commander, Gen John Harding, had been badly wounded by shellfire. He was replaced by Gen Bobbie Erskine who would lead the Division on to the Mareth Line and for the rest of its time in North Africa, then on into Italy and Northwest Europe, the second longest period in command of any 7th Armoured GOC. On 6 March came Rommel's first major counteroffensive which culminated in the Battle of Medenine. Here, the enemy for once was forced into making an ill-judged attack against strong, well-prepared positions, where the division's tanks and anti-tank guns were firmly located. The anti-tank guns, especially those of the Queen's Brigade, caused heavy casualties.

The division played only a small part in the subsequent battles of Mareth and Wadi Akarit, but was first into Sfax on 10 April. During the battle of Enfidaville, the division was suddenly switched (making a 300-mile journey on tank transporters) from the Eighth to the First Army, in order to attack from Medjez in the west towards Tunis and then to wheel north to link up with the Americans. On 6 May, two infantry divisions followed by two armoured divisions, one being 7th Armoured, all under the command of Gen Horrocks, with heavy artillery and air support, smashed their way through to Tunis in a highly successful "textbook" operation — a rewarding note on which to end a gruelling campaign.

After 2,000 miles and six months' hard fighting from Alamein to Tunis, in which the division had played so great a part, the Allies had succeeded in completely destroying the Axis forces and expelling them from North Africa. It was now time for a well-earned rest, before embarking on the invasion of Italy.

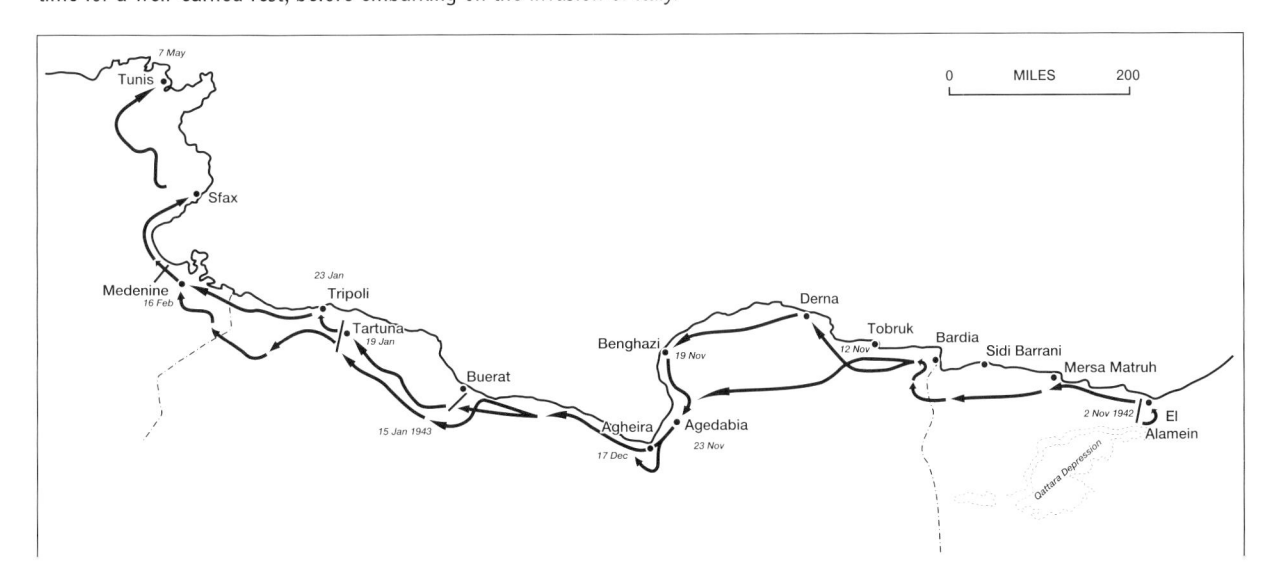

Right: "Fighting fit and fit to fight!" Whilst preparing for El Alamein, everyone had to undergo some tough training. This photo of how to deal with a sentry was on the front of the *Tough Tactics* pamphlet, the brainchild of Maj (later Lt-Col) Jerry Hedley of 7th Armd Div.

Below: Montgomery's Message to his Troops on the Eve of the Battle of El Alamein. "Monty" was a great one for getting his message down to every private soldier and issued communiqués like this one before each important event and battle.

EIGHTH ARMY
Personal Message from the ARMY COMMANDER

1 — When I assumed command of the Eighth Army I said that the mandate was to destroy ROMMEL and his Army, and that it would be done as soon as we were ready.

2 — We are ready NOW.

The battle which is now about to begin will be one of the decisive battles of history. It will be the turning point of the war. The eyes of the whole world will be on us, watching anxiously which way the battle will swing.

We can give them their answer at once, "It will swing our way."

3 — We have first-class equipment; good tanks; good anti-tank guns; plenty of artillery and plenty of ammunition; and we are backed up by the finest air striking force in the world.

All that is necessary is that each one of us, every officer and man, should enter this battle with the determination to see it through — to fight and to kill — and finally, to win.

If we all do this there can be only one result — together we will hit the enemy for "six," right out of North Africa.

4 — The sooner we win this battle, which will be the turning point of this war, the sooner we shall all get back home to our families.

5 — Therefore, let every officer and man enter the battle with a stout heart, and with the determination to do his duty so long as he has breath in his body.

AND LET NO MAN SURRENDER SO LONG AS HE IS UNWOUNDED AND CAN FIGHT.

Let us all pray that "the Lord mighty in battle" will give us the victory.

B. L. MONTGOMERY,
Lieutenant-General, G.O.C.-in-C., Eighth Army.

MIDDLE EAST FORCES,
23-10-42.

Above: A Sherman burns as British tanks advance into no man's land. Although the new American M4 Medium tanks, known as the Shermans, were in many ways superior to the obsolescent British cruisers, they still caught fire very easily, earning them the unfortunate nickname "The Ronson Lighter", as they were guaranteed to light first time. The Germans called them "Tommy Cookers" for the same reason.

Left: El Alamein: the long retreat begins. On the other side of the minefields, after a stubborn defence, Field Marshal Erwin Rommel, the "Desert Fox" and his *Afrika Korps*, had to begin a long, painful withdrawal that would end up with the Axis troops surrendering in Tunis. However, they conducted it extremely tenaciously and never allowed it to become a rout.

Opposite, Below: El Alamein. Lit by the eerie light of the massive artillery barrage, Sappers begin the difficult and dangerous job of gapping the German minefields — Rommel's "Devil's Gardens" as they were called. They used mine detectors to locate the mines, then they had to prod for them with their bayonets and finally lift them by hand.

Right: Tobruk recaptured. Men of the 1/6 Queen's enter Tobruk. After two sieges and many battles, the little port was at last in British hands for good and all! As seen here, even in an armoured division the infantry had to march quite a lot of the time.

Below: Victory parade in Tripoli. The Prime Minister, Mr Winston Churchill, passing through the main street in Tripoli inspecting the victorious troops. To his rear are the Crusader tanks of C Sqn 4 CLY. The A15 Crusader was the best of the early cruisers, much superior to the others although still armed with only a 2pdr gun as its main armament. However, the final production version, the Mark III, had a 6pdr plus additional armour on its hull and turret. *IWM — E22280*

Inset: On to Tunis! Stirring headlines of the *Tripoli Times* for 23 March 1943 as the 8th Army joins with the 1st Army on the last lap through Tunisia.

Left: The first British troops into Tripoli were the members of this 11th Hussars armoured car crew, commanded by Sgt Hugh Lyon. Having been first into both Tobruk and Benghazi, the "Cherry Pickers" could rightfully claim the triple crown, albeit if only by a short head from the troops advancing along the coast road!

Below: Whilst King George VI was visiting the division he inspected the "Cherry Pickers" on 21 June. He is seen here accompanied by the CO of 11 H, Lt-Col Smail, plus the Army commander ("Monty") and the GOC (Erskine). HM The King was their Colonel-in-Chief.

7th Armoured Division HQ

22nd Armoured Brigade
1RTR
5RTR
4CLY
1RB

131st (Queen's) Brigade
1/5 Queen's
1/6 Queen's
1/7 Queen's
C Coy 1 Cheshire (MMG)

Divisional Troops
11H
Div Sigs
3RHA
5RHA
15 LAA Regt, RA
24 Fd Regt, RA
65 Atk Regt (Nor Yeo)
69 Med Regt, RA
146 Fd Regt, RA
4 and 621 Fd Sqn, 143 Fd Pk Sqn, RE
5, 58, 67, 287, 432 and 507 Coys RASC
2 and 131 Fd Amb, 70 Fd Hygiene Sect, 21 Mobile CCS, 3 FSU, 7 Fd Transfusion Unit, 132 and 135 Mobile Dental Units RAMC
Div OFP RAOC
22 Armd Bde Wksp
131 Bde Wksp
15 LAA Wksp

Top: Organisation of the division in September 1943 (while in Italy).

Above: Loading for Italy: one of the ACVs belonging to the division being loaded for Italy. This was to follow the successful Allied amphibious landing on Sicily (Operation Husky, 10 July 1943). The British 8th Army landed on the "toe" of Italy (Operation Baytown) of 3 September, whilst the US 5th Army (which included the British 7th Armd Div) landed at Salerno (Operation Avalanche) on 9 September.

ITALY

After the surrender of the Axis forces in North Africa, instead of a wildly optimistic 2,000-mile "withdrawal", back to the fleshpots of Cairo and Alexandria, the division was extracted from Tunisia, to just along the coast of Tripolitania, for a period of relaxation, re-equipment and training. Homs, near the ancient city of Leptis Magna, was the chosen location in which it would spend the next three months. There were little signs of modern civilisation, but at least it was close to the sea, which made up for a lot and everyone swam daily. Here they prepared for a major amphibious assault on mainland Italy, as part of the US Fifth, who would take part in Operation Avalanche at Salerno on 9 September 1943. They had been left out of the earlier amphibious operation against Sicily (Operation Husky, 10 July 1943), but would soon be in the thick of it once again.

During this period there were further changes in organisation and — a tribute to the now flourishing Allied war machine — still more fresh weapons, vehicles and equipment. 22nd Armoured Brigade was brought back up to strength and was now composed almost entirely of M4 Sherman Medium tanks. 11th Hussars, the divisional armoured car regiment, was reorganised for the European theatre of operations, with an additional troop equipped with White scout cars to augment the mixed Daimler armoured car and Dingo scout car troops. The new support troop combined the roles of infantry and Engineers. The Jeep Troop was also replaced by an SP Gun Troop consisting of two 75mm SP guns, mounted in White half-tracks, to give close, immediate fire support. 5 RHA was equipped with self-propelled Priest 105mm guns, to work in close conjunction with the tanks of the armoured brigade.

The Engineers were trained to use the new Bailey bridges and tank-mounted scissors bridges for the first time. In the coming campaign they would enable the division to keep moving, by maintaining the difficult, mountainous roads in good working order and fording/bridging the various rivers and irrigation ditches which would otherwise hold up the advance at every turn.

Having landed successfully, the campaign that followed, although brief as far as the division was concerned, was complex, involving a tortuous advance into difficult terrain for the most part unsuited to armour. It was a mountainous area with fierce rivers and bad roads, which in wet weather could hold up an armoured division on their own. It definitely favoured the defenders who naturally exploited the local terrain to the full. Although Italy had just surrendered, the Germans had not and, as ever, were taking their fighting seriously, opposing the Allied attacks with their usual stubbornness, under their brilliant commander Field Marshal "Smiling Albert" Kesselring. They ensured that the Allied landings, both Fifth Army at Salerno and the slightly earlier Eighth Army landing on the toe of Italy (Operation Baytown, 3 September 1943), despite Allied air superiority, were hard fought, even managing to disable a warship with a new weapon — a radio-controlled glider bomb.

7th Armoured Division had begun landing on 15 September as the follow-up division of X Corps, behind 46th and 56th Infantry Divisions who had had their work cut out for them.

The Eighth Army had made better progress further south and by 16 September the two beachheads had linked up and were pressing on northwards together, Fifth Army in the west, Eighth Army in the east. Nevertheless, the Germans fought a masterly campaign as they withdrew slowly northwards from defensive line to defensive line.

After fierce fighting, in particular by 1/7th Queen's in order to take high ground just to the south of the main road, elements of 7th Armoured covered some 50 miles in a single day and attacked Scafati on the River Sarno. Fortuitously they managed to prevent the Germans from blowing the bridge and drove them out of the town, being rapturously greeted by the inhabitants.

As the advance continued across the river, the divisional Engineers built a Bailey bridge next to the existing Scafati roadbridge, in order to relieve congestion. For the next two days (28-9 September) the divisional advance was slow but steady across countryside heavily waterlogged by recent rains and defended stubbornly with mines, booby-traps and small hardcore rearguard units. Nevertheless, on 1 October forward elements of the division entered Naples.

Beyond Naples, the country opened out and was more suited to armour which was accordingly deployed up front. For the Motor Battalion (1 RB) it was a busy and slightly frustrating time, assimilating the limitations of the new terrain which lacked the desert's freedom of manoeuvre.

By 5 October the division had reached the River Volturno near Capua, only to find that all the bridges had been blown and the enemy was strongly established on the far bank. During the following week, energetic reconnaissance by 1/7th Queen's located most of these enemy positions. Although the main Allied attack on 12 October was to be made elsewhere by the infantry, 7th Armoured was to mount its own diversionary crossing in order to keep the enemy occupied. Despite fierce opposition, 1/7th Queen's eventually managed to secure and maintain a small bridgehead into which machine guns and anti-tank guns were then ferried and hauled up the far bank by hand. Behind them the Sappers began to bridge the river. Tanks of the armoured brigade in addition managed to locate a ford where, with the aid of bulldozers and by waterproofing the tanks, they effected a crossing and began mopping up enemy positions along the bank in both directions.

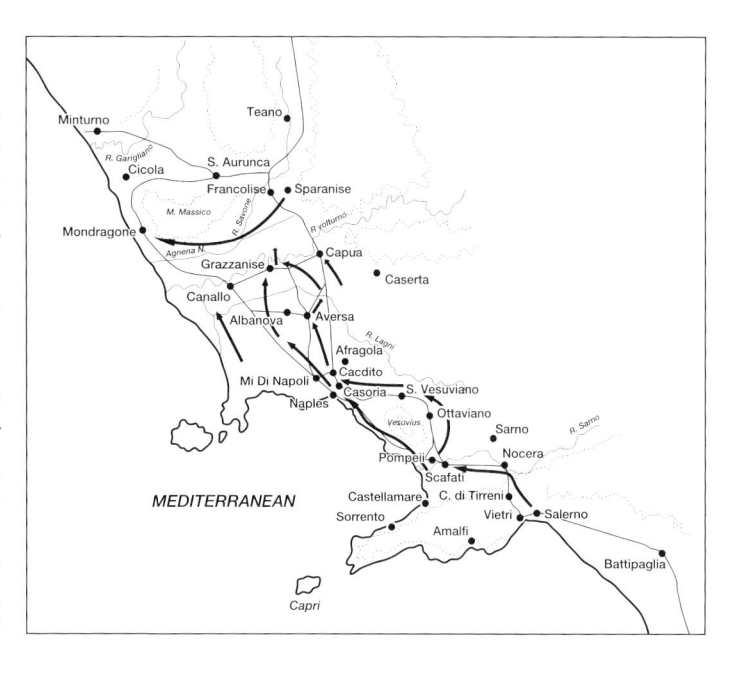

Top: 7th Armoured in Italy, September – November 1943.

Above: Col Pat Hobart, the GSO1, briefs 7th Armd Div HQ personnel during the voyage to Salerno. He went on to command 1st Royal Tank Regiment, in 22nd Armd Bde, and was awarded the DSO, OBE and MC. Postwar, he reached the rank of Major-General, as Director of the Royal Armoured Corps.

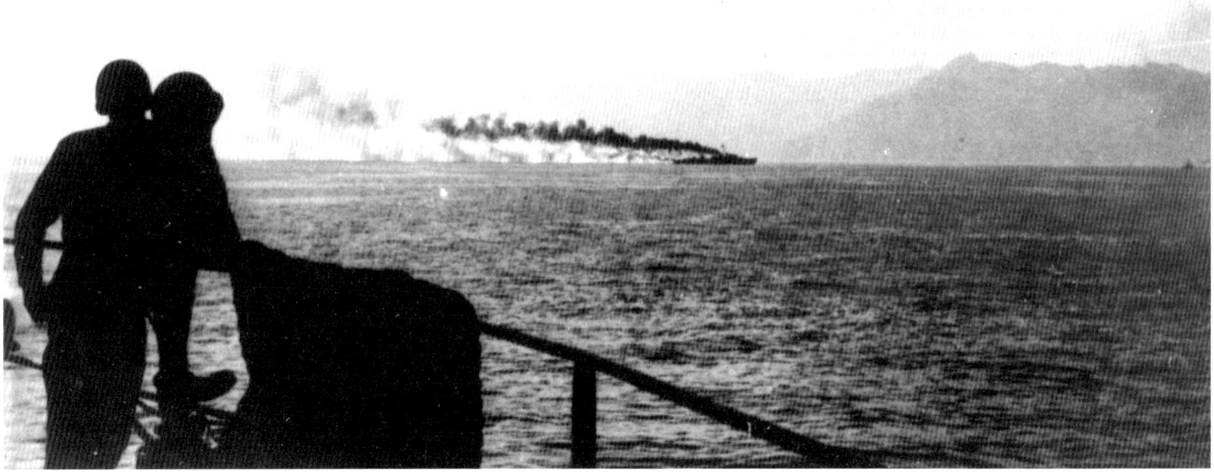

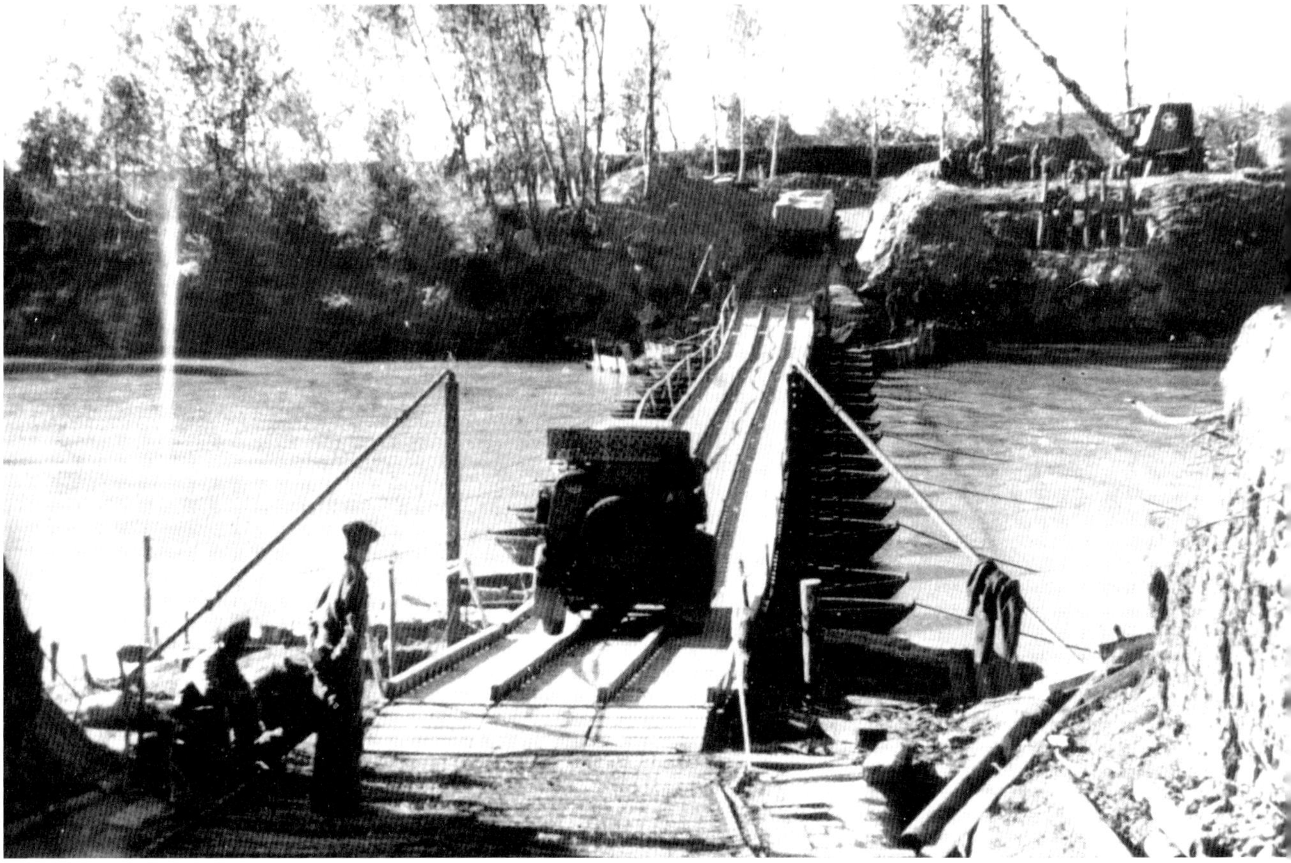

For the Germans, coupled with the success of the main Allied thrust by the infantry divisions, this was just too much, so they broke off contact and withdrew to their next defence line along the River Garigliano

MONDRAGONE

The division continued to advance down the valley of the Volturno, with the Germans demolishing and destroying everything in front of them, until the division was moved further downriver towards the coast, to a marshy plain overlooked by Monte Massico. There the enemy was in a well-established position and able to observe all movement. However, careful reconnaissance revealed a possible crossing place near the river's mouth, although it had been heavily mined. At dawn on 1 November the attack went in, with the mines cleared and 5 RTR making a successful crossing, while 1/6th Queen's attacked Mondragone further upriver, taking first the village and then going on to dislodge the enemy from his commanding ridge positions and to occupy the whole mountain. 1RTR then took Cicola after a brief but intense battle and the 22nd Armd Bde moved up to Sessa Aurunca to join up with 46th Division. This would be the division's last operation in Italy.

By 19 November, the division had been withdrawn back behind Monte Massico near the Volturno once more and an advance party had already set sail — destination England. The "Desert Rats", as one of the most experienced formations of the British Army, had been chosen to take part in the coming Allied invasion of Normandy. Having handed all their tanks and equipment over to the Canadian 5th Armoured Division, they made their way back to the docks in Naples, boarded troop transports, and reached the UK on 7 January 1944.

Above: Tanks of 5 RTR in the square at Sparanise, having cleared the surrounding area in late October 1943. The division's time in Italy was now almost over, as "Monty" had chosen it to be among the seasoned troops to return to the UK for the Normandy landings.

Above left: First sight of Italy, evening of 8 September 1943. The assault was led by British 46th Inf Div and 56th (London) Armoured Division of X Corps, with 7th Armoured Division as the follow-up force. They had heard the announcement that the Italians had surrendered and many thought the landing would be unopposed, but the Germans swiftly disarmed the Italians and took over their positions, so the assault was met with well-controlled enemy fire.

Left: Crossing the Volturno, 7 to 16 October 1943. The division first had to carry out an assault river crossing, establish a firm bridgehead in the area of the village of Grazzanise, then the Sappers were able to construct bridges over the fast-flowing river

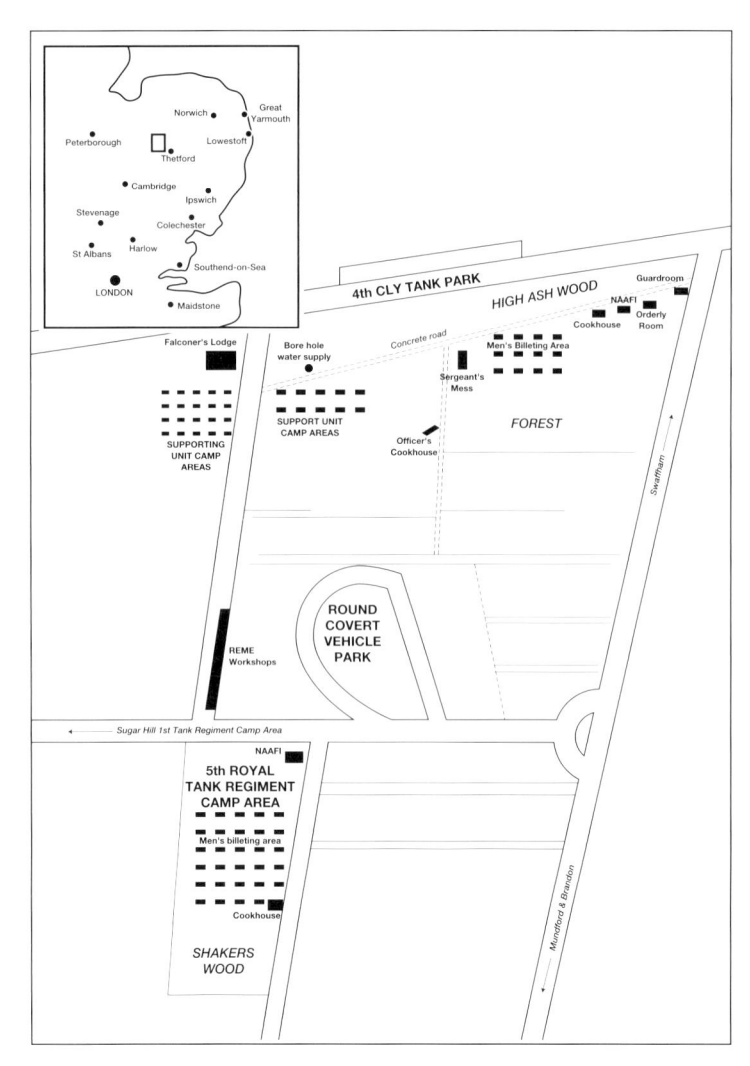

Above: Preparing for Normandy — 7th Armoured in the Thetford area, December 1943 to June 1944.

CONCENTRATION AND REORGANISATION IN BLIGHTY

After its well-deserved disembarkation leave, the division assembled in its allocated concentration area in Norfolk. The Queen's Brigade got the better choice of billets, being mainly quartered in "civilisation" around King's Lynn. 22nd Armoured Brigade units on the other hand were in the damp Thetford forests near Brandon, occupying "… groups of decayed Nissen huts clustered beneath tall pines". The 4 CLY camp was probably the worst of all, being both cold and wet, having been constructed well below the water level, whilst any form of heating was severely rationed! Here the division received its quota of new recruits to make units up to strength, whilst many of its old hands were cross-posted to other formations to give them a leavening of battle experience — in this way the "Desert Rats" lost the commander of their lorried infantry brigade, the senior staff officer of the division and the Chief Signals Officer. Many members of the division had been fighting since Italy first declared war in June 1940 and had been through both the entire North African campaign and Italy. Some of these old hands undoubtedly felt it was time that somebody else "had a go" and vocally expressed this opinion. This meant that the GOC, Gen Bobbie Erskine, had to pay considerable attention to the maintenance of morale during this preparatory period. The situation wasn't helped by the fact that, before pre-invasion training could be started, a complete scale of new equipment for the entire division had to be drawn up. This in itself was a major undertaking and it did not make matters any easier to discover that the armoured regiments were to be equipped with an entirely new cruiser tank — the A27M Cromwell. Fast (except in reverse gear), with a reliable Rolls-Royce engine, it was however thinly armoured and, with a 75mm main armament, undergunned. Many considered it, with justification, to be inferior to their well-loved Shermans. Erskine wrote: "We knew the Sherman inside out, but none of us knew the Cromwell — many of which suffered from minor defects, and the reputation of the tank did not improve as we had to repair the defects ourselves. The armoured regiments all had to go to Scotland (Kirkcudbright) to do their gunnery which was absolutely necessary, but took up much time on a form of training which could have been avoided if we had been given Shermans … We left for Normandy with a high state of morale, but it is no use concealing the fact that we felt we had been rushed. We were nothing like so well teamed up as we had been before Salerno."

Fortunately, alongside the Cromwells, each troop was issued with a Sherman Firefly, a British-modified Sherman mounting a 17pdr main gun which was one of the most effective Allied tank guns of the war. The divisional armoured car regiment (11 H) temporarily became corps troops, but later returned to under divisional control in Normandy, providing, as always, invaluable medium reconnaissance. Additionally, there was the divisional close reconnaissance regiment, the 8th Hussars, which had the same equipment (Cromwells and Stuarts) as the armoured regiments of 22nd Armoured Brigade. As a result, it tended to be used as a fourth armoured regiment, being allocated

IN ACTION

7th Armoured Division HQ

22nd Armoured Brigade	**131st (Queen's) Brigade**	**Divisional Troops**
1 RTR	(1)	8 H
5 RTR	1/5 Queen's	11 H
4 CLY (until Jul 1944)	1/6 Queen's	Div Sigs
5 RIDG (from Jul 1944)	1/7 Queen's	
	No 3 Sp Coy RNF	

Divisional Artillery	**Medical**	**Divisional Engineers**
3 RHA	2 Lt Fd Amb RAMC	4 Fd Sqn
5 RHA	131 Fd Amb	621 Fd Sqn
15 LAA RA	29 FDS	143 Fd Pk Sqn
65 Atk Regt RA	70 Fd Hygiene Sect	
(Norfolk Yeo)	134 Mob Dental Unit	

EME	**Divisional S&T**	**Ordnance**
7 Armd Tps Wksp	No 58 Coy RASC	Div OFP
22 Armd Bde Wksp	No 67 Coy RASC	22 Armd Bde OFP
131 Bde Wksp	No 507 Coy RASC	131 Bde OFP
15 LAA Wksp	No 133 Coy RASC (2)	

RAC
No 263 Fwd Del Sqn

Note 1. From Nov 1944 131 Bde comprised 1/5 Queen's, 2nd Devons and 9 DLI plus No 3 Sp Coy RNF.

Note 2. From Jan 1945

Left: Organisation of the division on 6 July.

Below: Handing over to the Canadians. 22nd Armd Bde workshops in the middle of its handover to its Canadian counterparts in 5th Canadian Armoured Division — conducted in a sea of mud! The brigade had to leave its Sherman tanks in Italy and would be re-equipped with Cromwells when it reached England.

to either the armoured or the infantry brigade as required. It differed only in that it had no Fireflies, but was eventually issued with a small number of A30 Challengers which also mounted the 17pdr. The Motor Battalion remained mounted in half-tracks and the Queen's Brigade in lorries; its supporting MMG company being replaced by one equipped with 4.2in mortars as well as Vickers machine-guns. All infantry anti-tank platoons now had the improved 6pdr anti-tank gun, firing discarding sabot ammunition, whilst infantry platoons had the PIAT (Projector Infantry Anti-Tank) — a close-range, hand-held weapon firing a hollow charge projectile.

The divisional artillery contained both towed and self-propelled guns, whilst the divisional anti-tank regiment (Norfolk Yeomanry) had two batteries of self-propelled 17pdrs, the rest being towed, first by half-tracks and later by converted Crusader tanks. Amongst the supporting services, the REME had been massively expanded, now having separate workshops for each brigade and divisional troops, along with Centaur or Cromwell armoured recovery vehicles, whilst the Sappers had "scissors" and Bailey bridges. Divisional communications had been considerably improved with the issue of new radio equipment based on the WS19.

As can be seen from these examples, Allied equipment procurement was running at full spate as everyone prepared for D-Day. The division was now a fully functioning all-arms formation, with a high level of "on call" air support. Nevertheless, the coming campaign would be another gruelling, hard-fought struggle against a determined enemy who had, despite shrinking resources, upgraded much of his own equipment. Throughout the war the Germans had led the field in tank design and their Tiger and Panther heavy tanks, though still somewhat mechanically unreliable, were massively better armoured and

Below: Gen Montgomery inspected every unit in the division on 16 and 17 February 1944. Here he inspects 4 CLY, now one of the armoured regiments in 22nd Armd Bde. He made a point of giving each unit a rousing speech. *IWM — H36004*

gunned than their Allied counterparts. Opposing the "Desert Rats" in Normandy was their old desert adversary — Field Marshal Erwin Rommel, the "Desert Fox" himself, who now, as the commander of Army Group "B", had done much to bolster the "Atlantic Wall" defences. Another important figure from the division's past actively commanding a frontline formation in Normandy was its creator, Gen Percy Hobart. After raising and training both 7th and 11th Armoured Divisions, he had gone on to create the revolutionary "Funnies" (79th Armd Div), whose specialised vehicles such as swimming tanks, flamethrowers, mineclearers and all manner of mobile bridges, Engineer vehicles etc would play such a major part on the British and Canadian beaches in overcoming of the enemy's defences.

A few weeks before D-Day everyone moved even deeper into the fir woods and camps were sealed, the soldiers spending most of their time waterproofing their vehicles. Eventually, the units moved down to their embarkation points — boarding the LSTs in a number of different places, then collecting into a convoy off Deal on the afternoon and evening of 5 June. By the evening of D-Day they had crossed the Channel and were in the vicinity of the landing beaches, but did not actually start to land until about 1100 hours on the 7th.

NORMANDY

7th Armoured Division landed successfully in France on 7 June after being delayed by bad weather. Fortunately, however, only a few vehicles were lost in the surf, and by that evening 22nd Armoured Brigade, less 1 RB, was safely in its concentration area. The following morning it was ready to support what were in the main, initially anyway, infantry operations. 5 RTR was first into action, supporting 56th Brigade in dealing with stubborn pockets of enemy at Sully and Port en Bessin. It would soon be involved in very different fighting in the thick bocage country of Normandy to what it had been used to in the Western Desert or even Italy. Now commanders were vulnerable at close-range from enemy snipers, whilst bypassed small groups of enemy were able to knock out AFVs with close-range, handheld anti-tank weapons such as the *Panzerfaust* (the German equivalent of the PIAT or Bazooka) — so death lurked around every corner.

The overall XXX Corps plan, Operation Perch, was that, having landed on Gold Beach, 50th Infantry Division would capture Bayeux, secure the road from there to Tilly sur Seulles, then break through the enemy positions in the area of Tilly, Juvigny, Hottot and la Senaudiere. The initial attacks would be supported by naval gunfire as well as close air support. Once the way was clear then 7th Armoured would pass through, take Villers Bocage en route, then press on to the important high ground around Evrecy. This last manoeuvre was to be supported by an airborne landing (codenamed Wild Oats). Having secured a firm base in the "Suisse Normande", the armour would then turn eastwards towards Thury Harcourt and the Orne River crossings.

Unfortunately, the airborne part of the operation never came to fruition, whilst 50th Infantry Division, after taking Bayeux

Below: France 7 June – September 1944 including Villers Bocage 12–14 June.

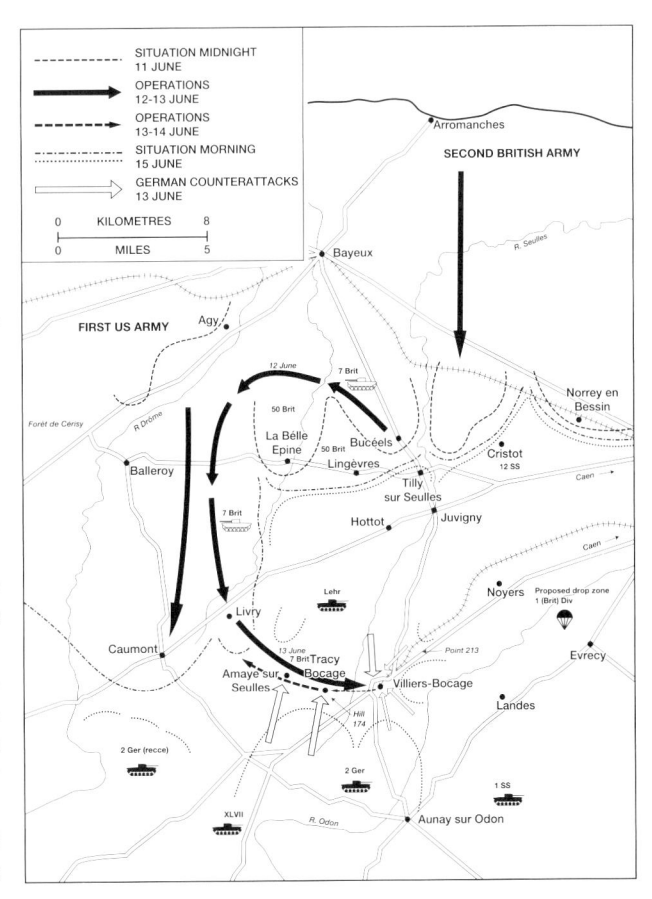

ELITE ATTACK FORCES: 7TH ARMOURED DIVISION

Left: Two of these three senior commanders helped to control the destiny of 7th Armd Div in the early days in Normandy. They were, left to right: Lt-Gen J. T. Crocker, GOC I Corps, Lt-Gen M. C. Dempsey GOC British 2nd Army and Lt-Gen G. C. Bucknall, GOC XXX Corps, in which 7th Armd Div served. Bucknall would be "sacked" by "Monty" after the Villers Bocage debacle. *IWM — B5326*

Below left: Into the bocage. A column of vehicles led by a Cromwell of 4 CLY moves down an unmade up road, to the south of Bayeux, as part of the "right hook" towards Villers Bocage. The patchwork of small fields, thick hedgerows and sunken roads, made the bocage ideal country for the defence.

Opposite, Above: Normandy. The division was not employed on D-Day, but landed on Gold Beach on 7 June. This photograph was taken during the journey across the Channel and shows some of the vast armada of ships sailing across the Channel.

Opposite, Below: A Crusader AA tank, belonging to 4 CLY, leaves the massive doors of the LST and makes its way ashore through the surf. There were three versions of AA Crusaders: the MkI with a single 40mm Bofors, the MkII with twin Oerlikons (as in the photo) and a few with triple Oerlikons. *IWM — B5129*

ELITE ATTACK FORCES: 7TH ARMOURED DIVISION

without too much trouble, got itself bogged down in its attack in the Tilly sur Seulles area, due mainly to the close, difficult, bocage countryside. Lack of progress led Montgomery to decide to modify his strategy and to send 7th Armoured on a daring "right hook" to capture Villers Bocage and the high ground to its northeast, then to push on to Evrecy.

Initially, all went well and, by 0900 hours 13 June, the division's advance guard (A Sqn 4 CLY/A Coy 1 RB) had motored virtually unhindered through Villers Bocage and reached the high ground to its northeast (Point 213). Unbeknown to it, however, part of 2 Kompanie, schwere SS-Panzer Abteilung 101, under the command of the redoubtable Panzer ace, Obersturmführer Michael Wittmann, was already leaguered there and, before 4 CLY could react, his heavy Tiger tanks created havoc among the lighter, underarmoured and undergunned Cromwells, Stuarts and half-tracks of the British force. In the ensuing battle Wittmann and his Tigers knocked out or captured the majority of the advance guard, before Wittmann's vehicle was itself knocked out and he had to escape on foot. After a fierce battle, 22nd Armd Bde Group withdrew from the little

Left: Devastation at Villers Bocage. This is one of the 4 CLY Cromwells that was knocked out by Michael Wittmann and his Tiger tank as it swept down the advance guard column from Point 213 and into the village. The tank belonged to Capt Paddy Victory. *IWM — B 8633*

Below left: Cromwell tanks and M10 tank destroyers of 22 Armd Bde in an open leaguer in their concentration area just before an attack east of the Orne River, July 1944. The M10 was an open-topped tank destroyer, mounting a 3in gun, that was based upon the Sherman hull. A British version, known as "Achilles", mounted a 17pdr, was only in service in limited numbers, but was highly successful.

Below: Two officers of 5th Inniskilling Dragoon Guards, the regiment which replaced 4 CLY in 22 Armd Bde after Villers Bocage (4 CLY was amalgamated with its sister regiment 3 CLY), inspect a knocked out German PzKpfw V Panther tank. This heavy Medium tank was one of the best produced by the Germans and owes much of its design to the Soviet T34. It was knocked out by C Sqn of the "Skins" south of Canville whilst attacking Mont Pincon, 14 August 1944.

Above: Obviously a vintage year! A "Skins" crew enjoying a local bottle of wine. 5 Innis DG quickly settled into 22 Armd Bde, with 1st and 5th RTR. The brigade would remain unchanged for the rest of the war.

town into a "brigade box" to the northwest, near Amaye dur Seulles, where it successfully held off enemy attacks that night and the next morning, until being withdrawn, after inflicting considerable casualties on the enemy.

The Villers Bocage battle would have considerable long-term effects on the division. For example, the weakened 4 CLY was some weeks later (30 July) combined with 3 CLY to form a single regiment and left 7th Armoured Division, their place being taken by the 5th Royal Inniskilling Dragoon Guards (5 DG). Additionally, the XXX Corps commander, Lt-Gen Bucknall, the divisional commander, Maj-Gen Erskine, 22nd Armd Bde commander, the eccentric Brig "Looney" Hinde, and the divisional CRA, Brig R Mews, were all "sacked" by "Monty". Maj-Gen G. L. Verney, a "no-nonsense" Guardsman, took over as GOC, whilst the popular and capable Lt-Gen Brian Horrocks once again became corps commander. These changes did not, however, actually take effect until late July.

For the rest of the month the division held the line a couple of miles from Caumont, running through Bricquessard and Torteval, with an ever-growing casualty list from being under continuous attack and shelling. Eventually it handed over to the American 2nd Armd Div at the end of the month, going to the rear for rest and refit. During three weeks of fighting in Normandy the division had lost 1,149 all ranks.

OPERATION GOODWOOD

The next operation was Goodwood — an attack by VIII Corps (now commanded by ex-WDF commander and escaped POW Gen Sir Richard O'Connor) to the south east from

Caen consisting of three British armoured divisions — 7th, 11th and the Guards Armoured. The express purpose of this action was to engage as much German armour and resources as possible in the area, thus helping the Americans to break out in the west (Operation Cobra). The countryside was more open than the bocage but there were a couple ridges and several railway embankments that were impassable for tanks, which meant that the deployment of the three armoured divisions over the Orne was an extremely complicated operation. The attack was preceded by a massive aerial and artillery bombardment. The armour began to advance on 18 July with the three armoured regiments of 11th Armd Div leading. Initially, the Germans were stunned after the massive bombardment, but gradually resistance stiffened, and at Cagny the attack was held all day. Slowly the division moved forward, fighting bitterly for every village and ridge — Le Poirier, Four, Soliers, Bras, Hubert-Folie, la Hogue. By the end of the day, divisional losses were substantial in both men and armour. However, in the morning the advance was resumed, but resistance became even stronger. On 20 July, 5 RTR took Bourguebus and 4 CLY cut the Caen-Falaise road, when massive rainstorms then brought all further operations to a halt. The division was now bunched up and within enemy artillery range, so suffered accordingly, even undergoing visits from enemy reconnaissance planes, then bombers. As much support as possible was given to the division from RAF rocket-firing Typhoons.

OPERATION SPRING

On 25 July, 7th Armd Div was ordered to support 2nd and 3rd Canadian Divisions in their assault on May-sur-Orne and Tilly-la-Compagne respectively. The May-sur-Orne attack started well but was heavily counterattacked in the evening and although this was repulsed, the use of hull-down enemy armour on the overlooking ridge made things very uncomfortable. The Tilly attack also ran into fierce resistance, however the aim of the operation had been successful — the enemy had been required to bring in reserves from all over to deal with what it thought was the main Allied thrust, consequently, the American Cobra breakout on the 25th was materially assisted. From 26 to 28 July the division remained in a defensive position supporting the Canadians, then was ordered to join XXX Corps in the Caumont sector.

FRANCE AND THE LOW COUNTRIES

In order to continue to take pressure off Cobra, "Monty" launched Operation Bluecoat, using both VIII and XXX Corps, towards Le Beny Bocage, Vire and Condé, into some of the densest parts of the bocage. 7th Armoured, as part of XXX Corps, had now replaced 4 CLY with 5 DG, but was not needed in the opening stages of the operation. However, it was concentrated near an increasingly congested Caumont. Moving up later, it entered the fray on 2 August, being directed to move on Aunay; with 8 H, 1 RTR and 5 DG leading. Having encountered growing opposition on the high ground northwest of Sauques, more infantry — the Queen's Brigade — were brought up for a successful night attack, although the Germans immediately responded with counterattacks. One particularly fierce armoured counterattack even overran some elements of 5 RTR and the Norfolk Yeomanry. However, with 8 H reinforcing them it was eventually beaten off, with great loss to the enemy in both tanks and men.

It was at this point that the division underwent the changes in command that have already been mentioned above, Maj-Gen G L Verney, latterly the commander of 6 Guards

---

ONE DAY'S WORK

The speed of the advance through France and into the Low Countries is highlighted by one exploit of B Platoon of the Division's Petrol Company.

It was used on an ammunition lift in Holland and Belgium travelling Eindhoven-Louvain-Waterloo-Eindhoven-Nijmegen.

At Louvain the company collected 25pdr rounds, and at Waterloo the drivers had to dig out of a wood a large number of shells — they had been hidden there since 1940 and all of them had to be carried 40 yards to the vehicles. Each driver loaded 4.5 tons of shells like this and then had himself to unload them at Nijmegen.

On this trip the platoon covered 240 miles in 19 hours over roads that were crowded with transports and in many places almost ruined by pot-holes and collapsed verges.

THE TOWN COUNCIL
and THE CITIZENS
of GHENT

express their real veneration and gratitude to the gallant

Officers and Men of the 7th Armoured Division

who, on the 6th September 1944, delivered our City from the bold and odious German enemy.
Glorify the heroic war-acts of the 7th Armoured Division on the African and the European continent,
Bow deeply for the sacrifices brought by the 7th Armoured Division for the liberty of our City and our Country,
Salute in the 7th Armoured Division the spirit of freedom and opposition against all kind of tyranny of the English people, who, alone resisted, in 1940, the strongest enemy and so made possible the final victory.

Long live the 7th Armoured Division !

Ghent, the 6th September 1945.

Burgomaster:
Town Council:

Town Secretary:

Above and Right: The liberation of Ghent. An illuminated address presented to 7th Armd Div by the town council and citizens of Ghent soon after their liberation on 6 September 1944, and a reciprocal plaque from the division to the town made by the division workshops.

Armd Bde, becoming GOC, whilst over 100 other long-serving officers and men were posted to other commands.

With fierce and continuous opposition being met in the centre of the division's advance, Gen Verney ordered a left-flanking movement by 22nd Armd Bde and 1/5th Queen's. This began on 4 September and by the 5th had reached Bonnemaison, then the high ground north of Hamars. Here it began to get bogged down because of difficulties navigating through an area of massive destruction caused by bombing, plus the considerable damage left after the ferocious fighting around Villers Bocage and Aunay, as well as enemy minefields and accurate defensive artillery fire. Nevertheless, the advance continued early on the 6th, edging north of Aunay, so as to make use of the still-intact road to La Vallée, which, although mined and defended, was cleared by nightfall. An artillery duel now ensued across the valley behind the village with the enemy on the slopes of Mt Pincon, whilst elsewhere the limitations of the terrain and the ferocity of the defence completely held up further progress. It was decided to mount another night assault to break the deadlock, which became a highly successful "textbook" operation featuring perfect "box-barrage" cooperation between the divisional infantry and artillery.

On 7 August the Germans in the west launched an unsuccessful counterattack against the Americans, in an attempt to contain them within the Cherbourg peninsula, which was destroyed primarily by Allied air power. The Americans then wheeled round to their left, with the aim of linking up with British and Canadians, so as to cut off some 50,000 enemy troops and much of his armour in the Falaise Pocket, and thus preventing further German attempts to contain the Allies in Normandy. As part of this operation, the division moved towards Condé in two columns, one (1 RTR and 1/7th Queens) along the Aunay-Condé road and the other (5 RTR, 5 DG, 1/5th and 1/6th Queens) from the direction of the recent breakthrough at La Vallée. This, its last battle in the bocage, would be a terrible one, because the terrain virtually precluded the use of armour and had therefore to be fought mainly by the infantry — who bore the brunt of the casualties, including CO 1/5th Queen's, Lt-Col J B Ashworth, as well as many other officers and men. In fact, because of the persistent drain on manpower and equipment over this period of high attrition, the division soon no longer had the resources to operate at such a pace — it needed a rest, resupply and a refit for its tanks. It was consequently taken out of the line on 10 August, except for 11 H, 3 and 6 RHA and 5 DG, who remained with XXX Corps.

However, the fighting continued, so rest was not for long — the division being summoned back to action on 17 August, when it was able to escape from the constricting bocage into considerably easier terrain which was more open going, where the armour could often, but not always, lead.

The "Desert Rats" then advanced east from Caen towards the River Seine but were held up by having to navigate over the Dives, Vie, Touques, Orbec and Risle rivers, with almost all their bridges blown and determined enemy rearguards making good use of them all. On 17 August, the division was directed to advance on Livarot and then Lisieux, the Queen's Brigade leading with 8 H and 11 H fanned out across a wide front, searching to find any bridges still standing or other potential crossing places over the River Vie, whilst the armoured brigade brought up the rear. After initially making good progress they were met with stiff resistance and over the next 48 hours the battle raged, with substantial casualties to both sides. On 19 August an old forgotten bridge was found intact by 11 H, the Vie was crossed and a bridgehead established towards Livarot. When the enemy realised what had happened he blew the main bridge into the town, cutting off some of his own forces. Nevertheless, the stubborn defence was eventually annihilated and the town taken. By the 21st the Engineers had re-bridged the Vie, brought across 22nd Armoured Bde and the division was now strung out along ten miles of road, fighting in three different places. At times its forward elements were cut off by enemy counterattacks, for the area around Lisieux was sufficiently well defended to prevent the bridgehead being further expanded.

Gen Verney now sought to find a way around the right flank, sending 1/7th Queen's and a squadron of 11 H across. However, resistance was too stiff and the going no good for armour. Finally, through dogged persistence, the enemy was worn down and wiped out. By mid-afternoon on 22 August, 1 RTR and 1/6th Queen's had penetrated well into the town — although it did not fall until the next day, under the combined weight of attacks from 51st Div from the south and 7th Armoured from the west.

The following day, despite counterattacks which were beaten back, the town was taken and the Orbec bridged. The advance then moved on to the next main German defensive line, based on the River Risle. As the division approached it was found that, although the road on either side of the bridge had been badly damaged by the RAF, Pont Authou was still standing, with the enemy established there in force. Further downstream the bridge at Montfort had been destroyed, but a forgotten and dilapidated old bridge was eventually found a mile beyond it. 5 DG then crossed over, attacked and took Pont Authou, which was then used as the main divisional route forward. Over the next three days, the division fought a series of piecemeal clearing actions against troops of varying quality, scattered over a wide area up to the River Seine, some of whom were tired and ready to surrender, while others were fresh, fanatical and well equipped. But the Battle of Normandy was drawing to a close, and on 28 August the division was pulled back for a quick rest and refit before the next stage of the long campaign, getting steadily nearer and nearer to the heart of the matter… Germany!

THE ADVANCE TO GHENT

7th Armoured was next to advance on Ghent as part of XII Corps under Lt-Gen Ritchie (a previous commander of Eighth Army in the desert). The Canadians were assigned to move along the coast on the left, with 11th Armoured Division on the right heading for Antwerp. The new British and Canadian tasks were firstly to move north and east, destroying "V-weapon" launching sites that were terrorising London; secondly, to take the major ports — in particular Antwerp — in order to shorten the Allied lines of supply. Having concentrated at Le Neuberg, and with 4th Armoured Brigade, the Royals and 10th Medium Regt, RA, all temporarily attached, the division's first task was to secure a bridgehead over

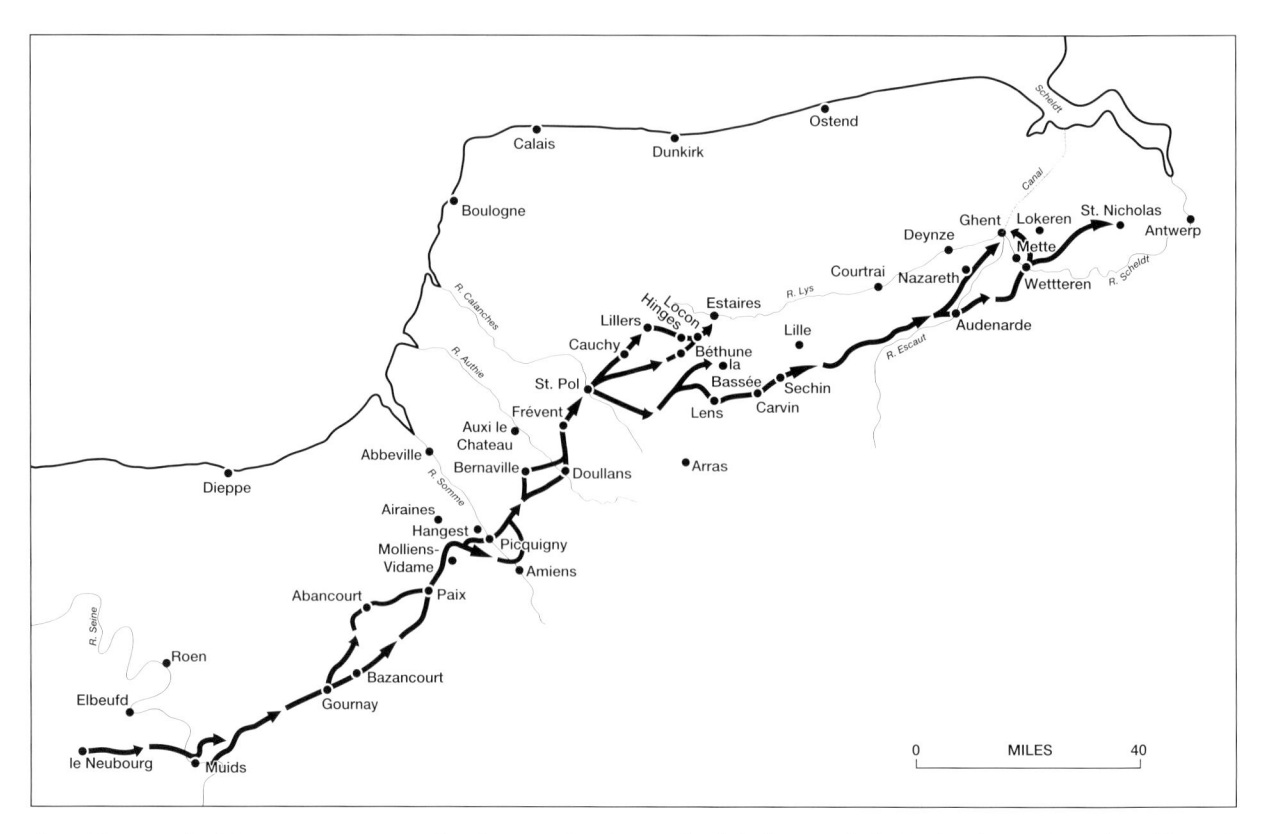

Above: Belgium & Holland, 6 September – 30 November 1944

Above right: Here is one of the dreaded PzKpfw VI Tiger tanks, with its massive 88mm gun and thick armour. Also on the photo (see 'X') is a *Panzerfaust* anti-tank weapon, the larger versions being able to penetrate 200mm of armour.

Right: Winter operations. 1 RTR and 2nd Devons took Echt and Hingen on 18 January 1945. Here infantrymen move carefully through the village at the beginning of the assault.

the Somme. Crossing north of Amiens on 1 September in pouring rain, with much congestion and coming up against a determined enemy rearguard, meant progress was tortuously slow. Because of these problems other routes were looked for and another bridge was found just out of the division's area of operations. With permission given to use it, the Engineers were also ordered to bridge the river on the site of the destroyed bridge at Picquigny. The Queen's Brigade, together with 5 RTR, now crossed over behind 4th Armd Bde and pushed on through the night to take the high ground near Bernaville, capturing a flying-bomb site en route. There was now a dangerous threat on the left flank from the German divisions in the Pas de Calais area, so the divisional attacks became a series of hooks into this defence line. The countryside was also better suited for armour and the speed of progress increased, although the river valleys ultimately focused on a few crossing places. The 8 H and 1/5th Queen's crossed the Authie northwest of Doullens, cleared Frévent and moved on to St Pol. However, at St Pol and at Auxi there was a strong German presence and when it was realised progress was easier further west, the emphasis of the advance changed accordingly.

By 4 September the division was now heading for the complicated canal and coalmining area just north of Lille, where the defence was well entrenched and there was especially fierce resistance. Fortunately, in order to get to Ghent on schedule, the division was given permission to circumvent this dangerous area to the south and it was left to 1 RTR, with help from some elements of 5 DG, 1 RB and the Maquis, to break down and overcome this stubborn defence.

Meanwhile, back at St Pol, on 3 September 11 H had fanned out on a three-squadron front, and found an intact bridge over the La Bassée Canal, which it crossed, and then assaulted the well-defended town of la Bassée. Then, while the rest of the division remained in the difficult Béthune/Lille area, keeping the centre line open, a mixed group of units from both brigades led by 11 H, made a dash for Ghent. They reached it the

IN ACTION

Above: Members of the tank troop that provided protection for Tac HQ 7th Armd Div, seen here in Holland during the winter 1944-5. All wear the zippered tank oversuit which kept crewmen warm and dry inside their tanks.

following day after securing Oudenarde and entered the city to a rapturous welcome from the inhabitants. The Germans slowly withdrew north and remained in control of the north bank of the Scheldt.

The division stayed around Ghent, securing the city, mopping up pockets of resistance and bridging the Scheldt at Wettern, whilst slowly bringing up the elements left at Béthune and liaising with the invaluable Belgian resistance. The battered German Fifteenth Army was still in the area with some 11 divisions still dangerous. Because it was trying to escape eastwards, fighting its way home through the division's area of operations, Gen Verney ordered the destruction of all bridges over the River Lys and preparation for the same on the River Escaut. However, in the end the Germans retired northwards across the Scheldt estuary.

At the close of this phase the division had covered 220 miles in a week, taken over 1,000 prisoners and lost far fewer men than in the bocage battles (less than 100 as compared with 1,300). However, the supply lines were now awesomely long and as a result the division was very stretched out. Once again it had fought itself almost to a standstill, expending its resources to achieve its objectives. Its armoured brigade was down to about two thirds of its tanks and its infantry strength had been reduced by half.

OPERATION MARKET GARDEN

The division was next moved to Malines for a brief spell, guarding the canal line between Herenthals and Antwerp, while other divisions (11th Armd and Guards Armd) forced strongly contested bridgeheads over the Albert and Escaut canals. Then on 17 September 1944 Operation Market Garden began. This operation was a daring gamble to foreshorten the war by means of a series of paratroop landings to capture vital bridges en route to Germany, being followed up by an armoured assault to link them all together. This was the reason for the "bridge too far" airborne landing at Arnhem. Unexpectedly strong enemy resistance, heavy casualties and bad weather all combined against the airborne troops, whilst the relieving ground forces failed to reach them. On 25 September, the battered survivors were pulled out. While the attempt to capture a bridge over the Lower Rhine had failed, the Allies still retained a valuable salient from which they would launch further assaults during the battle for Germany the following February. For the operation, XII Corps (of which the division was still a part) was moved into Holland with the task of guarding the western side of the attack corridor, while VIII Corps, with 11th Armoured Div, protected the eastern side. The terrain was very unsuitable for armour, with flat marshy "polder" and many dykes, as well as roads which

Above: Getting ammunition ready for this BL 5.5in gun/howitzer, which is supporting armoured operations in Holland. It had a maximum range of 16,200yd and the shell weight was 100lb.

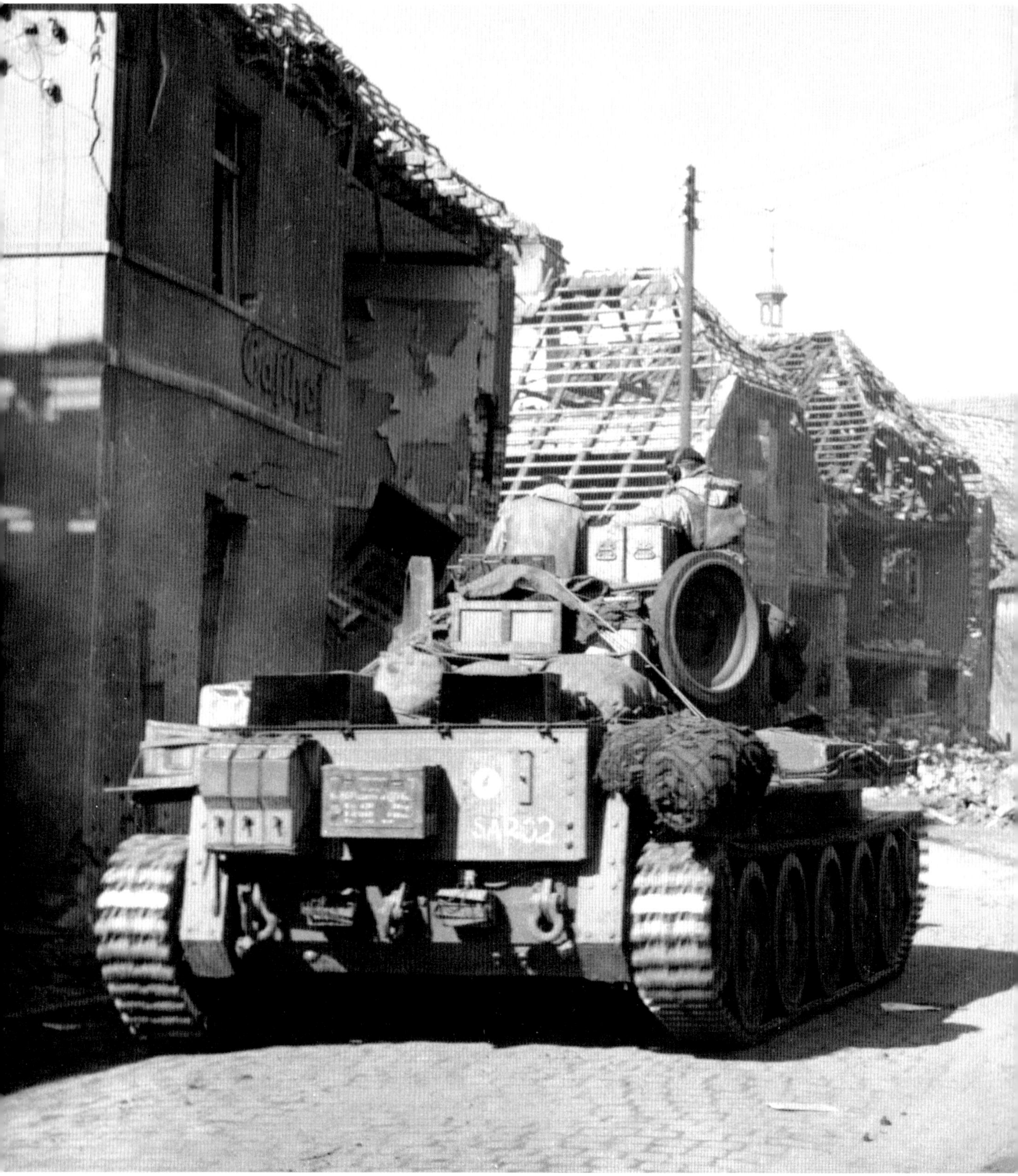

were both of poor quality and dangerously exposed to enemy fire. XII Corps was accordingly swung round westwards into Brabant to clear the northern shore and 7th Armoured instructed to push on to the River Maas. From 22 to 31 October, in a bitter, relentless attack, the division (Queen's Bde complete, 1 RTR, 8 H, 11 H and 1 RB), supported by minesweeping and flamethrowing tanks, slowly and deliberately eliminated the various strongpoints in that area and achieved its objectives, taking s'Hertogenbosch, Middelrode, Loop-on-Zond, Dongen and Oosterhout, then finally reaching the Maas.

Following these battles the division remained beside the Maas and was rested for 10 days. On 10 November it was moved to the eastern edge of the Second Army sector, taking over the line along the Maas and the Wessem Canal. The division then played a small part in the XII Corps offensive east of Wert, its task being to seize the lock gates at Panheel before the Germans destroyed them and flooded the area. In a ferocious battle with high casualties, involving 1/7th Queens and 8H, the lock gates were taken. The division was not involved in stopping the German Ardennes offensive of mid-December 1944, but instead remained on the Maas in freezing weather while it was rested, re-equipped and reorganised, and had its manpower brought back up to strength. The Queen's Brigade had suffered heavily in the previous months' fighting and the battalions

Above: HQ 22nd Armd Bde at Syke, on the southern approaches to Bremen in early April 1945. Note the temporary command post that has been set up, partly on one of the Cromwells, with two LOs/staff officers sitting outside the tank on chairs, numerous large aerials on the tank and behind it, and what looks like a skywave aerial on the roof of the nearby thatched cottage. *IWM — BU3348*

Left: A well-laden 7th Armd Div Cromwell passing through the ruined village of Borken, 30 March 1945. *IWM — BU 2895*

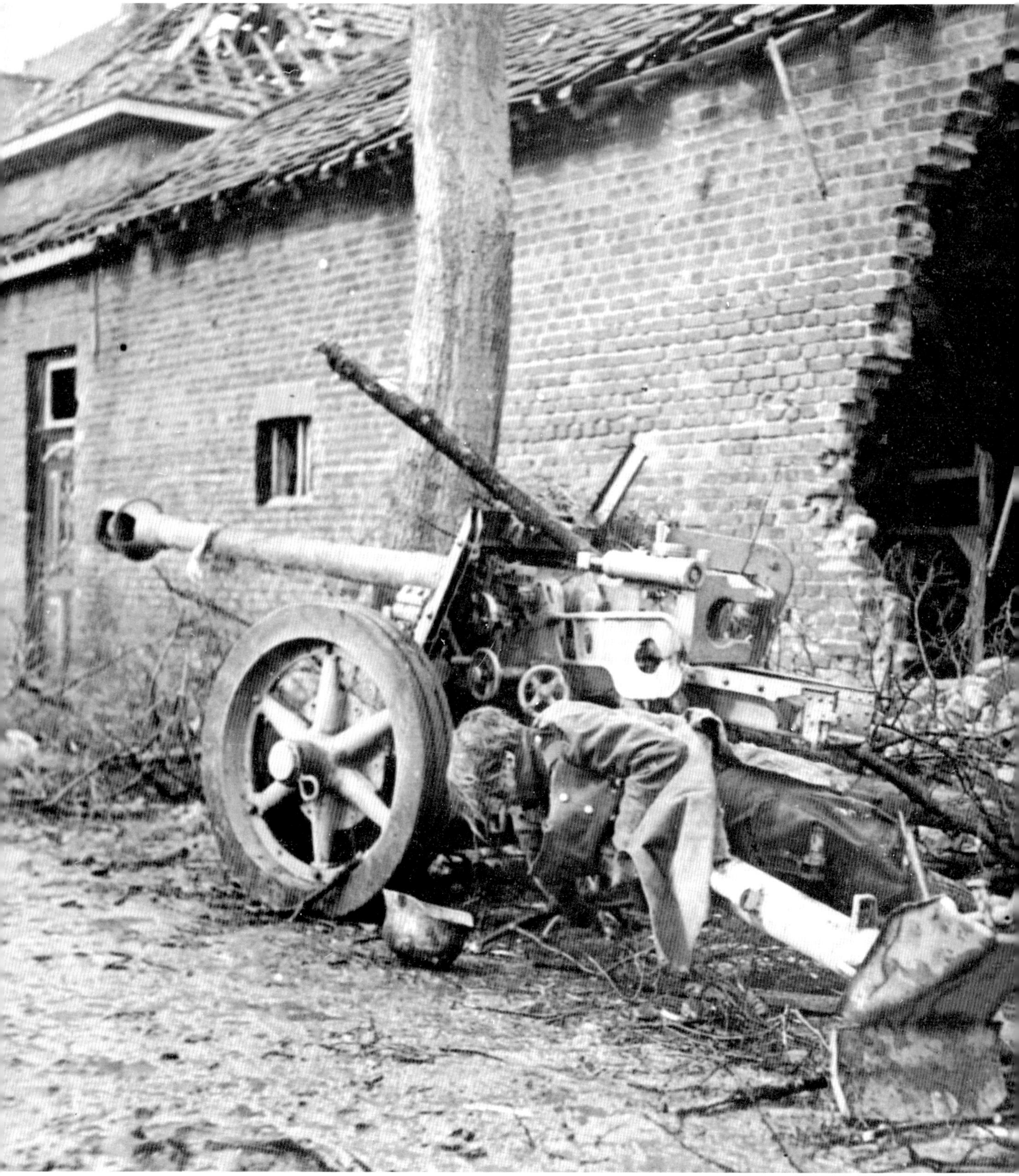

Left: Two members of 5 RTR looking at a knocked-out enemy anti-tank gun (a 7.5cm Pak 40 L/46) in Rethem on the Aller which they reached in early April 1945.

Above: Div HQ staff sorting through just some of the enormous numbers of maps that were needed to keep up with the rapid advance through Germany. One can imagine how difficult it was just folding a map in the confines of a tank turret — hence the need for some space to examine them properly. *IWM — BU3185*

Right: VE Day. D Sqn 11 H built this huge bonfire to celebrate "Victory in Europe", on 8 May 1945.

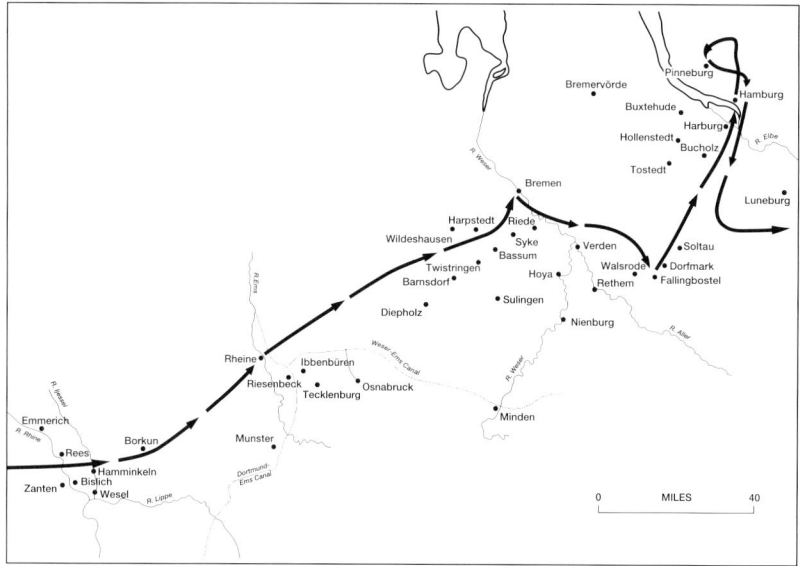

Above: Taking the war into the Reich. From the entry into Germany to end of the war, January 1945 – May 1945.

were therefore amalgamated, leaving only 1/5th Queen's in 131 Brigade, the other two battalions being replaced by 2nd Devons and 9th Durham Light Infantry, both from 50th Infantry Division. Maj-Gen L O Lyne, also from the Northumbrian Division, relieved Gen Verney and took over as GOC, whilst Verney went to Italy to command 6th Armoured Division.

ADVANCE INTO GERMANY

Designed to clear the area up to the River Roer, an operation (Blackcock) was conducted under the aegis of XII Corps and as a result 7th Armd had additional armour and troops temporarily attached — 8th Armd Bde and 155 Inf Bde from 52nd Infantry Division and later 1st Commando Bde.

The continuation of the freezing weather was essential to the operation's success, for a thaw and its muddy consequences would quickly bring an armoured division on the move to an abrupt halt.

On 13 January 1945 1/5th Queen's began the first preliminary attack, aided by flail tanks and an artillery barrage. The main assault went in on the 17th, with 9 DLI capturing Dieteren, the Queen's then leapfrogging forward to attack the next village — Susteren. An enemy counterattack was swiftly broken up by 3 RHA, with 1 RTR coming up in support, but the battle for Susteren was to be a costly affair in both armour and men and the next few days were a hard-fought and expensive struggle, winkling out defenders and forcing them to retreat or be killed. A partial thaw threatened to stymie the whole operation but the weather turned cold again and the ground refroze. On 18 January the Devons and 1 RTR captured Echt and the advance was continued northeastwards. On the 20th and 21st another fierce action was fought with high casualties by elements of 1 RB, 8 H and 9 DLI for possession of St Joost. On 22 January 5 DG and C Coy 1 RB moved on Montfort and later 1/5th Queen's with 5 RTR came up in support and the village was taken, along with many prisoners. On the 24th the division advanced along three axes, 1/5th Queens and 1 RTR to the east, aiming for Posterholt; the Devons and 5 DG in the centre, advancing northeast to the Roer; and 8 H with 1st Commando Bde in the west moving towards Linne. With the taking of all these objectives, Operation Blackcock was successfully concluded. The division was then rested until early February, holding the area it had taken whilst training for the next major operation — the crossing of the Rhine.

OPERATION PLUNDER

The plan was for Second Army to cross the Rhine at three points — at Rees with XXX Corps, and at Zanten and Wesel with XII Corps, of which 7th Armd was still a part. The specific divisional objective was Hamburg, approximately 200 miles away. By 26 March the river line had been taken and bridged and on the 27th 7th Armd Div, led by the ubiquitous 11 H, was the first British armoured division across. During the following week, it advanced to the Ems with the armoured brigade leading. Progress now slowed considerably, as each village and town had been so badly bombed they were often just rubble, and often, also, tenaciously defended. The Engineers were kept fully busy building fresh bridges and repairing roads, while the division now fought innumerable small-scale actions against ramshackle groups of the rapidly disintegrating German Army. On 1 April

Above left: End of the Third Reich. Men of 22nd Armd Bde display a pristine Nazi flag they have acquired. And by the look of the boxes on the back decks of their Cromwell, that isn't all they have liberated!

Below: Maj-Gen Lyne taking the salute at the dress rehearsal for the Victory Parade in Berlin

Above: Victory Parade, Berlin. Winston Churchill, accompanied by "Monty", Alanbrooke and Lyne, riding in an immaculate half-track, move slowly past Cromwells and their crews of the division. *IWM — BU9078*

Above right: Men of HQ 131 Bde and Signals Squadron marching towards the saluting base during the parade.

Right: OP tanks of 3 RHA move towards the saluting base.

the forward elements of the division, 5 DG and 9 DLI, broke into Rheine and the town was fully invested the following day. Meanwhile 11th Armd Div had crossed the Dortmund-Ems Canal on its way to Osnabrück, so 7th Armd now made use of this bridgehead to get 22nd Armd Bde across. 5 RTR also managed to seize a bridge over the Weser-Ems Canal and went on to take Diepholz, despite a rare attack by the Luftwaffe. 22nd Armd Bde was next tasked with the capture of Ibbenburen, but this proved to be a hard and costly nut to crack as it was ably defended by the diehard staff and trainees of a Wehrmacht officer training school, located in the town. Indeed it proved troublesome enough for the division to sidestep it and leave it to 53rd Infantry Div.

With the left flank now protected by a large marshy area and with 22nd Armd Bde leading, the division approached the next major obstacle of the River Weser. The bridge at Hoya was promptly blown on its arrival and the town was bristling with so many defenders and their artillery support that it was decided that the division would wheel north and attempt to cut off the German First Parachute Army rather than attempt to take the town or cross the river until sufficient forces had been concentrated there.

7 April saw 131 Brigade moving north towards Twistringen and then Bassum, which was heavily defended and did not fall until the following day under the combined weight of a converging two-pronged assault led by A Sqn 5 DG and A Coy 1 RB on the left and B Sqn 5 DG with a company of 9 DLI on the right. 155 Brigade then linked up with 131 Bde on 9 April at Bassum, having captured Barnstorf. Meanwhile, 22nd Armd Bde approached Bremen, 8 H and 1/5 Queen's taking Reide, while 11 H and 5 RTR captured Syke. By 10 April 9 DLI and 5 DG, plus a battery of Norfolk Yeomanry, had captured Harpstedt and Wildeshausen. All gains were held against counterattacks and consolidated. However, the battle for Bremen would be a more drawn-out affair and it was decided instead to send the division north to the Elbe and Harburg, to firstly cut the autobahn link with Hamburg, then assault that city itself. Once again the next 10 days were a bitter struggle against fanatical defenders pursuing a scorched earth policy of destroying everything, hiding and re-emerging behind the advance and making the most out of the heavily wooded and marshy terrain. They were also well equipped and supplied with all kinds of arms and plentiful ammunition from pre-prepared caches. However, the Allied war machine was now unstoppable and remorseless, and a surrounded and invaded Germany no longer had the resources to defend itself other than by these final desperate individual actions.

On 15 April 22nd Armd Bde crossed the Rethem bridgehead, by evening Walsrode had been occupied and the following day the brigade advanced in two columns on Soltau — one with 8 H along the main road and the other with 1 RTR across country further to the north. Opposition was stiff at Fallingbostel but it was comprehensively cleared by the

IN ACTION

Queen's and 8 H, who liberated nearby two large prisoner-of-war camps, one of which had already been taken over by the inmates and was being run with iron precision by a paratroop RSM.

On 17 April 22nd Armd Bde bypassed Soltau, leaving it to 5 DG and 7 RTR with their Crocodile flamethrower tanks, and moved across boggy ground towards Tostedt, which fell on the 18th. With Bucholz captured the next day by 131st Brigade, the First German Parachute Army had now been squeezed into a pocket between Bremen and Hamburg. The division again found itself somewhat spread out, with more than one task in hand. The prime aim was to still cut the autobahn between Bremen and Hamburg and capture Harburg; the secondary aim was to root out the last hardcore German forces hiding in the woods in the Soltau area.

The autobahn was cut at Hollenstadt on 19 April by 8 H and 1/5 Queen's, who then turned east and fought their way inch by inch into the Elbe valley. These final actions took place to the south and west of Hamburg, and involved rounding up or destroying ragtag groups of Nazi fanatics including police, army, SS, Gestapo, paratroops, marines, submarine crews and even stevedores, most of whom were determined to die with the end of the Third Reich

Above: When 7th Armd Div entered Berlin in the summer of 1945, it erected a stone monument at the end of the autobahn. Later, roadworks in the area made it necessary to move the monument, so it was taken to the UK and set up in the grounds of the RMA Sandhurst, where it remains today.

SURRENDER OF HAMBURG

On 29 April 1945 a deputation was sent to the British lines from Hamburg to begin the surrender negotiations for the city and, under the threat of a renewed air assault, the city quickly surrendered. Thus, on 3 May units of the Division drove unopposed into the shattered city. Two days later, on 5 May, the hostilities ceased at 8am. The Division now became an army of occupation, remaining in the area it was located when the fighting stopped and beginning to process the huge numbers of German troops that were coming west to surrender.

BERLIN PARADE 1945 AND CHURCHILL'S ADDRESS

On 21 June 1945 at 10am the guns roared out over ruined Berlin — British guns fired by 3 RHA, to signify the start of the "End of the War Parade". The "Desert Rats" were given the signal honour of playing a major role in this parade, which was a fitting epilogue after they had fought their way from the deserts of North Africa, through Italy and Northwest Europe, from Mersa Matruh to the Baltic — "a march unsurpassed through all the story of war," as Prime Minister Winston Churchill put it. What thoughts must have passed through the minds of the veterans as they saluted their great war leader! FLOREAT JERBOA!

Above: From February to May 1942, 7th Armoured Brigade conducted a heroic withdrawal through Burma acting as rearguard for the withdrawing British and Commonwealth forces for most of the way. 7 Hussars and 2 RTR were equipped with the small M3 Light "Honey" tanks and had to fight all their way back to the Chindwin River.

Left: On reaching the Chindwin, they then had to destroy their tanks to prevent them being used by the Japanese, so the engines were drained of oil and run until they seized. Then the crews had to make a long and dangerous trek into India, moving by night and hiding up by day. However, they made it safely and went on to fight against the Germans and Italians in Italy.

INSIGNIA, CLOTHING & EQUIPMENT

Above: This insignia denotes a major in 44 RTR. The major's crown has the yellow backing of the RAC/cavalry and sits atop a yellow and red regimental flash of the 44th Royal Tank Regiment. At the top of the sleeve sits the Desert Rat, properly the jerboa, in black and white, signifying 4th Armoured Brigade. Below that is the red and yellow service stripe of the Royal Armoured Corps. Last but not least is the "arm badge, tank" worn on the right sleeve by all ranks of the Royal Tank Regiment.

FORMATION INSIGNIA

The Red Rat
7th Armoured's initial emblem was inherited from the Mobile Division, being a plain white circle on a scarlet ground. However, soon after Gen O'Moore Creagh took command, he decided that the circle should contain some symbol that was truly representative of the division's desert background. He chose the Greater Egyptian Jerboa (Jaculus Orientalis), a tough little rodent that lived in the Arabian desert. It was sand coloured, with a long balancing tail and massive back legs which enabled it to leap six feet from a standing start! The next problem was to find a live one to copy, but after much searching one was located in Cairo Zoo and the first "Desert Rat Rampant" was drawn on a sheet of hotel notepaper by Mrs Creagh and Mrs Peyton (wife of the GSO3). This was transferred in flaming scarlet to the white circle on the divisional commander's flag by Peter Hordern (then serving as a liaison officer at Div HQ) and thence onto every vehicle and every topee flash.

The Green Rat
At the end of 1941, 7th Armoured Brigade left the division and went to Burma. It kept its jerboa emblem, but changed its colour to green — presumably to blend in with the jungle.

The Black Rat
When 4th Armoured Brigade also left the division (after the capture of Tobruk) it also kept its rat but not only changed its colour to black, but also put its tail up over its head. Not to be outdone, the Queen's Brigade used a black jerboa in a red oval as its vehicle sign.

The Stag's Head
Certain other armoured brigades also had their own brigade sign on their vehicles. Within 7th Armoured Division this applied only to the 22nd Armd Bde, whose red stag's head on a white square is sometimes to be seen on the opposite mudguard, balancing the divisional sign.

A Shoulder Patch
When the division was resting in the Homs-Tripoli area in the summer of 1943, after the Axis surrender in North Africa, the first shoulder patch appeared — it was the original scarlet jerboa on a khaki square, but it was not worn universally because it was in short

supply. Then when the division left Italy, the GOC gave orders that shoulder patches for the whole division should be produced and be ready for issue when they reached the UK. However, the clothing firm selected by the War Office to make them had its own ideas on what a jerboa should look like and the result was more akin to a kangaroo than a jerboa (hence some rude remarks from Aussie troops!). The powers that be were adamant that they were to be used, so the altered flashes had to be accepted, although the original scarlet rat was still used as the vehicle sign.

Ever since then the red/brown "kangaroo-like" jerboa on its black background has remained the emblem of the division and then, after the disbandment of the division, that of the 7th Armoured Brigade, while 4th Armd Bde has retained the black rat. To quote Gen Verney: "Whatever his shape, his colour or his attitude, the Jerboa remains the farthest travelled animal with the longest fighting record. Long may he be honoured. *FLOREAT JERBOA!*"

Vehicle Signs in the Desert
In addition to the divisional signs, there were other ways of recognising vehicles belonging to the division, for example:

a. Overall colour. In the early days of the war (1939-41), the standard camouflage painting for British AFVs was in straight-edged patterns of either black with green, or silver-grey with slate-grey, on top of a basic light stone colour. There might well also be the white/red/white or white/black/white British identification stripes painted on the side of the turret or body of the tank (perhaps on the side plates).

Above left: The original topee flash, which became the vehicle sign for the newly formed 7th Armoured Division, first drawn by Mrs Peyton, then in flaming scarlet by Lt (now Col Retd) Peter Hordern, who was at the time one of the LOs in HQ 7th Armd Div.

Above: Final divisional jerboa shoulder patch. This sign was introduced when the division reached the UK in December 1943 and was worn throughout the rest of the war and on until disbandment. It is now worn by 7th Armd Bde.

b. Unit Identification. Units were identified by two numerals in white on a red, green, or green and white square, for example:

Div HQ:		a red square containing the divisional sign above a white "99" on a black square
Armd Car Regt:	11H	black "14" on a square (top half green, bottom half white)
7th Armd Bde:	1RTR	white "24" on a red square
	8H	white "25" on a red square
	3H	white "26" on a red square
4th Armd Bde:	7H	white "28" on a green square
	2RTR	white "29" on a green square
	6RTR	white "30" on a green square

Vehicle Signs in Northwest Europe

By the time the division landed in Northwest Europe, the standard vehicle colour was olive drab and camouflaged patterns had largely been discontinued (however, during the winter of 1944/5, many AFVs were painted with whitewash to help them blend in with the snowy scenery). Unit identification numbers were still being used, but had changed (see table below), as had the colour of the background squares, both of which had now been standardised within the British Army as a whole.

Examples of Standard Vehicle Markings as used in NW Europe

Unit	Number	Arm or Service Colour of Background
HQ Armd Div (incl FSS and Int Sect)	40	Black
Armd Recce Regt	43	Green/blue horizontal
Armd Car Regt (Corps Tps)	44	Green/blue horizontal
Field Regts RA	64, 65	Red/blue horizontal
Atk Regt	77	Red/blue horizontal
LAA Regt	73	Red/blue horizontal
Field Sqns RE	41, 46	Blue
Fd Pk Sqn	42	Blue
HQ Armd Bde	50	Red
3 x armd regt	51, 52, 53	Red
Mot Bn	54	Red
HQ Inf Bde	60	Green
3 x inf bns	61, 62, 63	Green
Armd Bde Coy RASC	81	Red/green diagonal
Inf Bde Coy RASC	83	Red/green diagonal
Div Tps Coy RASC	84	Red/green diagonal
Fd Amb	90	Black
Lt Fd Amb	89	Black
FDS	93	Black
Fd Hygiene Sect	92	Black
Ord Fd Pk	97	Blue/red/blue
Armd Bde Wksp	99	Blue/yellow/red horizontal
Inf Bde Wksp	100	Blue/yellow/red
Pro Coy	43	Black
Postal Unit	44	Black
Sigs	*	Blue/white horizontal

* carry number of formation/unit to which they are attached

Above: A group of fitters, belonging to A Squadron, 5 RTR, pose on top of one of their vehicles, a heavy utility 4 x 2 Canadian Ford C11ADF that was widely used in North Africa, often with the complete top removed. Note both the divisional sign and the "A" Sqn triangle (also the mixture of dress/undress — typical fitters!).

Above right: A excellent shot of an "acquired" Mercedes-Benz 170VK staff car. Note that as well as the "Desert Rat" sign, there is also the 22nd Armd Bde Stag's Head on the opposite mudguard, plus "53" which signifies that it belongs to the junior armoured regiment in the brigade, namely 5 RTR.

Right: War Imminent! NCOs of 1 RTR wearing the two-piece black denims, plus in most cases solar topees, as they are briefed on 24 August 1939. Note also the black hose-tops, worn by the SSM in KD, goggles (on the sergeant with the beret) and the slung respirators which some are carrying.

Other Vehicle Signs
Squadron signs as used throughout the war by all formations were the normal diamond (HQ), triangle (A Sqn), square (B Sqn) and circle (C Sqn), sometimes with troop numbers inside. Initially, in the desert, the senior regiment in the brigade had its signs in red, the second senior yellow and the junior regiment blue. Colour was, however, often dispensed with and they appeared in white or black.

Tank Names
These normally followed a standard pattern as laid down within regimental standing orders, although on occasions crews might choose their own names. For example, RTR regiments used names beginning with the appropriate letter of the alphabet for the regiment, eg in 1 RTR all tank names began with "A", in 2 RTR with a "B" and so on. However, there were many variations and especially at times of stress new tanks were often unnamed.

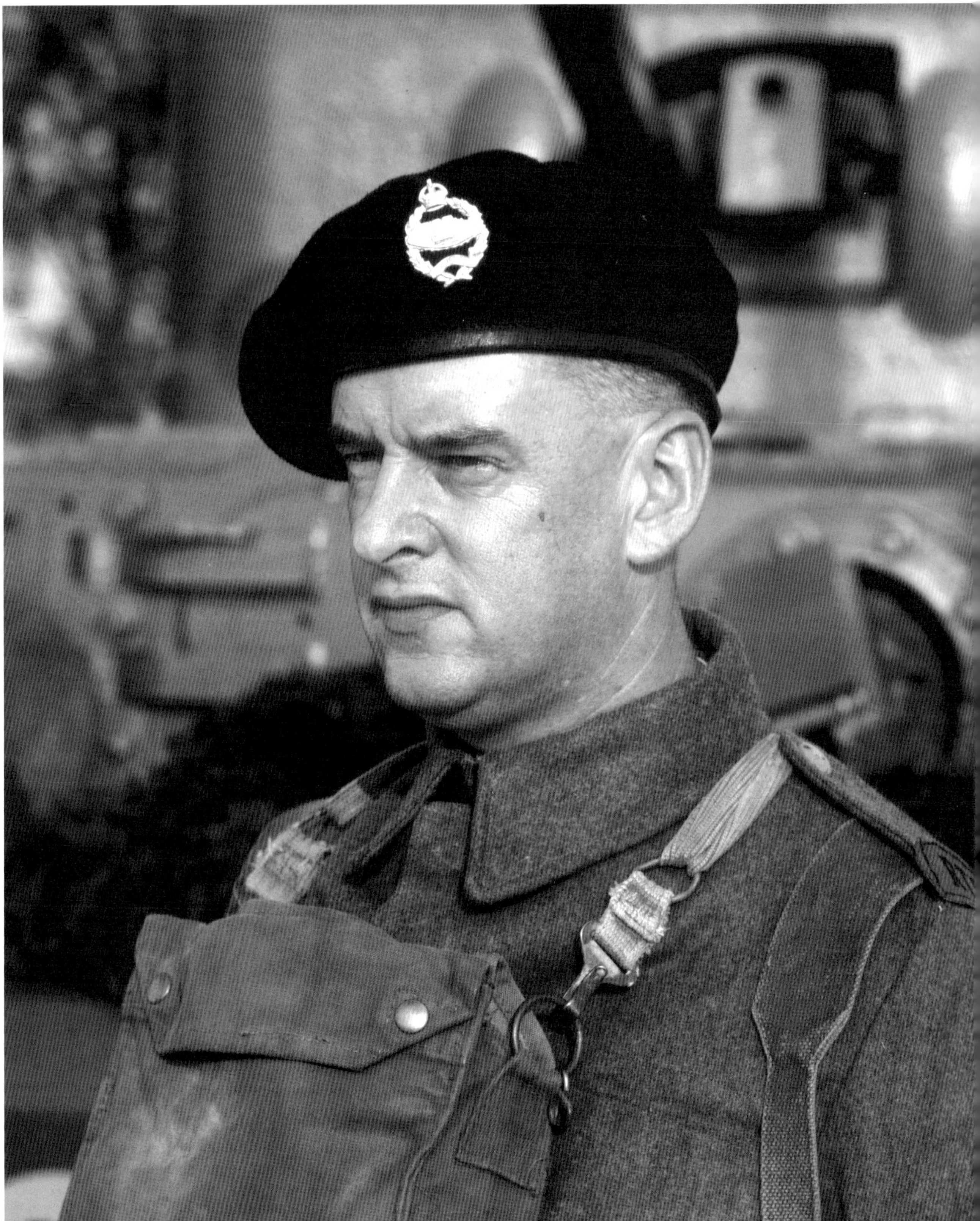

INSIGNIA, CLOTHING & EQUIPMENT

Opposite: The distinctive black beret and silver cap badge of the RTC/RTR. The cap badge with its scroll reading 'Fear Naught' dates from 18 October 1923. The beret was copied from the WWI headgear worn by French chasseurs alpins. The entire Royal Armoured Corps took to wearing black berets with individual regimental badges in 1940. Note also the service respirator worn in the ready position on the chest.

Left: RAC crash helmet, 1939 issue. Made from a number of panels it sported ventilation holes with rubber grommets. The helmet gave no protection from bullets or shrapnel, only bumps from the tank.

Below left: Hard fibre RAC crash helmet, 1941. This gave increased protection with a padded front section.

Below: Side view of the hard fibre RAC crash helmet with an additional side flap for wireless operators. This one has earphones wired for the WS19, 15 watt AFV wireless.

Right: The crew of this A13 cruiser tank belonging to 2 RTR have just fought the Battle of Beda Fomm, so are relaxing. Note the leather jerkins worn by the commander sitting by the bivvie and his gunner (with beard). They knocked out 20 Italian tanks that day! The gunner wears his pistol in a low-slung holster, with the strap around his upper leg. All wear denims and RTR berets.

UNIFORMS, PERSONAL EQUIPMENT AND PERSONAL ARMS

Uniforms

When war was declared the introduction of the new battledress (BD) and the new range of webbing equipment was still in progress. This uniform was, of course, primarily designed for wear in temperate climates, so during the division's initial years in North Africa and Italy, khaki drill uniform was worn — which comprised lightweight sand-coloured khaki tunics or shirts, long/short trousers worn with boots or shoes, long stockings and hose-tops (with shorts). This is not to say that BD was never worn in the Middle East — it was certainly most welcome during the bitterly cold desert nights or in the mountains of Tunisia and Italy, where even greatcoats and cap comforters were often worn. In addition, the officers in particular added various items of unofficial dress — suede desert boots with crepe rubber soles, coloured silk scarves, sheepskin coats and the like. Indeed, such items became synonymous with the "Desert Rats", thanks to the unforgettable "Two Types" cartoons by Jon and the example set by their C-in-C, "Monty"! Once they returned to Northwest Europe, BD became the order of the day, although coloured scarves still could be seen. The colder the weather became, the more essential became winter clothing. AFV crewmen were fortunate to have a special zipped oversuit to keep them warm and dry, whilst the stout brown leather sleeveless jerkin which had its beginnings in the Great War was much sought after. Prewar headgear, such as the solar topee, lasted for a few months in the Western Desert, but was soon replaced, either by the regular pattern steel helmet, or individual unit headgear — berets, for example, being much more convenient to wear inside a tank. In short, the soldiers of the division wore most of the normal types of British Army uniforms appropriate to the theatre of operations, their individuality being maintained by their "Desert Rat" flashes, their unit headgear and cap badges, and for some, their unofficial items of dress.

Below: An excellent photograph of HQ Support Group staff, 7th Armd Div, in the desert in 1940. In the centre of the rear row with his hands on chest is Brig "Strafer" Gott. Most wear KD shorts and shirts, some wear suede desert boots, RTR berets, forage caps and one an issue pullover (see his solar topee on the table behind the group). I would give them nought out of 10 for their camouflage on their Command Vehicle!

VEHICLES, WEAPONS AND EQUIPMENT

The same general rule applied to personal weapons. Pistols, rifles, light machine guns, grenades etc were all standard British Army issue, although of course, in some cases, American weapons and equipment were used — eg the Browning machine gun (.30 and .50 calibre) and the Thompson sub-machine gun.

Tanks

Main Types of Tanks Used by 7th Armoured Division

Yrs of main use	Type	Name/Nomenclature	Weight (tons)	Crew	Armament
1939-40	Medium	Vickers Mark III	13.5	5	1 x 3pdr, 3 x MG
1939-41	Light	Vickers Mark VI	5.5	3	1 x hy MG, 1 x MG
1939-41	Cruiser	Mark I (A9)	12	6	1 x 2pdr, 3 x MG
1939-42	Cruiser	Mark II (A10)	13.75	4	1 x 2pdr, 1 x MG
1939-42	Cruiser	Mark III (A13)	14.75	4	1 x 2pdr, 1 x MG
1941-3	Cruiser	Mark VI (A15)	19	5	1 x 2pdr, 2 x MG

(The Crusader III was 0.75-ton heavier, mounted a 6pdr gun and had two less crewmen)

1941-5	Light (US)	Stuart I ("Honey")	12.5	4	1 x 37mm, 2 x MG
1942-4	Medium (US)	M3 (Grant I)	28.5	6	1 x 75mm, 1 x 37mm, 1 x MG
1942-5	Medium (US)	M4 (Sherman)	30	5	1 x 75mm, 2 x MG
1944-5	Medium (US/UK)	Sherman VC (Firefly)	32	4	1 x 17pdr, 1 x MG

(This was the British upgunned Sherman and was issued on a scale of one per tank troop)

1944/45	Cruiser	A27M (Cromwell)	19	5	1 x 6pdr, 2 x MG
1945	Cruiser	A34 (Comet)	35.2	5	1 x 77mm, 2 x MG

Examples of Other Types of AFVs Used

Type	Name/Nomenclature	Weight (tons)	Crew	Armament
Scout Car	Daimler Dingo	2.8-3.15	2	1 x LMG
Scout Car	Humber	3.39	3	1 x LMG
Armoured car	Rolls (1924 pattern)	3.8	4	1 x MG
Armoured car	Morris CS9/LAC	4.2	4	1 x MG, 1 x Boys
Armoured car	Humber	6.85	3	1 x hy MG, 1 x MG (MkIV had 1 x 37mm gun)
Armoured car	Daimler	6.8	3	1 x 2pdr, 1 x MG
Carrier	Bren No 2	3.75	3	1 x LMG or 1 x atk rifle
Carrier	Scout	3.3	3-4	1 x LMG or 1 x atk rifle

ELITE ATTACK FORCES: 7TH ARMOURED DIVISION

INSIGNIA, CLOTHING & EQUIPMENT

Opposite: Tank crew overalls were introduced in 1942. Made of unlined heavy cotton they had a water repellant finish and adjustable wrist and ankle buttoned tabs. A zipped vent on both sides above the hip gave access to clothing underneath, above each is an open top pocket closed with a press stud. On the right hip is an additional dressing pocket. On the left thigh is a map pocket and on the upper right thigh a shaped flap for a revolver.

Left: This group of four infantrymen all wear KD shirt and shorts, together with boots, webbing gaiters and long stockings, plus webbing belts, ammunition pouches, service respirators and steel helmets. All are armed with the Rifle No 1 MkIII, SMLE (Short Magazine Lee Enfield) rifle as used in World War I. One of the finest rifles ever produced, it could be fitted with a long, 18in, bayonet.

Below left: Two members of a Sherman tank crew lift down the tank's coaxially mounted .30-cal M1919 Browning machine gun for cleaning. The M1919 had an air-cooled barrel, a rate of fire of 400-500rpm and was fed by a 250-round belt.

Below: Tank crewman holding a brew and a 9in cruciform bayonet as fitted to the SMLE's successor, the Rifle No 4 MkI. He is armed with the usual tank crewman's .38in six-shot Pistol, Revolver, No 2 MkI which was taken into service in 1932.

"B" Vehicles

Whilst the division used the standard range of British wheeled vehicles as can be found in any similar British formation serving in the same theatre, the early command vehicles (CVs) as used in the Western Desert deserve special mention. The bodies of the orginal CVs were made of 5-ply wood with a zinc covering. When they were sent back to Cairo to be armoured, the wood was removed, angle iron clamped on to the chassis and South African boiler plate then bolted on using thousands of 3/16in bolts. Consequently, there were myriad bolt ends sticking through the armour — a most uncomfortable arrangement for those inside!

ARTILLERY

During the wartime years the division used the full gamut of British Army artillery as far as field, anti-tank and light anti-aircraft weapons were concerned. The table below lists the main types in each category.

Anti-tank

Description	Max Effective Range	Rate of Fire	Comments
Ordnance QF 2pdr	600yd	20-22rpm	heavy gun, so had to be towed or carried "portee"
Ordnance QF 6pdr	5,500yd	10rpm	by 1943 it could not penetrate the frontal armour of heavy enemy tanks
Ordnance QF 17pdr	10,000yd	10rpm	very effective, could penetrate 130mm of armour at 1,000yd

Anti-aircraft

Description	Effective Ceiling	Rate of Fire	Comments
Bofors 40mm	5,000ft	120rpm	Highly effective, widely used. (Swedish-designed). By 1945, the British had three main Marks, six specialised and two lightweight mountings and five different firing platforms.

Field

Description	Max Range	Shell Weight	Comments
Ordnance QF 18pdr	11,100yd	18.5lb	In widespread service prewar
Ordnance QF 25pdr MkI and MkII	12,000yd (MkII — 13,400yd)	25lb	Rugged and dependable. By 1944, most were MkII

(Both the 18 and 25pdrs were towed by a Field Artillery Tractor 4 x 4 — at first the Guy "Quad" Ant, then the Morris C8 "Quad".)

Medium

Description	Max Range	Shell weight	Comments
QF 4.5in Howitzer	6,600yd	34.5lb	In service prewar, a few saw action in desert
BL 5.5in MkIII Gun	16,200yd	100lb	One of the best British field guns

INSIGNIA, CLOTHING & EQUIPMENT

Above left: 'That bint from the Sweet Melody promised she'd write!' Jon's jaunty 'Two Types' were famous for their eccentricities of dress — the suede boots, silk scarves, corduroy trousers, sheepskin coats and all the rest; however, such garments did have a serious, practical side as well. For example, the scarves gave the wearer protection against the choking clouds of dust that swiftly caked everything during a sandstorm, including eyes, nostrils and throat, whilst the sheepskin coats kept out the bitter cold of the desert nights far better than the average army issue greatcoat. And all these goods were temptingly on display in the shop windows in Cairo — with no need for clothing coupons either! Even when they left the desert sands for the rainstorms of Italy, the Desert Rats still kept wearing their trademark garments, as did Monty, who always had an eye for wearing comfortable, practical, slightly eccentric clothes, that were not always exactly the King's uniform.

Above: This RAOC fitter is hard at work, wearing BD and a battered, almost shapeless, SD cap. All Ordnance Corps fitters automatically became craftsmen in the Corps of Electrical & Mechanical Engineers when the new corps was formed in May 1942.

Left: This 6 RTR crew was photographed at Burg el Arab in October 1942. Note the mixture of KD and one-piece denims being worn. The crew stands in front of its American Grant M3 Medium tank, which had its 75mm main gun in a side sponson and only a 37mm in the turret.

169

ELITE ATTACK FORCES: 7TH ARMOURED DIVISION

INSIGNIA, CLOTHING & EQUIPMENT

Left and Below: Tank crewman of the 1st King's Dragoon Guards wearing his camouflaged oversuit. Designed towards the end of the war for operating in temperate climates, it has two full length zips running down the front for quick dressing and easy access to wounds. The left chest pocket has pencil loops.

Opposite, Above left: The denim tank suit had integral braces which allowed the top half of the suit to be opened up and dropped to the waist while still being supported. The suit also had a rear hip pocket unique to the denim overalls.

Opposite, Above right: The "Pixie Suit" (properly Tank Crew Oversuit, 1943). Made of heavyweight cotton and fully lined with wool fabric, it had two throat-to-ankle zips and adjustable wrist and ankle tabs. It had two internal supporting braces and seven external patch pockets, two side pockets and three internal pockets.

Opposite, Below left: The RAC steel helmet gave better protection from shrapnel and bullets than previous headgear. The epaulettes are of strengthened cloth to supply a useful handhold when necessary.

Opposite, Below right: An RTR radio operator on top of a Sherman. In his pocket is a hand-held microphone and around his neck the headphones for his W519 wireless set. He is looking at a Fallschirmjäger helmet.

PEOPLE

Above: First and last. Field Marshal Viscount Montgomery talks to Gen Percy Hobart and Gen "Pip" Roberts, who were the actual first and last commanders of the 7th Armoured Division, although neither commanded the division during the war. When the photo was taken (in Berlin at the Victory Parade) Hobart was GOC 79th Armd Div and Roberts was GOC 11th Armd Div. *IWM — BU10669*

PERCY "HOBO" HOBART (1885–1976)

Major-General Sir Percy Cleghorn Stanley Hobart KBE, CB, DSO, MC — "Hobo" as he was known to all — was responsible for the initial training of the Mobile Division and thus the architect of much of its greatness. After being unfairly "retired" because he had fallen out with those in higher authority who knew nothing about tanks and armoured warfare, he was rescued from obscurity (a LCpl in the Home Guard!) by Winston Churchill and would later go on to form and train both 11th Armd Div and 79th Armd Div. As historian Sir Basil Liddell Hart said of him: "To have moulded the best two British armoured divisions of the war was an outstanding achievement, but Hobart made it a "hat trick" by his subsequent training of the specialised 79th Armoured Division, the decisive factor on D-Day."

"DICKIE" CREAGH (1892–1970)

Major-General Sir Michael O'Moore Creagh, KBE, MC led the division through its earliest triumphs against the Italians, including its first major battle at Sidi Barrani in 1940. His tenure of command was the longest during the war. It was he who took the bold decision to send a "Flying Column" (Combe Force) southwest across the virtually unmapped Libyan Desert to cut off the Italians at Sidi Saleh/Beda Fomm. This daring stroke led to the surrender of the *entire* Italian Tenth Army on 5-7 February 1941.

"STRAFER" GOTT (1897–1942)

Lieutenant-General W. H. E. "Strafer" Gott CB, DSO, MC began his career in the division as its first wartime GSO 1; later he commanded the Support Group. After commanding 7th Armd Div he went on to become commander XIII Corps and in August 1942 was appointed to command the Eighth Army. Tragically, whilst flying back to Cairo from the battle area a few days later, his aircraft was shot down by a German fighter. He survived the crash, but was killed by machine gun fire whilst rescuing others from the wreckage.

"JOCK" CAMPBELL (1894–1942)

Major-General J. C. Campbell VC, DSO, MC was perhaps the most famous of all "Desert Rats", his name being a byword for courage through the division. He was awarded the

Victoria Cross at Sidi Rezegh in November 1941, whilst commanding the Support Group. It was he who conceived the idea of forming mobile columns to harass the Italians — called "Jock Columns" after him. He was killed when his staff car overturned on a clay road near Halfaya Pass.

FRANK MESSERVY (1893–1974)

Lieutenant-General Sir Frank Walter Messervy CB, DSO took over the division after commanding 4th Indian Division. Known as the "Bearded Man" because he tended not to shave in battle. Knew little about tanks and was commanding when Div HQ was captured by the Germans, but managed to bluff them into believing he was a batman, escaped with other members of his staff and rejoined Div HQ the following day! He went on to command IV Corps in Burma.

"WINGY" RENTON (1898–1972)

Major-General James Malcolm Leslie Renton CB, DSO, OBE was known as "Wingy" Renton because he had lost an arm whilst commanding 2RB during the battle at Sidi Saleh in 1941, later commanded the Support Group, 7th Motor Bde, during the Gazala battles.

LORD HARDING (1896–1989)

Field Marshal, The Lord Harding of Petherton GCB, CBE, DSO, MC took over command after serving as Chief of Staff to Gen Sir Richard O'Connor and his successors in the early days in the desert. Fearless and brilliant, he was responsible for the division's breakout at El Alamein in October 1942. Badly wounded near Tarhuna on 20 January 1943, he recovered and continued a distinguished career, becoming C-in-C Far East (1949-51), C-in-C BAOR (1951-2), CIGS

Top: "Strafer" Gott being driven by "Jock" Campbell. Both men would command the division and be killed in accidents in the desert. *IWM — E7401*

Above: Frank Messervy—the "Bearded Man", as he was known—was captured and escaped during one fluid operation in the desert by pretending to be a private soldier. *IWM — E7506*

Right: The longest-serving member of HQ 7th Armd Div was Capt "Richie" Richardson BEM, who served continuously with Div HQ from August 1939 to January 1957, under no fewer than 16 GOCs! He is being congratulated by Gen Sir John Hackett. Note the board of GOCs behind them.

(1952-3), then Governor and C-in-C Cyprus (1955-7). Montgomery called him "that little tiger".

"BOBBIE" ERSKINE (1899–1965)

General Sir George W. E. J. Erskine GCB, KBE, DSO commanded during the memorable advance from Tripoli to Tunis and throughout the short campaign in Italy. He also launched the division into Northwest Europe. A man of great integrity and considerable physical and moral courage, he was commanding during the debacle at Villers Bocage in June 1944 and was "sacked" by Montgomery along with the corps commander, Gen Bucknall. Nevertheless, he went on to become C-in-C East Africa during the Mau Mau rebellion and, on retirement, Lt Governor and C-in-C Jersey.

GERALD VERNEY (1900–1957)

Major-General Gerald Lloyd Verney, DSO, MVO was personally appointed by "Monty" to take command of the Desert Rats in Normandy on 4 August 1944, after the division's disappointing showing in the bocage. Verney commented, in the history of the division (which he wrote postwar), that before the battles of Caumont he had been warned to look out for the transport of the 7th Armoured on the road, because its march discipline was "non-existent!" He also said that they "greatly deserved the criticism they received". A no-nonsense Guardsman, Verney soon had them "firing on all cylinders" again. He left in November 1944 to command 6th Armoured Division.

"LEW" LYNE (1999–1970)

Major-General Lewis Owen Lyne CB, DSO took over command of the division on 22 November 1944, when Gen Verney went to Italy to command 6th Armoured Division. Gen Lyne had commanded 50th Northumbrian Division in Normandy, when Gen Graham was injured, until it became a training division in the UK. He would then command the "Desert Rats" on the final lap through the Siegfried Line, into Germany and on to the surrender of Hamburg and the end of the war. Postwar he was the first Military Governor of the British Zone of Berlin, then Director Staff Duties at the War Office, before retiring in 1949.

"PIP" ROBERTS (1906–1997)

Major-General George Philip Bradley Roberts CB, DSO, MC was a charismatic wartime commander of 11th Armoured Division, and rated the best British armoured divisional commander of the war, Gen "Pip" Roberts was the first (and only) peacetime commander of 7th Armoured Division. He was no stranger to the division, having been the DAQMG when the Italians invaded Egypt in 1940, GSO2 during the Brevity and Battleaxe operations, CO of 3 RTR, commander 22nd Armoured Brigade and had

Top: Field Marshal The Lord Harding of Petherton, GCB, CBE, DSO, MC, late SLI. The "Little Tiger" as "Monty" called him, was a brilliant and fearless commander. *IWM — E9612*

Above: Gen Sir George Erskine GCB, KBE, DSO, late KRRC. Bobbie Erskine commanded at the end in North Africa, all through Italy, back to the UK and on into France on D+1, making him the second longest-serving GOC. *IWM — NA7450*

commanded the division for four days (20–24 January 1943) when Gen Harding was wounded. He would command the "Desert Rats" through the early postwar days to their first disbandment in March 1948. He then became Director of the Royal Armoured Corps and retired from the Army in September 1949. His book *From the Desert to the Baltic* is a very readable account of all his wartime battles.

"MONTY" (1887–1976)

In addition to those already mentioned above, there were a number of senior officers — corps and army commanders mainly — whose actions had a direct bearing on the fortunes of the division. I have tried to mention these VIPs in the main body of the text. However, there is one who must be mentioned here as his influence on the "Desert Rat" was greater than that of anyone else. This was of course "Monty" — Field Marshal Bernard Law Montgomery, 1st Viscount of Alamein — who was probably Britain's most well known and charismatic senior commander of World War II. He was also one of the longest-serving and most successful Allied field commanders, coming into prominence when he took over the Eighth Army in North Africa and subsequently winning the battles of Alam Halfa and El Alamein. His further success in North Africa, Sicily and Italy made him the obvious choice to command 21st Army Group in Northwest Europe and he deliberately selected 7th Armoured Division to add battle experience to the largely untested Allied forces that would follow-up the initial landings in Normandy, bringing it back from Italy for that specific purpose. Therefore, he was understandably annoyed by its initial disappointing showing in the difficult bocage country in Normandy. He took drastic action to solve this problem by changing the corps, divisional and brigade commanders, whom he considered were responsible. He continued to command 21st Army Group throughout the battle in Europe. Postwar he was CIGS and deputy supreme commander of NATO Forces.

Above left: Maj-Gen G. L. Verney DSO, MVO, late Brigade of Guards, who took over the "Desert Rats" from Erskine soon after the Villers Bocage debacle, seen here with "Monty", his "Desert Rat" very visible. *IWM — B 10387*

Above: Maj-Gen L. O. Lyne CB, DSO, last wartime commander of the division, took the division into Germany and all the way to Berlin. Here he tries out a bridge built by divisional Sappers at Nienburg over the River Weser on 13 April 1945. *IWM — BU 3440*

GENERAL OFFICERS COMMANDING 7th ARMD DIVISION

From	Status	Name
03.09.1939	GOC	Maj-Gen P. C. S. Hobart
16.11.1939	acting GOC	Brig J. A. L. Caunter
04.12.1939	GOC	Maj-Gen. M. O'M. Creagh
01.04.1941	acting GOC	Brig J. A. L. Caunter
13.04.1941	GOC	Maj-Gen. Sir M. O'M. Creagh
03.09.1941	GOC	Maj-Gen W. H. E. Gott
06.02.1942	GOC	Maj-Gen J. C. Campbell
23.02.1942	acting GOC	Brig A. H. Gatehouse
09.03.1942	GOC	Maj-Gen F. W. Messervy
19.06.1942	GOC	Maj-Gen. J. M. L. Renton
14.09.1942	GOC	Maj-Gen A. F. Harding
20.01.1943	acting GOC	Brig G. P. B. Roberts
24.01.1943	GOC	Maj-Gen G. W. E. J. Erskine
04.08.1944	GOC	Maj-Gen G. L. Verney
22.11.1944	GOC	Maj-Gen L. O. Lyne

VICTORIA CROSS WINNERS

During World War II members of the 7th Armoured Division won three Victoria Crosses. All three were awarded for conspicuous bravery during the battle of Sidi Rezegh on 21 November 1941. Here are details of their citations:

Above: Brigadier (Acting) John Charles Campbell DSO MC, Royal Horse Artillery.

Above right: 2nd Lieutenant George Ward Gunn MC, Royal Horse Artillery.

Right: Rifleman John Beeley, 1st Battalion The King's Royal Rifle Corps.

"JOCK" CAMPBELL (1894–1942)

Brigadier (Acting) John Charles Campbell DSO, MC of the Royal Horse Artillery's citation reads:
"On November 21st 1941, Brigadier Campbell was commanding the troops, including one regiment of tanks, in the area of Sidi Rezegh ridge and the aerodrome. His small force holding this important ground was repeatedly attacked by large numbers of tanks and infantry. Wherever the situation was most difficult and the fighting hardest he was to be seen with his forward troops, either on his feet or in his open car. In this car he carried out general reconnaissance for counter-attacks by his tanks, whose senior officers had all become casualties early in the day. Standing in his car with a blue flag, this officer personally formed up tanks under close and intense fire from all natures of enemy weapons.

"On the following day the enemy attacks were intensified and again Brigadier Campbell was always in the forefront of the heaviest fighting, encouraging his troops, staging counter-attacks with his remaining tanks and personally controlling the fire of his guns. On two occasions he himself manned a gun to replace casualties. During the final enemy attack on November 22nd he was wounded, but continued most actively in the foremost positions, controlling the fire of the batteries, which inflicted heavy losses on enemy tanks at point-blank range, and finally acted as loader to one of the guns himself.

"Throughout these two days his magnificent example and his utter disregard of personal danger were an inspiration to his men and to all who saw him. His brilliant leadership was the direct cause of very heavy casualties inflicted on the enemy. In spite of his wound he refused to be evacuated and remained with his command, where his outstanding bravery and consistent determination had a marked effect in maintaining the splendid fighting spirit of those under him."

GEORGE GUNN (1912–1941)

2nd Lieutenant George Ward Gunn MC — Royal Horse Artillery.
"On November 21st 1941, at Sidi Rezegh, 2nd Lt Gunn was in command of a troop of four anti-tank guns which was part of a battery of 12 guns attached to the Rifle Brigade Column. At ten o'clock a covering force of enemy tanks was engaged and driven off, but

an hour later the main attack by about 60 enemy tanks developed. 2nd Lt Gunn drove from gun to gun during this period in an unarmoured vehicle encouraging his men and reorganising his dispositions as first one gun and then another were knocked out. Finally, only two guns remained in action and were subjected to very heavy fire. Immediately afterwards one of these guns was destroyed and the portee of the other was set on fire and all the crew killed or wounded except the sergeant, though the gun remained undamaged. The battery commander then arrived and began to fight the flames. When he saw this, 2nd Lt Gunn ran to his aid through intense fire and immediately got the one remaining anti-tank gun into action on the burning portee, himself sighting it whilst the sergeant acted as loader. He continued to fight the gun, firing between 40 and 50 rounds regardless alike of the enemy fire which was by then concentrated on this one vehicle and on the flames which might at any moment have reached the ammunition with which the portee was loaded. In spite of this, 2nd Lt Gunn's shooting was so accurate at a range of about 800 yards that at least two enemy tanks were hit and set on fire and others were damaged before he fell dead, having been shot through the forehead."

JOHN BEELEY (1918–1941)

Citation of Rifleman John Beeley, 1st Battalion The King's Royal Rifle Corps

"On the 21st November 1941, during the attack at Sidi Rezegh, against a strong enemy position, the company to which Rifleman Beeley belonged was pinned down by heavy fire at point-blank range from the front and flank on the flat, open ground of the aerodrome. All the officers but one of the company and many other ranks had either been killed or wounded. On his own initiative, and when there was no sort of cover, Rifleman Beeley got to his feet carrying a Bren gun and ran forward towards a strong enemy post. He ran thirty yards and discharged a complete magazine at the post from a range of twenty yards, killing or wounding the entire crew of the anti-tank gun. The post was silenced and Rifleman Beeley's platoon was able to advance, but Rifleman Beeley fell dead across his gun, hit in at least four places.

"Rifleman Beeley went to certain death in a gallant and successful attempt to carry the day. His courage and self-sacrifice were a glorious example to his comrades and inspired them to further efforts to reach their objective, which they eventually captured, together with 700 prisoners."

POSTWAR

1945-8

During the initial postwar years 7th Armoured Division remained an integral part of the British Army of the Rhine (BAOR), with its units spread around North Rhine Westphalia and its divisional headquarters in the village of Bad Rothenfelde. Maj-Gen "Pip" Roberts CB, DSO, MC had been commanding since January 1946 and had guided the division through the initial, difficult period of "Army of Occupation" duties. Although Gen "Pip" had commanded 11th Armoured Division in the latter stages of the war, he was no stranger to 7th Armoured, having been a "Desert Rat" for most of the North African campaign, his last appointment with the division being as commander of 22nd Armoured Brigade at the time of the capture of Tripoli. The *Army Quarterly* of the day described him as being: "the living embodiment of all that has been best in the Division", therefore it was sad that he should have been commanding when, for the first time, the division was disbanded in March 1948.

In his farewell message to his "Desert Rats" Gen Roberts had expressed the hope that the division would be reformed and, fortunately, his words proved to be prophetic. About the time of the end of the Berlin airlift and the beginning of the Cold War (mid-1949), the division was reformed and went on to serve with distinction in BAOR until 16 April 1958, when it was yet again disbanded. However, on this occasion it was a change of title only, being redesignated first as the "5th Division" and then under a year later as the "1st Division" — the inner workings of the MOD never fail to amaze! A leader in *The Times* newspaper, published on the day following its disbandment, extolled the virtues of the remarkable "Desert Rats", stating that they had: "… won more renown than any other division has ever gained in the history of the British Army", then going on to explain why this was the case as they had been "first in and last out", being on active operations in the Western Desert at the start of the war. Winston Churchill certainly had a soft spot for his "Dear Desert Rats" as he called them, however, this did not save them and, as *The Times* ended its leader: "Public Relations are important, in war as in anything else. The nickname of the 'Desert Rats' caught on. It is a lesson which the unimaginative generals who had decreed the end of this famous fighting force should take to heart."

COLD-WAR DAYS

But of course that was not the end, because you cannot keep a good "Rat" down for long! The "Desert Rats" went on living in the shape of 7th Armoured Brigade (now wearing the Red Rat), still in BAOR, with its headquarters at Soltau. All "Rat" property, silver, pictures and relics were kept there and annually the Brigade celebrated the Battle of Sidi Rezegh

Above: Postwar, Soltau in North Germany, near a large British-run training area on the Lüneberge Heide, south of Hamburg, became the "Desert Rats" HQ location for many years once 7th Armd Bde assumed the 7th Armd Div Rat as its shoulder flash in place of the Green Rat. Now, with the slimming down of British forces in Germany, the Bde HQ has been moved to Hohne, where much of the British armour is concentrated.

Above right: A "Desert Rat" tank commander in his turret during Operation Desert Sabre, in which 7th Armd Bde was in the British 1st Armoured Division as part of the United Nations forces which went to the rescue of Kuwait. The main ground assault began at 0400hrs on 24 February 1991, the British and American armour swiftly making short work of Saddam Hussein's much vaunted Republican Guard.

on 22 November. Also, a 7th Armoured Division Officers Dinner Club was formed and met regularly each year in London. It seemed as though the "Rat" was indestructible although the "Powers that Be" certainly tried their best! In 1975 the Defence White Paper announced that brigades would be no more, but fortunately this was never put into practice thanks to the Cold War.

For the next quarter of a century war was prevented by the certain knowledge of the terrible consequences that would follow any attack by either side, in the shape of the subsequent nuclear exchange. The "Shield and Sword" of NATO contained tanks as an essential component of both, as did its Warsaw Pact potential enemies. With the demise of the Iron Curtain it had been hoped that disarmament talks would produce a great turning of "swords into ploughshares" once both sides had agreed to drastic arms limitations. However, whilst the head-to-head West versus East Europe problems have lessened, the modern world has proven to be just as dangerous a place, especially in the two major problem areas of the Middle East and the Balkans. Both have involved the United Nations in either peace-keeping operations or all-out war. The invasion of Kuwait in early August 1990, led first to Desert Shield, followed by Desert Storm, with a massive build-up of Coalition forces in the Gulf in order to take on Saddam Hussein's militant Iraq, in what he promised would be the "Mother of All Battles". A major part of the British contingent was 1 (British) Armoured Division, which comprised both 4th Armoured (The Black Rat) and 7th Armoured (The Red Rat) as its main components. Thus it was that the little jerboas were back in their desert setting. Both brigade groups had whirlwind success in the battle, which turned out to be something of a "damp squib", the Iraqi forces — estimated at the time to be the fourth largest army in the world — caving in, once the ground attack began in earnest. It was estimated that some 4,000 enemy tanks were destroyed in the 100-hour battle that brought the 43-day campaign to a close, the sheer professionalism of the two British brigades showing that they had still all the skills that had made their forefathers so successful.

OPERATION TELIC

The second Gulf War lasted from 19 March to 20 April 2003, the end result being the collapse of the Saddam Hussein regime. This time the Coalition forces went "all the way", effectively destroying Saddam's power base. Leading the assault on the second most important city in Iraq — Basra — was the 7th Armoured Brigade, its Challenger 2 tanks once again emblazoned with the little red desert rat that has come to symbolise all that is best in armoured warfare

Above: The "Desert Rat" in Bosnia. As the millennium closed, units of 7th Armd Bde went off to Bosnia on Operation Agricola. Here the crew of a 2 RTR Scimitar keeps a sharp lookout for interlopers from an OP on high ground some 800m from the Macedonian-Kosovo border. *Tank*

The Scarlet Rat is there again! This time the brigade sign is emblazoned on the front of the commanding officer of 2 RTR's Challenger 2, as it is photographed near Podujevo in Bosnia, February 2001. *Tank*

ASSESSMENT

WORLD WAR II

Apart from the one hiccup at Villers Bocage and its aftermath, the 7th Armoured Division had a wartime record second to none. Other divisions may well have felt that this was unfair, that they had won equally glorious victories and fought under even worse conditions, but the 7th Armoured was undoubtedly the only armoured division to acquire a reputation in the Army equivalent to that of "The Few" in the RAF. Indeed, the entire Eighth Army was happy to bask in its reflected glory and to call themselves "Desert Rats", despite the fact that only the units that were bona fide members of the division actually wore the little red jerboa. "The Desert Rats preserved a shining spirit," wrote the leader writer in *The Times* newspaper, on the day after the division was initially disbanded in March 1948. He continued: "rightly or wrongly, the concept of chivalry was retained among them in the circumstances of modern war. They were a light-hearted and happy division. Sir Winston Churchill in his memoirs recounts how, listening in London to a relay of one of the early desert battles, he heard with delight a squadron leader report: 'I am now at the second "B" in Buq Buq.' They exemplified the attitude of the British to war at its most dangerous, which found a response among the British people." They were clearly also helped by the inspired choice of emblem, the symbolism was there from the very start and remains as fresh today as it was in the early desert days. 7th Armoured Division was further immortalised by Jon's unforgettable cartoons — there was clearly only one division that the "Two Types" could have served in, and thus its reputation was enhanced by humour. And rightly so.

Below: Travels of the "Desert Rat" during WW2 are shown on this map

In North Africa, after helping to dispose of the inept Italians, the "Desert Rats" had found themselves up against other highly professional soldiers in the shape of the *Deutsches Afrika Korps*. In some ways they were very similar — was there, for

PETROL CONSUMPTION
During periods of heavy fighting the RASC carried 300 tons of ammunition and 150 tons of petrol each day. During periods of fast movement, ammunition was reduced to 150 tons and petrol raised to 360 tons per day. Even when the division was completely static it used 30,000 gallons of petrol per day. The Petrol Company lifted 69,245 tons of petrol between D-Day and 5 May 1945, which was an average of 466 lifts per lorry. B Platoon of the Petrol Company, which was equipped with four and a half ton Mack lorries, covered 462,000 miles, which was an average of 14,000 miles per vehicle.

AMMUNITION EXPENDITURE
General Verney, in *The Desert Rats*, identified these figures for ammunition expenditure 6 June 1944–5 May 1945.

RHA 25pdr HE
June–September: 295,700 rounds (average 51 per gun per day)
October–December: 104,400 (average 28 per gun per day)
January–May: 149,168 (average 26 per gun per day)
Total: 549,268

Tanks 17pdr HE
June–September: 13,000 rounds (average 3,250 per month)
October–December: 19,807 (average 6,602 per month)
January–May: 18,918 (average 4,729 per month)
Total: 51,725

4.2in Mortar HE
June–September: 5,248 rounds (average 1,312 per month)
October–December: 5,024 (average 1,674 per month)
January–May: 10,056 (average 2,514 per month)
Total: 20,328

.303in Rifle
June–September: 306,300 rounds (average 76,575 per month)
October–December: 376,000 (average 125,333 per month)
January–May: 464,300 (average 116,075 per month)
Total: 1,146,600

example, another senior German general who, like Rommel, wore a check scarf with his uniform, not unlike the gaudy, but very sensible, neckerchiefs, worn by many officers of the "Desert Rats"? The mutual respect which each side had for the other was undoubtedly matched by the chivalry that was so often displayed. The British respected Rommel, the "Desert Fox", and his men, and this was reflected by the DAK.

Villers Bocage
I have deliberately not laboured the disastrous action at Villers Bocage, principally because a full explanation deserves far more space than I can give in this short book. However, it is only fair to state the background facts as they apply. First and foremost, one must remember the situation that pertained in the UK when 7th Armoured Division arrived home from Italy in late 1943. Many of the soldiers had not been home since before the war and had just fought an extremely hard campaign in North Africa and again in Italy, while the rest of the "D-Day Army" had been training in the relative safety of the United Kingdom. Some of them undoubtedly felt that it was time for others to take the risks and said so, which did not go down well, raising a tricky morale problem for Gen Erskine. Add to this the fact that a fair number of the division's most experienced officers and men were taken away to provide battle-experience within other units and formations. Additionally, and probably most worrying of all, the division had been forced to exchange its tried and trusted Sherman Medium tanks for much smaller, less-well armoured cruisers, ie the Cromwell, of which most soldiers were deeply suspicious — it was less mechanically reliable and did not even mount a decent larger-calibre gun, so they would still be outgunned by the enemy. The Sherman Firefly, with its highly effective 17-pounder, was issued only on the scale of one per troop, so it was 3 to 1 against it being in the right place at the right time unless it always led. Thus, whilst Michael Wittmann's almost complete destruction of 7th Armoured Division's entire advance guard at Villers Bocage, was a superlative piece of individual tank commanding, the Cromwells were "sitting ducks" as compared with the massive 56-ton Tiger and its highly lethal 88mm gun that could easily penetrate the front armour of a Cromwell at long range, yet was impervious to its return fire, even at very short range.

Fighting in the bocage. 7th Armoured also found itself in a very different environment to the desert, or for that matter to Italy, and took time to adapt, as Gen Sir Brian Horrocks commented in his autobiography: "Another disturbing feature was the comparative lack of success of the veteran 7th Armoured and 51st Highland Divisions. Both came again later on and finished the war in magnificent shape, but during the Normandy fighting they were not at their best. ... after being lionised in the UK, (they) came out to Normandy and found themselves faced with an entirely different type of battle, fought under different conditions of terrain. And they began to see the difficulties all too clearly. A racing enthusiast once described this condition to me as 'like an old plater who won't go in the mud'. All the more credit to them that they eventually staged a come-back and regained their Middle East form." However, the division's problems did not entirely end with Villers Bocage and dragged on for some weeks. The outcome was that "Monty" had to remove the XXX Corps commander (Bucknall) and two divisional commanders — Erskine of 7th Armoured and Bullen-Smith of 51 Infantry, as he put it in a letter to a friend: "I have had to get rid of a few people you know. Bucknall could not manage a Corps once the battle became mobile and I have Jorrocks (General Horrocks) in his place in XXX Corps. Bullen-Smith could do nothing with 51 Div so had to go; Thomas Rennie is there now and the Division is quite different under him. 7 Armd Div went right down and failed badly; so I removed Bobbie (Erskine) who had become very sticky and put in Verney of the Gds Tank brigade. I also had to remove Loony Hinde; I have put Mackeson to 23 Armd Bde." In an earlier letter he had written to US Gen Simpson: "The old desert divisions are apt to look over their shoulders and wonder if all is OK behind or if the flanks are secure and so on. 7 Armoured Div is like that. They want a new General who will drive them headlong into and through gaps torn in enemy defence — not worrying about flanks or anything ... We want Generals now who will put their heads down and go like hell."

That then is the only minor blemish on the "Desert Rats'" escutcheon and, once "sorted" by Montgomery's drastic action, they recovered superbly.

POSTWAR

Postwar, the little "red rat" has done it again, especially in the second Gulf War, the latest "war by television", during which all ranks of the 7th Armoured Brigade have exuded sheer professionalism and quiet confidence. Whenever they have been asked to talk "On the Box", their ancestors would be proud of them! Challenger 2 is, of course, a far more sophisticated animal than a Sherman or Comet of World War II, however, it has warmed the heart of this old "tankie" to see that they still at times look more like "tinkers carts" than sleek, lethal weapons of war because of all the added "goodies" that the crews have acquired to make desert life just that little bit more comfortable as they go "Up the Blue". Undoubtedly, the general public has once again taken the "Desert Rats" to its heart, giving their exploits much well-deserved coverage.

Below: "Dear Desert Rats!" Prime Minister Winston Churchill addresses some of the division at the opening of its club in Berlin. *IWM — BU9111*

CONCLUSION

Perhaps the best way in which to close this book is with the words of Winston Churchill when he spoke to men of the division in Berlin after the Victory Parade on 21 July 1945, at the opening of the "Winston Club": "It is not without emotion that I can express to you what I feel about the 'Desert Rats'. Dear 'Desert Rats'! May your glory ever shine! May your laurels never fade! May the memory of this glorious pilgrimage of war which you have made from Alamein, via the Baltic to Berlin, never die! It is a march unsurpassed through all the story of war so far as my reading of history leads me to believe. May the fathers long tell the children about this tale. May you all feel that in following your great ancestors you have accomplished something which has done good to the whole world; which has raised the honour of your own country and which every man has a right to be proud of."

REFERENCE

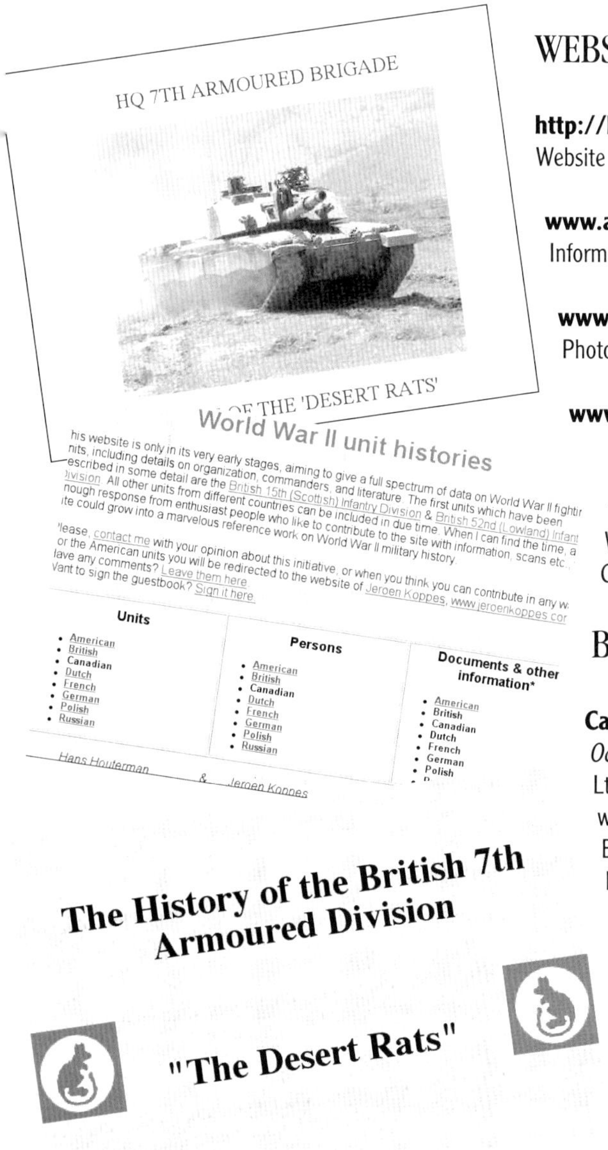

WEBSITES

http://houterman.htmlplanet.com/7Armd Div.html
Website giving unit histories, in this case 7th Armoured.

www.army.mod.uk/7bde/
Information on the modern "Desert Rats" — 7th Armoured Brigade.

www.fmdinning.freeserve.co.uk
Photos and information on the Thetford Forest Memorial.

www.btinternet.com/~ian.a.paterson/main.htm
Website devoted to the history of the "Desert Rats".

www.regiments.org/milhist/uk/lists/badivxref.htm
Website that gives details of the "Land Forces of Britain, the Empire and Commonwealth" including divisional histories.

BIBLIOGRAPHY

Carver, Lt-Col R. M. P.: *A Short History of the Seventh Armoured Division, October 1938–May 1943*, Printing & Stationery Services MEF, 1943.
Lt-Col (Later Field Marshal, Lord) Mike Carver, late Royal Tank Regiment, served with HQ 7th Armd Div early in the war and later commanded 1 RTR in 22 Armd Bde, so his knowledge of the division was second to none. He was also a brilliant historian and has written many books. His memoirs, *Out of Step* (Hutchinson, 1989), are well worth reading, especially as much of the book is relevant to the "Desert Rats".

Cordingley, Maj-Gen Patrick: *In the Eye of the Storm — Commanding the Desert Rats in the Gulf War*, Hodder & Stoughton, 1996.
A good, honest, first-hand account of his brigade's part in the first Gulf War, when he was commanding 7th Armd Bde.

Delaforce, Patrick: *Churchill's Desert Rats, from Normandy to Berlin with the 7th Armoured Division*, Allan Sutton Publishing, 1994.
Churchill's Desert Rats 2: 7th Armoured Division in North Africa, Burma, Sicily and Italy,

REFERENCE

Alan Sutton Publishing, 2002.
Delaforce, a Horse Gunner, served in 11 Armd Div during the war, then joined 7th Armoured (3 RHA) postwar. He has since written many books, mostly in the same style, that is to say, full of fascinating reminiscences and glimpses of battle, all providing very useful background reading.

Ellis, Chris: *Spearhead 1 21st Panzer Division — Rommel's Afrika Korps Spearhead,* Ian Allan Publishing, 2001.
Good all-round coverage of the principal opponent to the Desert Rats, the German 21st Panzer Division which fought through the desert before being destroyed around Tunis in 1943. It would be reconstituted to fight in Normandy after D-Day and was annihilated at Falaise.

Forty, George: *Desert Rats at War — North Africa,* Ian Allan Publishing, 1975.
Desert Rats at War — Europe, Ian Allan Publishing, 1977.
Tank Commanders, Knights of the Modern Age, Firebird, 1993.
Tanks across the Desert — the war diary of Sgt Jake Wardrop, Sutton Publishing, 2003.
Again, these are mainly "I was there"-type reporting, with lots of relevant, private photographs and first-hand accounts. *Tank Commanders, Knights of the Modern Age,* however, covers the entire history of armoured warfare from the invention of the first tank to the first Gulf War in 1990-1.

Lindsay, Capt Martin and Johnston, Capt M. E.: *History of 7th Armoured Division, June 1943–July 1945.* Originally published and printed in BAOR in 1945. Reprinted in 2001 by DP&G on behalf of the Tank Museum, which is now the copyright holder for this book.
This is really the continuation of Mike Carver's book and is a straightforward, factual account of the history of the "Desert Rats" from Italy up to the end of the war. The photographs are only photocopies, but the originals are available via the IWM Dept of Photos.

Neillands, Robin: *The Desert Rats: 7th Armoured Division, 1940-45,* Weidenfeld & Nicolson, 1991.
A good, general account of the wartime history of the 7th Armoured Division by a well-known military author.

Pearce, Nigel: *The Shield and the Sabre: the Desert Rats in the Gulf 1990-91,* HMSO, 1992.
Background reading, specifically about the Gulf War.

Sandars, John and Chappell, Mike: *British 7th Armoured Division 1940-45,* Osprey Vanguard series No 1, 1977.
Osprey — Vanguard1, published in 1977. This early volume in a well-loved series of flexiback books, gives a brief, but valuable, potted history of the division and all its works, with the usual emphasis on badges and insignia.

Verney, Maj Gen G L: *The Desert Rats,* Hutchinson, 1954. Reprinted in hardback, with new Introduction by General Sir John Hackett, in 1996 by Greenhill Books. Reprinted in paperback by Greenhill Books in 2002.
Without doubt, the best and most comprehensive "straight" history of the division,

Above: The battered walls of Fort Capuzzo, one of the desert forts, situated to the west of Sollum and the south of Bardia. It was built by the Italians prewar and changed hands many times. Here scout carriers of 1 KRRC, 7th Armd Div Support Group, congregate outside one of its gateways.

Right: A9 cruisers of 1 RTR, moving through the outskirts of Cairo on their way "Up the Blue", 30 May 1940. Although the majority of the vehicle's tell-tale signs have been blotted out by the censor on this photograph, the Mobile Division's white circle on its scarlet background is still visible.

written by one of its GOCs. Verney was a "no-nonsense" Guardsman and his book provides a first-rate, detailed history of the "Desert Rats" in World War II.

Additional books which contain information or reminiscences about 7th Armd Div units are listed below. They can provide valuable detail if needed, but many are detailed Regimental Histories and contain a lot of irrelevant information. *Take These Men* by Cyril Joly, however, is without doubt one of the best books about tank crews in action in wartime and is highly recommended.

Bolitho, Hector: *The Galloping Third*, John Murray, 1963.

Clark, Dudley: *The Eleventh at War*, Michael Joseph, 1952.

Crawford, Robert: *I was an Eighth Army Soldier*, Victor Gollancz, 1944.

Davy, George: *The Seventh & Three Enemies*, Heffer, 1952.

Evans, Roger: *The Story of the Fifth Royal Inniskilling Dragoon Guards*, Gale & Polden, 1951.

Foster, R. C. G.: *History of the Queen's Royal Regiment Volume 8*, Gale & Polden, 1956.

Hart, B. Liddell: *The Tanks, Volume 2*, Cassell, 1959.

Hastings, R. H. W. S.: *The Rifle Brigade in the Second World War 1939-1945,* Gale & Polden, 1949.

Joly, Cyril: *Take these Men,* Constable, 1955.

Nicol, A. A.: *My Moving Tent: Diary of a Desert Rat,* Pentland, 1994.

Watt, Maj Robin: *A Soldier's Sketch-book: with the British Army in the Gulf,* National Army Museum, 1994.

Woolley, A. D.: *The History of the KDG,* Privately published, 1946.

MEMORIALS

The Memorial Stone
In addition to the still-operational 7th Armoured Brigade, there are some other tangible reminders of the "Desert Rats", one being a memorial stone detailing the countries through which the division fought on its triumphal path from El Alamein to Berlin (1939-45). It was erected at the end of the autobahn near Berlin when the division entered the city in the summer of 1945. However, it was moved to the grounds of the Royal Military Academy, Sandhurst, where it still stands.

The Thetford Forest Memorial
At the entrance to the Covert site near Swaffham, Norfolk, stands a tank memorial to the "Desert Rats". The site is close to their wartime camp in which they spent the period January-May 1944, preparing for the D-Day invasion of Normandy. The memorial comprises a Cromwell tank, from which footpaths connect to the campsites at High Ash Wood, Shakers Wood and Sugar Hill.

Glossary

German	English
Abteilung	Battalion/Detachment
Armee	Army
Artillerie	Artillery
Aufklärung	Recce
Ausbildung	Training
Bataillon	Battalion
Begleit	Escort
Einheiten	Units
Ersatz	Replacement
Feldersatz	Field replacement
Flak	AA gun
Geschütz	Gun
Grenadier	Rifleman
Heer	German Army
Infanterie	Infantry
Kampfgruppe	Battle group
Kavallerie	Cavalry
Kompanie	Company
Kraftfahrpark	Maintenance depot
Lehr	Training
Leichte	Light
Luftwaffe	German Air Force
Motorisiert	Motorised
Nachrichten	Signals
Nebelwerfer	Grenade launcher (multi-barrel)
Panzergrenadier	Armd infantry
Panzerjäger	Anti-tank infantry
Pionier	Engineer
Sanität	Medical
Schütze	Rifleman
Schwer	Heavy
Stab	Staff (HQ)
Stamm	Cadre
Stellung	Position/static
Sturmgeschütz	Assault Gun
Truppe	Troop
Versorgungstruppen	Service troops
Wache	Guard
Wehrmacht	German armed forces
Zug	Platoon

Abbreviations

Abbr	Meaning
2IC	Second-in-Command
AA	Anti-aircraft
ACV	Armoured Command Vehicle
ADC	Aide de camp
ADMS	Assistant Director Medical Services
Armd	Armoured
Arty	Artillery
Atk	Anti-tank
BD	Battledress
Bde	Brigade
BM	Brigade Major
Bn	Battalion
Brig	Brigade
Bty	Battery
'Cherry Pickers'	11th Hussars
Cheshires	Cheshire Regiment
CIGS	Chiefs of the Imperial General Staff
C-in-C	Commander-in-Chief
CLY	County of London Yeomanry
CO	Commanding Officer
Col	Column
Coy	Company
CRASC	Commander Royal Army Service Corps
CV	Command Vehicle
DAK	Deutsches Afrika Korps
DAQMG	Deputy Assistant Quartermaster General
Derbys Yeo	Derbyshire Yeomanry
Det	Detachment
Devons	Devonshire Regiment
DG	Dragoon Guards
DLI	Durham Light Infantry
DMT	Director Military Training
DR	Dispatch Rider
EME	Electrical and Mechanical Engineers
Engrs	Engineers
Fd Amb	Field Ambulance
Fd Coy	Field Company
Fd Hygiene Sect	Field Hygiene Section
Fd Pk Sqn	Field Park Squadron
Fd Regt	Field Regiment
FDS	Field Delivery Squadron
Fd Sqn	Field Squadron
Fd Transfusion Unit	Field Transfusion Unit
FSS	Field Security Section
FSU	Field Surgical Unit
Fwd Del Sqn	Forward Delivery Squadron
GOC	General Officer Commanding
GSO	General Staff Officer
H	Hussars
Hy	Heavy
Ind Div	Indian Division
Innis	Inniskilling
Int Sect	Intelligence Section
KDG	King's Dragoon Guards
KRRC	King's Royal Rifle Corps
LAA	Light Anti-aircraft
le FH	leichte Feldhaubitze (light field gun)
LMG	Light Machine Gun
LO	Liaison Officer
LST	Landing Ship Tank
Lt	Lieutenant; light
Lt Fd Amb	Light Field Ambulance
Lt Hygiene Sect	Light Hygiene Section
Maint	Maintenance
MC	Motorcycle
Med Regt	Medium Regiment
MELF	Middle East Land Forces
MG	Machine Gun
MMG	Medium Machine Gun
Mobile CCS	Mobile Casualty Clearing Section
Mob Dental Unit	Mobile Dental Unit
Mor	Mortar
Mot	Motor
Mot Inf	Motorised infantry
Mtrel	Materiel
M&V	"Meat and Veg" = Beef
Stew	
NAAFI	Navy, Army, Air Force Institutes = canteen/general stores
Nor Yeo	Norfolk Yeomanry
OFP	Ordnance Field Park
OKH	Oberkommando des Heeres
OKW	Oberkommando der Wehrmacht
OP	Observation Post
Ord	Ordnance
Pak	Panzerabwehrkanone (anti-tank gun)
PIAT	Projector Infantry Anti-tank
Pl	Platoon
Pro Coy	Provost Company
PU	Pick-up
PzBefWag	Panzerbefehls-wagen (armd comd vehicle)
PzGr	Panzergrenadier
PzJr	Panzerjäger
PzKpfw	Panzerkampfwagen
QM	Quartermaster
QMG	Quartermaster General
RA	Royal Artillery
RAC	Royal Armoured Corps
RAMC	Royal Army Medical Corps
RAOC	Royal Army Ordnance Corps
RASC	Royal Army Service Corps
RB	Rifle Brigade
RE	Royal Engineers
Recce	Reconnaissance
REME	Royal Electrical and Mechanical Engineers
RGH	Royal Gloucestershire Hussars
RHA	Royal Horse Artillery
RHQ	Regimental Headquarters
RIDG	Royal Inniskilling Dragoon Guards
RMA	Royal Military Academy
RNF	Royal Northumberland Fusiliers
R Scots Greys	Royal Scots Greys
RSM	Regimental Sergeant Major
RTC	Royal Tank Corps
RTR	Royal Tank Regiment
SAAC	South African Armoured Corps
SD	Service Dress
Sect	Section
SG	Scots Guards
Sigs	Signals
'Skins	5th Royal Inniskilling Dragoon Guards
SMLE	Short Magazine Lee Enfield (rifle)
SOME	Staff Officer Mechanical Engineering
SP	Self-propelled
Sp Coy	Support Company
Sqn	Squadron
SSM	Squadron Sergeant-Major
S&T	Supply & Transport
Tac	Tactical
TCV	Troop Carrying Vehicle
Tk	Tank
Tps	Troops
Veh	Vehicle
WDF	Western Defence Force
WH	Wehrmacht Heer
Wksp	Workshops

INDEX

Abyssinia, 6, 7, 40

Agedabia, 21, 22, 23, 26

Alam Halfa, 58, 59

Alexandria, 37

Arnim, J. von, 62

Ashworth, J. B. 142

Auchinleck, Sir Claude, 40, 41, 54, 58, 115, 116

Avalanche, Operation 128

Bardia, 9, 29, 42, 55

Battleaxe, Operation 114-115

Baytown, Operation 129

Bayeux, 68

Beda Fomm, 18, 22, 111, 113, 164, 172

Beeley, John 116, 177

Belhamed, 51

Ben Gania, 23

Benghazi, 9, 18, 22, 24, 25, 55

Beresford-Pierse, Sir Noel, 37, 40, 110, 114

Bismarck, G. von, 56, 58, 59, 84, 86–87

Blackcock, Operation 153

Böhles, 42

Böttcher, K., 54, 84, 86

Bouarada, 62

Brauchitsch, W. von, 8, 21, 32, 37, 41

Brevity, Operation 114-115

British and Commonwealth units:

   Armies — Western Desert Force, 9, 18, 37, 40, 41; First, 123; Eighth, in passim 40–62, 115, 119, 123, 128, 129, 143, 173, 181; **Brigades** — 1st Army Tk Brig, 41; 32nd Army Tk Brig, 41; 3rd Armoured, 25; 1st Commando 152, 153; 4th Armoured 38, 41, 48, 49, 50, 51, 52, 101, 103, 106, 110, 111, 114, 115, 116, 118, 143, 144, 158, 159, 179; 4th Light, 122; 7th Armoured, 35, 50, 51; 8th Armoured, 152; 9th Armoured, 59; 22nd Armoured, 35. 38, 41, 115, 116, 117, 122, 128, 129, 131, 132, 133, 134, 135, 139, 140, 142, 143, 149, 154, 156, 158, 160, 175, 178; 131st (Queens), 122, 123, 128, 133, 141, 144, 147, 149, 152, 156, 158; 155th Infantry, 152; 1st Guards Brig, 41; **Corps** — I, 137; VIII, 140, 147; X, 129, 131; XII, 143, 147, 149, 152, 153; XIII, 18, 41, 48, 49, 50, 53, 59, 110, 115, 116, 117, 131, 142, 143, 172; XXX, 41, 48, 49, 51, 59, 116, 117, 135, 137, 140, 141, 142, 153, 182; **Divisions** — Australian 6th, 110; 9th, 25, 112; Canadian 2nd, 141; 3rd, 68, 141; 5th 131; New Zealand 1st, 41; 6th, 53; South African 1st, 41; 2nd, 41; British — Guards Armoured, 68, 141, 147; 2nd Armoured, 21, 26, 112; 3rd, 26, 68; 6th Armoured, 149; 7th Armoured 9, 21, 22, 35, 38, 39, 41, 46, 47, 49, 51, 52, 53, 56, 58; 11th Armoured 141, 147, 172, 173, 175; 22nd Armoured, 52; 46th Infantry, 129, 131; 50th Infantry 135, 149; 51st Infantry 143, 182; 52nd Infantry, 152; 53rd Infantry, 154; 56th Infantry, 129, 131; 79th Armoured, 172; Indian — 3rd , 26; 4th, 38, 107, 110, 114, 118, 173; **Regiments and Battalions** — 1 KRRC, 99, 100, 112, 177; 1 RTR, 28, 29, 31, 34, 98, 100, 101, 104, 105, 107, 129, 131, 140, 141, 142, 143, 144, 147, 152, 160, 161; 1 RTC, 98; 2 Devons 144, 149, 152; 2 RB 101, 173; 2 RTR, 35, 36, 51, 157, 160, 161, 164, 179, 180; 3 CLY 140; 3 Coldstream Guards 36, 112; 3 H 112; 3 RHA, 98, 100, 101, 142, 152, 154, 156; 4 CLY 134, 137, 140, 141; 4 RHA, 100, 101, 108; 4 RTR, 35, 36, 38, 114; 1/5 Queens 142, 144, 149, 152, 153, 154, 156; 5 Inniskilling Dragoon Guards, 139, 140, 141, 142, 143, 144, 153, 154, 156; KDG, 20, 21, 25, 28; LRDG, 24; 5 RHA, 128; 5 RTR, 24, 26, 118, 131, 135, 140, 141, 142, 144, 151, 153, 154, 160; 1/6 Queens 131, 142, 143; 6 RHA, 142; 6 RTR, 24, 51, 98, 100, 110, 112, 114, 169; 7 Queens Own Hussars, 98, 100, 157; 7th Hussars, 51; 11th Hussars, 35; 1/7 Queens 129, 142, 143, 149; 7 RTR, 28, 34, 36, 38, 40, 110, 114, 156; 8 Kings Royal Irish Hussars, 98, 100, 110, 132, 141, 144, 147, 149, 153, 154, 156; 9 Durham Light Infantry, 149, 152, 153, 154; 10

Medical, 143; 11 H (Prince Albert's Own) 98, 100, 101, 104, 108, 111, 112, 122, 127, 128, 132, 142, 143, 147, 151, 153, 154, 156, 158, 160, 175, 178; 1 RB, 144, 147, 153; 25th (NZ) Bn, 54; 60th Field Regt, RA, 51

British Operations:

Acrobat, 56; Avalanche, 128; Battleaxe, 37–40, 46, 48, 114–115; Baytown, 129; Blackcock, 153; Bluecoat, 68; Brevity, 35–37, 114–115; Cobra, 141; Compass, 107, 108–110; Crusader, 48–55, 115; Husky, 128; Lightfoot, 59; Market Garden, 147–152; Perch, 135; Plunder, 153; Supercharge, 59; Venezia, 118

Brooke, Sir Alan 154

Bucknall, Gerald 137, 140, 174, 182

Caen, 65

Campbell, Jock, 52, 108, 116, 118, 173, 176

Capuzzo, 29, 36, 38, 39, 86

'Cauldron', The, 56, 57

Caunter, "Blood" 101, 172

Chater, Robin 99

Churchill, Winston, 18, 37, 40, 100, 114, 118, 126, 154, 156, 172, 181

Cobra, Operation 141

Compass, Operation 107, 108–110

Creagh, Michael O'Moore 100, 101, 158, 172

Crocker, Sir John 137

Crusader, Operation 115

Crüwell, L., 42, 50, 51, 53

Cunningham, Sir Alan, 40, 41, 53, 54, 115, 116

Cyrenaica, 7, 9, in passim 18–59, 87

D-Day, 65, 137

Dempsey, Sir Miles 137

Derna, 22, 23, 25, 26, 29, 32, 33, 56

Dietrich, S., 68

Egypt, 8, 9, 21, 29, 35, 47, 55, 58, 59

El Agheila, 18, 20, 23, 56

El Alamein, 56, 57, 58, 59, 84, 87, 95, 107, 119, 122–125, 173, 175, 183, 187

Erskine, Sir George 132, 140, 174, 182

Falaise Pocket, 68

Feuchtinger, E., 65, 68, 84, 88

Fliegerkorps XI, 9

Freyberg, B., 54

Gabr Saleh, 49, 50

Gambier-Perry, M. D., 22, 26

Gambut, 47, 48, 52, 53

Gariboldi, I., 24, 41

Gatehouse, Alec 173

Gause, Alfred, 41, 423

Gazala, 25, 33, 35, 55, 117, 118–122, 173

Gebel Akhbar, 23, 24, 25, 28, 49

German High Command, 6, 7

German Units

15th Army, 146; 2nd MG Bn, 12, 17, 23, 29, 42, 43; 3rd Pz Div, 8, 10, 12, 72; 3rd Recce Bn, in passim 10–43, 49, 50; 5th Lt Div, in passim 10–42, 70, 72, 80, 85, 95, 112, 114; 5th Pz Div, 12; 5th Pz Regt, 12, in passim 17–62, 76; 7th Pz Div, 7, 84, 85; 7th (Ghost) Panzer, 112; 8th MG Bn, 12, 17, in passim 21–30, 43; 8th Pz Regt, 36, 39; 10th Pz Div, 10; 12th SS Pz Div, 68; 15th MC Bn, 34, 42, 86; 15th Pz Div, in passim 10–62, 112, 114; 15th Pz Regt, 12; 16th Luftwaffe Fd Div, 68; 21st Pz Div, 13, in passim 42–68, 72, 86, 87, 88, 90, 92, 94, 95, 122; 22nd Pz Regt, 68, 88; 33rd Flak Regt, 17, 38, 42; 39th Panzerjäger Bn, 10, 17, 43, 62; 75th Arty Regt, 17; 90th Lt Div, 42, 56, 57, 58, 62; 100th Pz Regt, 65, 68; 104th PzGr Regt, 86; 104th Rifle Regt, 42, 43; 112th Pz Brig, 68; 125th PzGr Regt, 65; 155th Arty Regt, 42, 43, 62; 155th Rifle Regt, 52; 192nd PzGr Regt, 65; 200th Rifle Regt, 52; 200th Sturmgeschütz Bn, 65; 220th Pz Pioneer Bn, 65; 305th Army Flak Bn, 62,

65; 605th Panzerjäger Bn, 12, 17; 606th Flak Bn, 12; 606th SP Flak Bn, 17; 931st Fast Brigade; Artillery Group Böttcher, 52; Battle Group Gruen, 62; Battle Group Pfeiffer, 62, 64; Battle Group Schuette, 64; Battle Group Stenkhoff, 64; Battle Group Stephan, 51; Combat Group Knabe, 35, 36; Deutsches Afrika Korps, in passim 9–42, 72, 77, 84, 87, 90, 91, 94, 95, 112, 117, 123, 125, 181, 182, 185; Panzerarmee Afrika, 62–64, 88; Panzergruppe Afrika, 41–62; Wireless Intercept Sect, 36
Gordon-Finlayson, Sir Robert 99, 100
Gott, W. H. E. "Strafer", 35, 36, 112, 115, 118, 164, 172, 173
Graziani, Marshal, 8, 9
Grolig, O., 68, 84, 88
Gunn, George 116, 176

Hafid Ridge, 38, 39, 40
Halder, F., 9, 18, 32, 41
Halfaya Pass, 29, 36, 38, 39, 40, 46, 47, 90
Harding, Lord, of Petherton 123, 174
Hart, Sir Basil Liddell 172
Hauser, 10, 21, 30
Hedley, Jerry 124
Heuduck von, 42
Hildebrandt, H.-G., 64, 84, 87–88
Hitler, Adolf, 6, 7, 8, 9, 24, 68, 83, 84, 112
Hobart, Pat 129
Hobart, Sir Percy 98, 99, 100, 108, 135, 172, 173
Horrocks, Sir Brian 123, 140, 182
Hülsen, H.-H. von, 64, 85, 88
Husky, Operation 128
Hussein, Saddam 179

Italian Units:
    Armies —Tenth, 111; **Divisions**—Ariete Ariete (Armd) Div, 23, 25, 26, 32, 42, 53, 56, 59, 112, 116; Bologna Div, 42; Brescia Div, 22, 28, 42, 112; Pavia Div, 42; Trente Div, 32, 42; Trieste (Mot) Div, 42; XX (Mob) Corps, 42; XXI Corps, 41, 42

Kasserine Pass, 62, 64
Kesselring, Albert 129
Kidney Ridge, 59
Kirchheim, H., 22, 28, 31, 32
Kluge, G. von, 10
Knabe, G.-G., 54, 84, 86

Lungerhausen, Carl-Hans, 59, 84, 87
Lyne, Lewis 149, 153, 154, 174, 175
Lyon, Hugh 127

March, John 111
Mareth Line, 62
Market Garden, Operation 147–152
Mechili, 23, 24, 25, 26, 27, 29, 30, 38
Mersa Brega, 21, 56
Mersa Matruh, 6, 8, 35, 57, 58
Messervy, Frank 118, 173
Mews, R. 140
Mirrles, W. H. B. 100
Montgomery, Bernard, 20, 59, 119, 122, 124, 134, 139, 154, 175
Morshead, L., 25, 27, 28, 31
Msus, 23, 24
Mussolini, Benito, 7, 8, 9, 23, 49, 98, 102

Neame, P., 22, 25
Neumann-Silkow, W., 37, 39
Normandy, 64–68, 72, 84, 88, 95

Operations see British Operations
O'Connor, Sir Richard, 9, 18, 22, 25, 100, 107, 108, 110, 111, 112, 140, 174
OKH (Army Command), 6, 9, 16, 18, 21, 22, 31, 32, 41
OKW, 6, 32, 35

Olrich, 23, 31, 36, 37

Paulus, F. von, 32, 33, 35
Perch, Operation 135
Plunder, Operation 153
Ponath, G., 25, 28, 30, 31
Prittwitz und Gaffron, H. von, 28–29

Qattara Depression, 58

Randow, H. von, 59, 62, 84, 87
Ranville, 68
Ras al Madawar, 32, 33–35
Renton, "Wingy" 173
Rigel Ridge, 56
Ritchie, Sir Niel, 54, 55, 116, 118, 143
Ravenstein, J. von, 37, 39, 47, 49, 52, 54, 84, 85–86
Roberts, "Pip" 173, 174, 175, 178
Rommel, Erwin, 7, 9, 16, 18, in passim 20–68, 72, 77, 82–84, 85, 86, 89, 90, 91, 95, 112, 113, 115, 116, 117, 118, 119, 122, 123, 125, 135, 180, 185
Russell, H. E. 98, 100
Ruweisat Ridge, 58

Sbiba, 62
Schmidt, H. W., 27, 31
Schmundt, R., 9, 20
Schwerin, G. Graf von, 23, 24, 25
Seebohm, A., 36
Sidi Omar, 39, 46, 47, 48, 49
Sidi Rezegh, 50, 51, 52, 53, 54, 55, 107, 115, 116, 117, 119, 173, 176, 177, 178
Sidi Suleiman, 40
Sidra Ridge, 56, 57
Sirte, 20; Gulf of, 18, 20
Smail, A. J. 127
Sollum, 26, 29, 36, 38, 86

Storch liaison aircraft, 23, 25, 26, 27
Streich, J., 12, in passim 21–37, 84, 85, 86, 95
Suez Canal 98, 112, 119

Thoma, W. Ritter von, 8
Tobruk, 9, in passim 23–55, 85, 86
Tripoli, 9, 12, 16, 18, 20, 29, 32, 33, 56, 57, 87
Tripolitania, 18, 20, 21, 23
Tunisia, 62, 95

Ultra, 18, 21, 35, 49, 94
US Army Units: 1st Armd Div, 62; Fifth, 128, 129

Venezia, Operation 118
Verney, Gerald 101, 103, 140, 141, 142, 143, 146, 149, 159, 174, 175
Victoria Cross 108, 116, 173, 176–177
Victory, Paddy 139
Villers-Bocage, 68, 135, 137, 139, 140, 142, 174, 175, 181, 182

Watkins, "Boomer" 100
Wavell, Sir Archibald, 18, 22, 35, 37, 40, 100, 107, 111, 112, 114, 117
Wendt, W., 36, 39
Western Desert Force 100, 103, 108, 110
Westhoven, F., 68, 84, 88
Williams, E. T., 20
Wilson, "Jumbo" 100
Wittmann, Michael 139

Zollenkopf, H., 68, 84, 88